CUSTOM WOODWORKING

The Small Shop

CUSTOM WOODWORKING

The Small Shop

By the editors of *Woodsmith* magazine

CONTENTS

CUSTOM WOODWORKING

The Small Shop

SHOP STORAGE 6

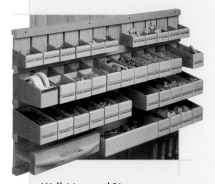

Wall-Mounted Bins

WORK STATIONS

Revolving Tool Station

BENCHES & CABINETS

Drop-Down Tool Tray

SHOP STORAGE

Organization is especially important if you want to get the most from a small shop. When the shop is organized, it seems that every project goes more smoothly and every hour spent there is more rewarding.

By helping you organize tools, hardware, lumber, and accessories, these seven projects will also help you carve out valuable space in your shop, so you can spend less time searching for a particular tool or fastener and more time actually working wood.

Pegboard Storage

At first glance, this cabinet appears to be just some framed pegboard hung on the wall. But its secret is revealed once you open up the doors and find plenty of hidden room to hang tools and accessories.

When I first showed this rack to a friend, his initial reaction was a simple, "Looks nice." But then I swung open the door to reveal two more pegboard panels inside. His eyebrows rose a bit. Then, when I swung the rear door open to reveal a fourth pegboard panel, plus storage on the wall behind the rack, he finally said, "Wow!"

All told, there is almost 22 square feet of pegboard and wall space in this rack that takes up less than seven square feet on the wall.

DOORS. The doors are just simple wood frames with pegboard screwed in place on each side. They pivot on a pair of bolts at the top and bottom corners. To allow access to both sides, the doors swing out in opposite directions (see the photos below).

MATERIALS. You should be able to pick up all the materials you need at the local lumberyard. The frame is made from "two-by" material. A ³/₄"-thick plywood top and bottom help brace the frame so it will support a load of tools hung on the doors. And a full sheet of pegboard provides the door panels.

SHOP LAYOUT. This project creates a convenient place to store tools and accessories. But there's more to getting the most out of your shop space than just having a place to put things. For tips on how to best lay out your shop, see the Shop Info article on pages 12-13.

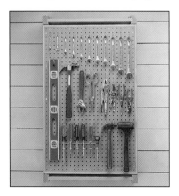

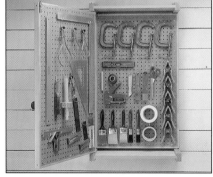

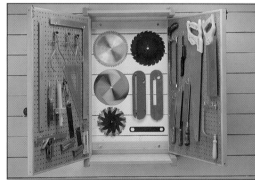

EXPLODED VIEW

OVERALL DIMENSIONS:
24W x 10½D x 41¾H

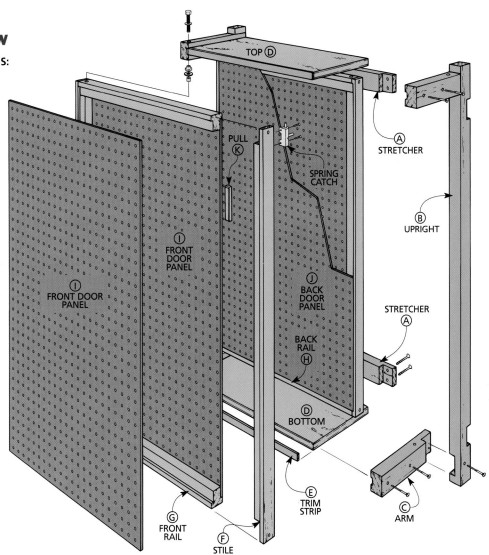

MATERIALS LIST

WOOD

A	Stretcher (2)	1½ x 2 - 24
B	Uprights (2)	1½ x 2 - 41¾
C	Arms (4)	1½ x 2 - 10½
D	Top/Bottom (2)	¾ ply - 10¼ x 21½
E	Trim Strips (2)	¼ x ¾ - 21½
F	Stiles (4)	1½ x 1½ - 36
G	Front Rails (2)	1½ x 1½ - 23
H	Back Rails (2)	1½ x 1½ - 22
I	Front Door Panel (2)	¼ pgbd. - 23 x 35
J	Back Door Panel (2)	¼ pgbd. - 22 x 35
K	Pull (1)	¾ x ½ - 5

HARDWARE SUPPLIES

(80) No. 10 x ½ " Fh woodscrews
(16) No. 8 x 2½ " Fh woodscrews
(8) No. 8 x 1¾ " Fh woodscrews
(8) No. 8 x 1¼ " Fh woodscrews
(4) ¼ " x 3½ " lag screws
(4) ¼ " x 2½ " hex bolts
(4) ¼ " T-nuts
(4) ¼ " washers
(4) ¼ " fender washers
(4) ¼ " x ½ "-long bronze bushings
(2) Left-hand spring catches

CUTTING DIAGRAM

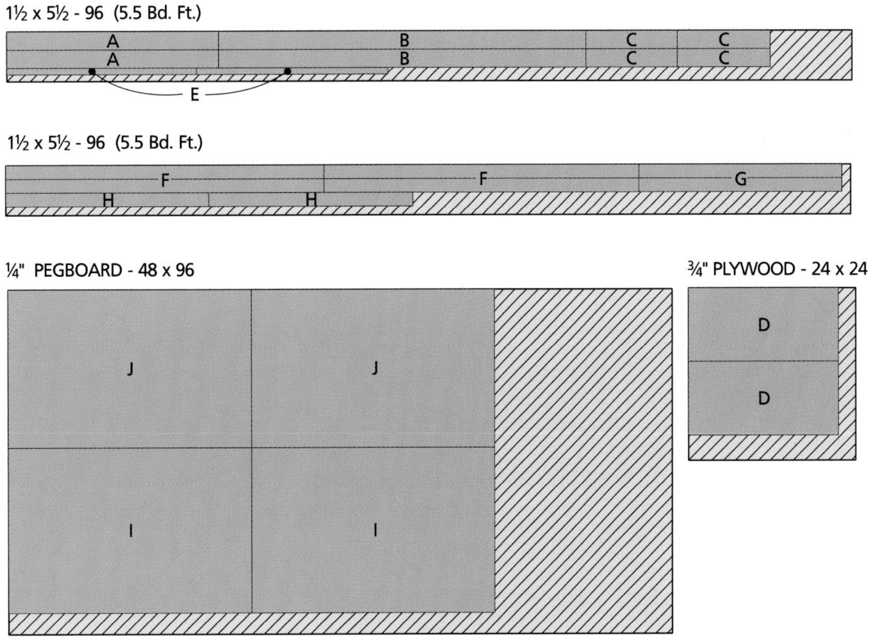

1½ x 5½ - 96 (5.5 Bd. Ft.)

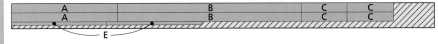

1½ x 5½ - 96 (5.5 Bd. Ft.)

¼" PEGBOARD - 48 x 96

¾" PLYWOOD - 24 x 24

I started construction of the storage unit by cutting the pieces for the U-shaped frame that supports the two swinging doors.

FRAME. This sturdy frame is made from "two-by" material that's been ripped to a width of 2". (I used Douglas fir.) A 3/4"-thick plywood top and bottom provide extra strength to support the doors *(Fig. 1)*. The frame is held together with simple (yet strong) lap joints. This joint is easy to make with a dado blade in the table saw by cutting a series of notches in the frame pieces.

The first pieces to make are a pair of stretchers (A) used to attach the rack to the wall. Once they are ripped to width (2") and cut to length (24"), the stretchers are rabbeted on each end to leave 3/4"-thick tongues *(Fig. 2)*.

Next, cut two uprights (B) to a finished length of 41 3/4". Then, to accept the tongues on the stretchers, dadoes are cut in the back edge of the two uprights (B). These dadoes are 3 1/2" from each end of the upright *(Fig. 2)*.

Another pair of 2"-wide dadoes are cut on the inside face of each upright to accept a pair of short arms (C) *(Figs. 1 and 2)*. The doors are attached to these arms later.

Once the dadoes are cut in the uprights, all four of the arms are rabbeted on one end to leave a 3/4"-thick tongue *(Fig. 2)*.

Before assembling the frame, it's easiest to drill a 1/4"-dia. hole in each arm for a pin that will allow the doors to pivot *(Fig. 3)*. Note that the holes are located toward the front of the left arms, and to the rear of the right arms. I used the drill press to make sure the holes were straight up and down.

After the holes are drilled, a shallow groove is cut in each arm to accept the 3/4"-thick plywood top and bottom added later. These grooves are centered on the inside faces of the arms, opposite the rabbets cut earlier.

ASSEMBLY. Now that all the joinery is cut, you can assemble the frame. The stretchers, uprights, and arms are held together with glue and screws.

To add rigidity to the frame, the plywood top and bottom (D) are cut to fit between the grooves in the arms. But before gluing and screwing them in place, I added hardwood trim strips (E) to cover their front edges *(Fig. 1)*.

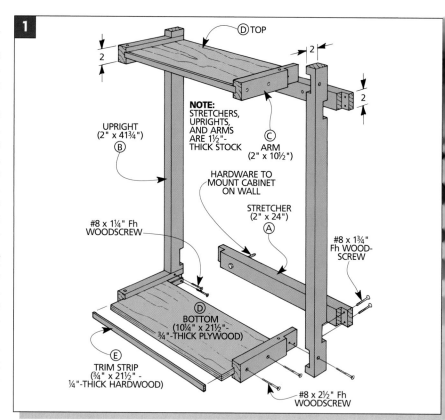

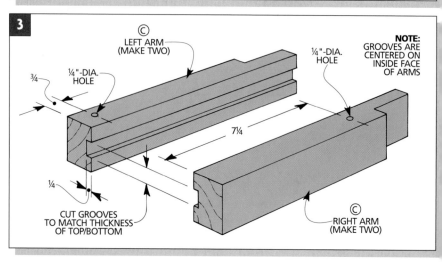

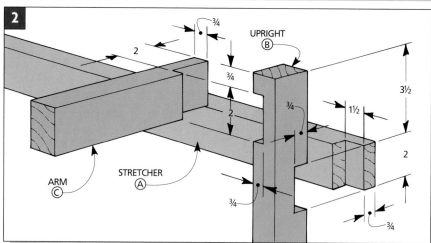

With the frame complete, you can start working on the doors. They're just simple wood frames that are rabbeted on both sides to accept the pegboard panels *(Fig. 4)*.

The overall height of the doors is the same. But the back door is 1" narrower so it swings past the front door when you open it *(Fig. 4d)*.

Determining the length of the frame pieces is easy. The stiles (F) on each door are identical in length. They are cut to provide ⅛" clearance at both the top and the bottom. (Mine were 36" long.) But the front rails (G) are 1" longer than the back rails (H). (This takes into account the overall width of the doors and the joinery that holds them together.)

With the frame pieces cut to length, matching rabbets are cut on both sides for the pegboard panels *(Fig. 4a)*. And notches in the ends of the stiles accept the rails *(Fig. 4b)*.

Once the frames were assembled, I eased the edges by routing ¹⁄₁₆" chamfers around the frames *(Fig. 4)*.

PANELS. After screwing the frame pieces together, it's just a matter of cutting front (I) and back door panels (J) to fit between the rabbets.

Note: Cut the pegboard so the holes are ½" from the outside edge *(Fig. 4c)*.

Next, a scrap pull (K) is glued to the front of the back door. The pull is just a ½" x 5" piece, cut from ¾"-thick stock.

ATTACH DOORS. All that's left is to attach the doors. They pivot on two hex bolts that pass into bronze bushings installed in the top and bottom edges of each door *(Figs. 5 and 5a)*. These bolts pass through holes in the arms (drilled earlier) and thread into T-nuts in the inside faces of the arms.

Finally, to lock the doors in place, a hole is drilled in each upper arm for a spring-loaded catch *(Fig. 6)*.

Note: One catch mounts to the back of the front door. The other is on the front of the back door *(Fig. 4)*.

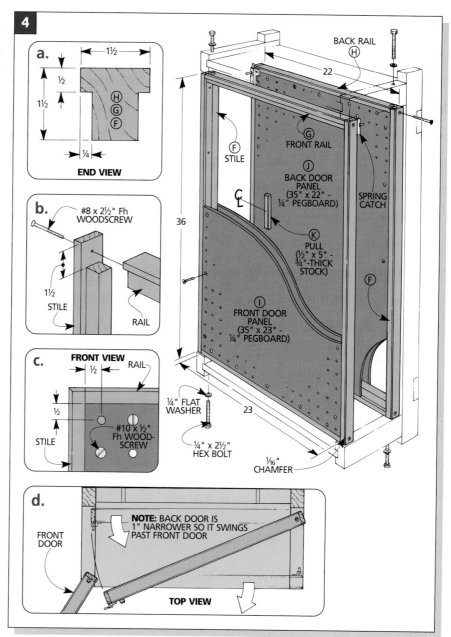

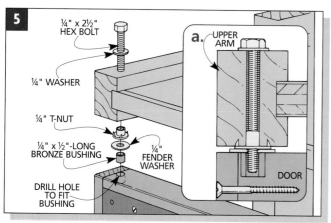

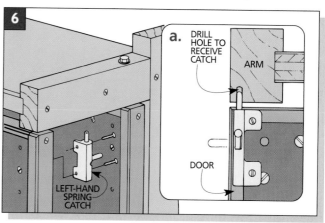

SHOP INFO ... *Shop Layout & Storage*

The ideal shop always has room for one more tool. And nothing gets in the way of anything else. But in all the shops I've set up, space (or the lack of it) has always been a consideration.

With all the tools and materials required for a project, a small shop can soon get crowded and cramped. Even so, there's no reason a small workshop can't work smoothly and efficiently. All it takes is a little planning.

WORK FLOW. The key to this planning is to think about how a typical project "flows" through the shop. Then establish an area for each part of the process.

For instance, when I bring lumber into the shop, it's handy to have a space to break it down into manageable pieces (see Breakdown Area in drawing below). This can be as simple as a pair of sawhorses and a circular saw. And if possible, I position tools used for stock preparation (like the jointer, table saw, and thickness planer) right nearby.

Once the stock is flat, straight, and square, the next step is to cut the joinery and shape the pieces. To make this go smoothly, I position the drill press, router table, and band saw near the workbench. By locating the work-

bench out in the open, there's access on all sides, making it easy to assemble the project and apply the finish.

Besides the way a project moves from one area to the next, there are a few other things to keep in mind as you lay out a shop. Is there any benefit to grouping tools together? What type of space requirements does each tool have? Where will you provide space for storage? And will each power tool have access to an electrical outlet? I find the best way to answer these questions is to plan a shop layout just as I would a project. And that process begins on paper.

LAYOUT

Rather than dragging heavy tools back and forth across the floor, it's much easier to shuffle paper to decide what arrangements will and won't work.

SCALE DRAWING. This is just a matter of drawing a floor plan of your shop to scale. Then cut paper templates of each of your tools (also to scale) and position them around the "shop."

When sliding the templates around, one thing that can make a small shop

work "big" is to group tools together.

JOB. One way of grouping that makes a lot of sense is to arrange tools by the job they do. For example, the table saw, jointer, and planer are all used during stock preparation, so it's convenient to cluster them together.

SUPPORT. You can also use tool groups to provide support for large workpieces. To give side support when crosscutting a long workpiece on the

table saw, for instance, you can set your jointer next to it (see left photo on the opposite page.)

Or if your router table is the same height as (or a bit shorter than) your table saw, the top can double as an outfeed support.

SPACE. While a group of tools may look alright on paper, don't start muscling them into place just yet. Each tool also has space requirements.

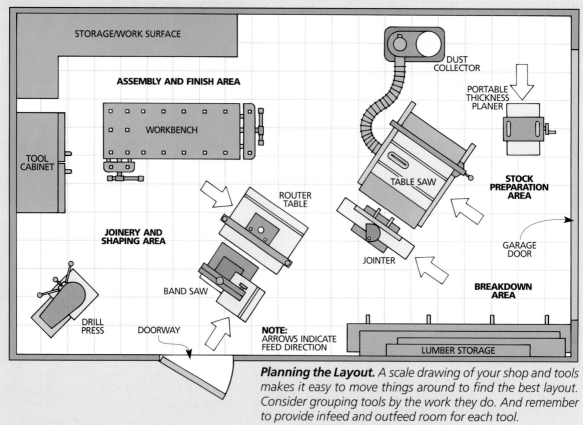

Planning the Layout. A scale drawing of your shop and tools makes it easy to move things around to find the best layout. Consider grouping tools by the work they do. And remember to provide infeed and outfeed room for each tool.

This isn't just the visible "footprint" of the tool. You need to include enough room to walk around and between tools as you move through the shop. And when you're laying out the shop on paper, it's easy to forget the extra space that's needed so the workpiece that feeds in (or out) of one tool doesn't bump into another one.

CENTER STAGE. Take the table saw, for instance. Because of the clearance required in front, back, and at the sides when cutting large workpieces, it usually claims more than its fair share of space in the center of the shop. Even so, you can still work around these space requirements. Sometimes it's just a matter of positioning the table saw at an angle so workpieces feed into an open area of the shop (see drawing on opposite page).

The table saw isn't the only tool that can gobble up space. When running long pieces through the jointer, band saw, router table, or planer, you might also need a sizable "run" at each end of the tool.

OVERLAP. One way to provide this space is to overlap the infeed and outfeed areas of two tools. For example, position a planer so the outfeed passes in front of the table saw.

Overlapping areas also works well with tools where the tables are at different heights. For instance, I park my band saw right next to the router table.

This way, a workpiece feeding off the band saw passes above the shorter router table (see middle photo below).

DOORS AND WINDOWS. When planning infeed/outfeed requirements, don't overlook an opening provided by a door or window. Positioning a band saw or table saw near a door may be just the ticket for those extra-long pieces (see drawing on opposite page).

CORNERS. One last note. The corners of a shop often get filled with clutter. But tucking a tool like a drill press into a corner can take advantage of wasted space. You can still drill holes in a long workpiece because of the distance between the adjoining walls (see right photo below).

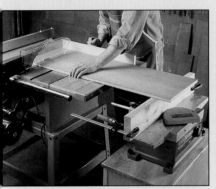

Support Work With Another Tool. *A board clamped to the jointer fence supports workpieces on the table saw.*

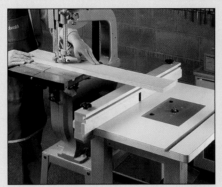

Overlap Tool Heights. *Take advantage of different table heights by overlapping infeed/outfeed areas.*

Use Corners. *Even with this drill press tucked in a corner, you can still work with long workpieces.*

STORAGE

Finally, don't overlook the need for storage when arranging your shop.

WALLS. The most obvious place to store things is to hang them on the walls. But even here, you can make the most out of that space with a cabinet such as the Pegboard Storage rack on pages 8-11.

Placement. *For efficiency, it just makes sense to position a tool cabinet next to your workbench.*

AROUND TOOLS. Most stationary tools should have some storage nearby for accessories. This storage can often utilize space that would otherwise be wasted. The Drill Press Caddy beginning on page 18 and the Saw Cabinet on page 102 are a couple of examples.

AROUND THE BENCH. One of the most important "tools" in the shop is my workbench. But it doesn't do me much good if I have to walk across the shop to get tools. Situating a cabinet near the bench gives me easy access to both hand and power tools (see photo at left).

Another way to keep tools handy is to take advantage of the space below the bench. On page 112, you'll find plans for a Drop-Down Tool Tray that fastens to the legs on one side of the bench. You can also use the floor space below your bench as shown in the photo at right.

OVERHEAD. Besides looking below for storage, you can usually carve out a lot of space up above. The Overhead Racks on pages 34-36 offer several ideas for storing lumber up out of the way.

SMALL TOOLS. And since you don't use all your tools all the time, consider tools that can be stored out of the way when they aren't in use. Two ideas are the Benchtop Router Table on page 70 and the Miter Saw Station on page 52.

Unused Space. *A wheeled box under your bench provides easily accessible storage for cutoffs or accessories.*

Hardware Bin

Don't be afraid to fill these drawers with hardware. The interlocking joinery can handle the load. Optional dividers let you customize the drawers to provide the type of storage you need.

This small Hardware Bin can make a big difference in the clutter that tends to pile up in a shop. Although it's only about as big as a tackle box, it still holds enough drawers to organize lots of loose parts and hardware. The drawers are built to fit tight in the case to keep dust out. And the bin's small size and simple construction mean you could build several and put them in a number of spots where you need quick access to hardware or parts.

JOINERY. The joinery for the case is simply dadoes and rabbets with a few nails to reinforce the corners. The drawers feature locking rabbet joints in the front, and tongue and dado joints in the

back. That may sound complicated, but everything is cut easily on the table saw with just a few setups.

OPEN BACK. One thing about this case that's a bit different is that it has no back. So even though the drawers fit tight, they close easily. Air that normally would be compressed inside the case as you push in a tight-fitting drawer goes right out the open back.

But don't worry about losing the drawers out the back of the case. A stop behind each one keeps the fronts flush with the front of the case.

PULLS. All those drawers wouldn't be nearly as useful if you always had to pull them open first to find out what was

inside. So I found some brass pulls with label holders to go on each door. These not only tell you what's inside at a glance, they also give you a handy way to open the drawer. I also think they add a touch of class. (*Woodsmith Project Supplies* offers these pulls. See Sources on page 126 for details.)

OPTIONAL DIVIDERS. An entire drawer may be too much space for storing smaller hardware. Or you may prefer to store several sizes of the same item in one drawer. The solution here is to divide the drawer into smaller compartments. A quick way to do this, by adding hardboard dividers, is detailed in the Designer's Notebook on page 17.

EXPLODED VIEW

OVERALL DIMENSIONS:
14⅛W x 9D x 11½H

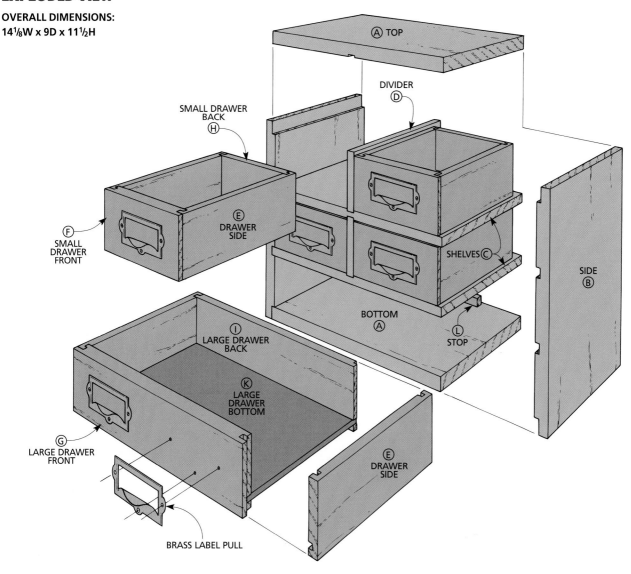

- Ⓐ TOP
- DIVIDER Ⓓ
- SMALL DRAWER BACK Ⓗ
- Ⓔ DRAWER SIDE
- Ⓕ SMALL DRAWER FRONT
- SHELVES Ⓒ
- SIDE Ⓑ
- BOTTOM Ⓐ
- Ⓘ LARGE DRAWER BACK
- Ⓚ LARGE DRAWER BOTTOM
- Ⓖ LARGE DRAWER FRONT
- Ⓛ STOP
- Ⓔ DRAWER SIDE
- BRASS LABEL PULL

MATERIALS LIST

WOOD

A	Top/Bottom (2)	¾ x 9 - 13⅛
B	Sides (2)	¾ x 9 - 11½
C	Shelves (2)	½ x 9 - 13⅛
D	Dividers (2)	½ x 9 - 3¼
E	Drawer Sides (10)	½ x 2¹⁵/₁₆ - 8
F	Sm. Drwr. Fronts (4)	¾ x 2¹⁵/₁₆ - 6
G	Lg. Drwr. Front (1)	¾ x 2¹⁵/₁₆ - 12⁹/₁₆
H	Sm. Drwr. Backs (4)	½ x 2¹⁵/₁₆ - 5½
I	Lg. Drawer Back (1)	½ x 2¹⁵/₁₆ - 12¹/₁₆
J	Sm. Drwr. Btms. (4)	¼ hdbd. - 7¼ x 5½
K	Lg. Drwr. Bottom (1)	¼ hdbd. - 7¼ x 12¹/₁₆
L	Stops (6)	½ x ½ - 1

HARDWARE SUPPLIES

(16) 4d (1½"-long) finish nails
(6) Brass label pulls w/ screws

CUTTING DIAGRAM

¾ x 10¼ - 72 (5.1 Bd. Ft.)

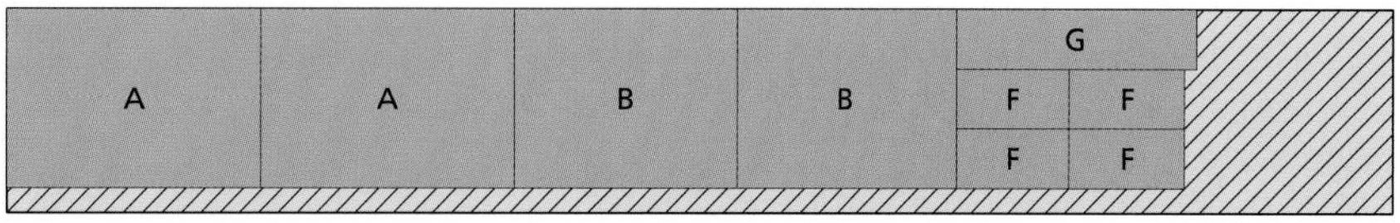

A	A	B	B	F	F
				G	
				F	F

½ x 7¼ - 72 (3.6 Sq. Ft.)

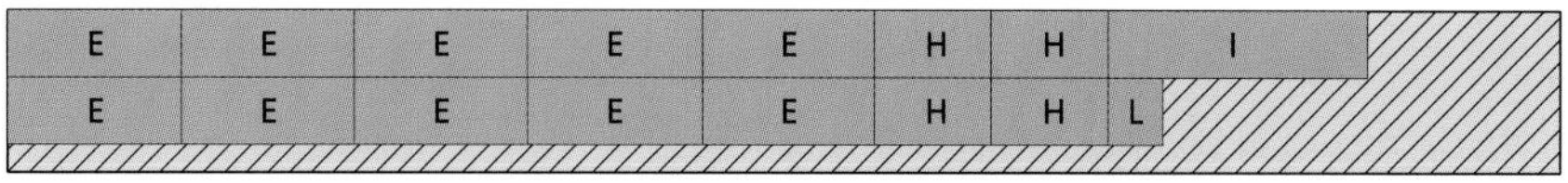

E	E	E	E	E	H	H	I
E	E	E	E	E	H	H	L

½ x 10¼ - 48 (3.4 Sq. Ft.)

C	C	D	D

ALSO NEED:
24" x 24" HARDBOARD
FOR DRAWER BOTTOMS

CASE

I started on the Hardware Bin by making the case. It starts out as a top and bottom (A) that are held together by two sides (B) *(Fig. 1)*. I used ³/₄"-thick pine, but most any wood will work.

After cutting ¹/₄"-deep rabbets in the sides (B) to accept the top and bottom (A), I then cut dadoes in the top and sides for a set of ¹/₂"-thick shelves and dividers added next *(Fig. 1)*.

SHELVES AND DIVIDERS. The shelves and dividers support the drawers and create a separate compartment for each one. To create openings for a large drawer on the bottom and four small drawers above, I cut two shelves (C) from ¹/₂"-thick stock. Then, after cutting shallow dadoes centered on the length of the shelves, a pair of ¹/₂"-thick dividers (D) can be cut to fit.

Now you can assemble the case. It's held together with glue and 4d (1¹/₂") finish nails at the corners. The shelves and dividers are glued in place.

DRAWERS

With the case complete, the drawers can be built to fit the openings. The drawers are held together with two simple, yet strong joints — a locking rabbet at the front corner and a tongue and dado joint at the back *(Fig. 2a)*. The first thing to do is to cut the drawer pieces to size.

THICKNESS. To allow for the locking rabbet, I used ³/₄"-thick stock for the drawer fronts *(Fig. 2)*. But to keep the weight of the drawers down, the sides and back pieces are ¹/₂" thick.

WIDTH. Regardless of the thickness, each piece is ripped to the same width. To keep the drawers from binding, they're ¹/₁₆" narrower than the height of the openings (2¹⁵/₁₆" in my case). But the length of the pieces will vary.

LENGTH. To determine the length of the sides (E), measure the depth of the case and subtract 1" *(Fig. 2)*. (This allows for the locking rabbet and the stops that are added later.)

Next, the small (F) and large drawer fronts (G) are cut ¹/₁₆" shorter than their openings. And to allow for the tongue and dado joint, you'll need to cut the back pieces (H, I) ¹/₂" shorter than the drawer fronts.

CUT JOINERY. Now you can cut the drawer joints.

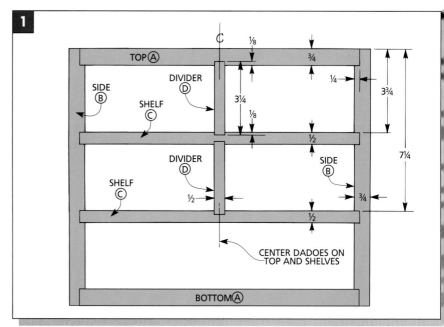

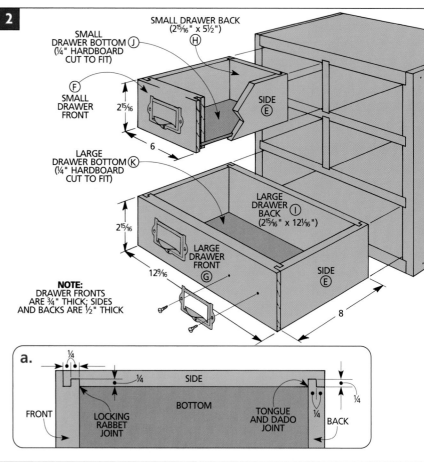

To do this, I set up a ¹/₄" dado blade in the table saw, with the blade ¹/₄" above the table's surface. Then I set the fence ¹/₄" from the blade.

First, make a pass on each end of the drawer sides (E) to cut matching dadoes *(Fig. 2a)*.

Then raise the blade to ¹/₂" above the table. Stand each drawer front (F, G) on end with its inside face against the fence and cut a slot in each end.

Safety Note: Use a zero-clearance insert to keep the workpiece from tipping into the opening around the blade.

Next, you'll need to trim $\frac{1}{4}$" from the length of the back tongues on the drawer front. This way, the drawer side sits flush with the end of the drawer front *(Fig. 2a)*. To do this, first lower the blade so it's just over $\frac{1}{4}$" above the table. Then, using the miter gauge to push the piece through the blade, sneak up on the final length of the tongue.

And finally, cut a $\frac{1}{4}$" rabbet on each end of the drawer back. You want to end up with a tongue that fits the dado in the drawer side *(Fig. 2a)*.

BOTTOMS. Since I used $\frac{1}{4}$"-thick hardboard for the drawer bottoms, I cut the grooves for the bottoms next. Then cut the bottoms (J, K) to fit.

Note: If you want to add dividers to the drawers (see the Designer's Notebook below), cut the slots for them now before gluing up the drawers.

STOPS. After the drawers have been assembled, you can glue stops (L) near the back of the drawer openings *(Figs. 3 and 3a)*. These are just small scrap blocks that keep the drawers flush with the front of the case.

PULLS. Finally, I screwed brass pulls to the drawer fronts, then made labels for each one so I knew what was in each drawer *(Fig. 2)*. ■

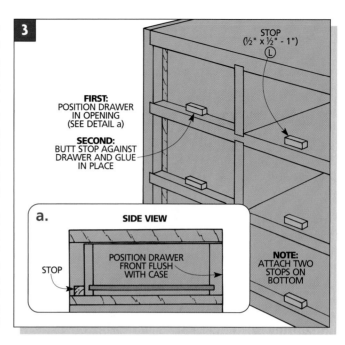

3

STOP ($\frac{1}{2}$" x $\frac{1}{2}$" - 1")
L

FIRST: POSITION DRAWER IN OPENING (SEE DETAIL a)

SECOND: BUTT STOP AGAINST DRAWER AND GLUE IN PLACE

a. SIDE VIEW

STOP

POSITION DRAWER FRONT FLUSH WITH CASE

NOTE: ATTACH TWO STOPS ON BOTTOM

DESIGNER'S NOTEBOOK

While you're set up to cut the joinery for the drawers, just a few more cuts lets you add dividers.

CONSTRUCTION NOTES:

■ The removable dividers (M, N) are made from $\frac{1}{4}$" hardboard. They fit into dadoes cut in the drawers. I divided a couple of the small drawers from side to side and the large drawer from front to back (see drawing).

■ The grooves for the drawer bottom and the dividers are the same size, so the same dado blade setup can be used. You simply need to adjust the position of the rip fence to cut the different slots.

■ On the small drawer, a dado is cut in each drawer side (E), centered on the length of the side (see drawing).

■ To divide the large drawer into three compartments, two dadoes are spaced evenly across the drawer front (G) and back (I) (see drawing).

■ The dividers (M, N) are cut to fit between the dadoes and flush with the top of the drawer.

■ Use a jig saw or band saw to cut an arc

in the top of each divider (see drawing).

■ Then the dividers just slide into position in the drawers.

MATERIALS LIST

NEW PARTS
M Small Dividers	$\frac{1}{4}$ hdbd.	- $2\frac{7}{16}$ x $5\frac{1}{2}$
N Large Dividers	$\frac{1}{4}$ hdbd.	- $2\frac{7}{16}$ x $7\frac{1}{2}$

Note: Cut as many as desired.

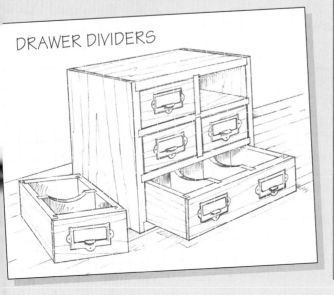

DRAWER DIVIDERS

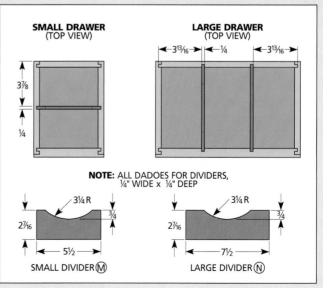

SMALL DRAWER (TOP VIEW)

$3\frac{7}{8}$

$\frac{1}{4}$

LARGE DRAWER (TOP VIEW)

$3\frac{13}{16}$ $\frac{1}{4}$ $3\frac{13}{16}$

NOTE: ALL DADOES FOR DIVIDERS, $\frac{1}{4}$" WIDE x $\frac{1}{4}$" DEEP

$3\frac{1}{4}$ R $\frac{3}{4}$

$2\frac{7}{16}$

$5\frac{1}{2}$

SMALL DIVIDER (M)

$3\frac{1}{4}$ R $\frac{3}{4}$

$2\frac{7}{16}$

$7\frac{1}{2}$

LARGE DIVIDER (N)

Drill Press Caddy

By clamping to the drill press column, this caddy uses wasted space to keep your bits and other accessories close at hand. The trays pivot out for access, then swing back in place to keep dust out.

Storing drill bits and accessories in a place convenient to my drill press has always been a problem. It's nice to be able to put them in a drawer or cabinet below the tool. That way, they're kept clean and organized. But if you're using a floor-model drill press, there isn't room to put a drawer.

A tray mounted to the drill press is more convenient, but you run the risk of having things fall off, or of sweeping away drill bits along with the shavings.

To solve this problem, I combined the benefits of the enclosed drawer with the convenience of a column-mounted tray — the result is the shop-made Drill Press Caddy shown above.

The design is very simple. It's just a pair of trays (one shallow and one deeper) sandwiched between a top and a base. Using a carriage bolt as a pivot, the trays swing open to provide access. Dust can't get in, and your accessories are just an arm's reach away.

SIZE. The caddy may look small, but it holds more than you might think. There's room for a collection of larger bits, like Forstner bits. You'll also have plenty of space to store your regular bits along with accessories, such as a circle cutter or sanding drums.

MATERIALS. You can probably make this project from scrap material you have on hand. The sides, top, bottom, and back of the trays are $1/2$"-thick stock. This helps keep the weight of the unit down. (I used maple for my caddy.) However, the fronts of each tray are made from $1^1/2$"-thick stock. This is needed to provide enough thickness to hold the carriage bolt that serves as a pivot for the trays. (Regular "2 by" lumber could be used for these parts.)

CLAMP. The caddy is held securely to the drill press column by a simple shop-made clamp that starts as part of the caddy's oversized top cover. After the clamp is cut from the cover, the two pieces are screwed back together with the column between them.

POWER TOOL SELECTION. A drill press (with or without a caddy) is just one of several tools that can be useful for a small shop. For help in selecting the most appropriate tools for your space and budget, see the Shop Info article on pages 22-23.

EXPLODED VIEW

OVERALL DIMENSIONS:
10½W x 11D x 6H

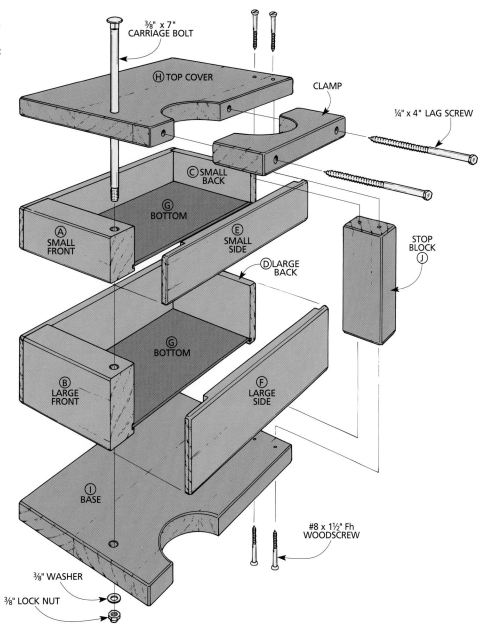

- ⅜" x 7" CARRIAGE BOLT
- Ⓗ TOP COVER
- CLAMP
- ¼" x 4" LAG SCREW
- Ⓒ SMALL BACK
- Ⓖ BOTTOM
- Ⓐ SMALL FRONT
- Ⓔ SMALL SIDE
- Ⓓ LARGE BACK
- STOP BLOCK Ⓙ
- Ⓖ BOTTOM
- Ⓑ LARGE FRONT
- Ⓕ LARGE SIDE
- Ⓘ BASE
- #8 x 1½" Fh WOODSCREW
- ⅜" WASHER
- ⅜" LOCK NUT

MATERIALS LIST

WOOD

A	Small Front (1)	1½ x 1¾ - 5½
B	Large Front (1)	1½ x 2¾ - 5½
C	Small Back (1)	½ x 1¾ - 5½
D	Large Back (1)	½ x 2¾ - 5½
E	Small Sides (2)	½ x 1¾ - 11
F	Large Sides (2)	½ x 2¾ - 11
G	Bottoms (2)	⅛ hdbd. - 5¼ x 9¼
H	Top Cover (1)	¾ x 10½ - 11
I	Base (1)	¾ x 10½ - 11
J	Stop Block (1)	1½ x 2 - 4½

HARDWARE SUPPLIES

(4) No. 8 x 1½" Fh woodscrews
(2) ¼" x 4" lag screws
(1) ⅜" x 7" carriage bolt
(1) ⅜" washer
(1) ⅜" lock nut

CUTTING DIAGRAM

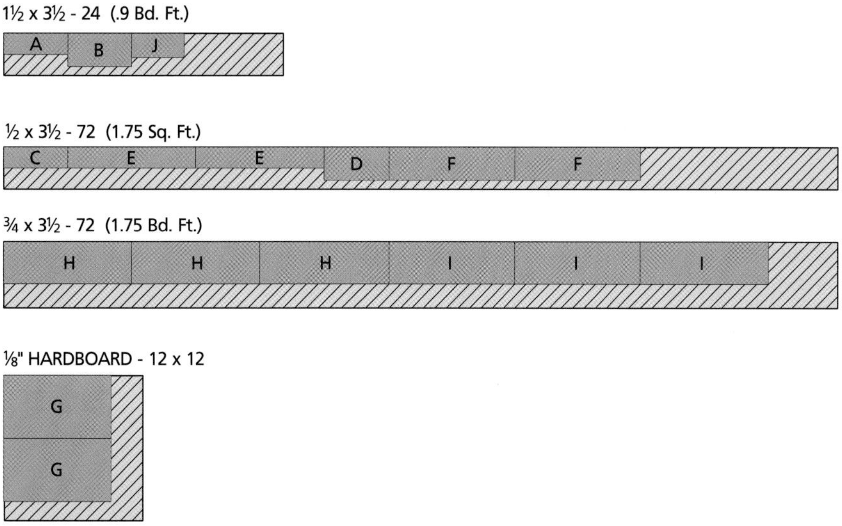

1½ x 3½ - 24 (.9 Bd. Ft.)

A	B	J

½ x 3½ - 72 (1.75 Sq. Ft.)

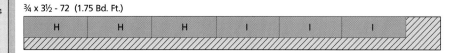

C	E	E	D	F	F

¾ x 3½ - 72 (1.75 Bd. Ft.)

H	H	H	I	I	I

⅛" HARDBOARD - 12 x 12

G
G

To build the caddy, start by making the two trays. The upper tray is shallow, while the bottom tray is deeper.

The only unusual thing is that the front of each tray is thicker than the sides and the back. This provides extra strength for the carriage bolt that passes through the fronts of the trays as a pivot pin.

FRONTS. The first step is to make the $1\frac{1}{2}$"-thick fronts (A, B). The length of both fronts is the same ($5\frac{1}{2}$"). The only difference is the width (height) of these pieces *(Fig. 1)*.

BACKS AND SIDES. With the fronts cut to size, the next step is to make the backs and sides. To keep the trays as light as possible, I cut the backs (C, D) and sides (E, F) from $\frac{1}{2}$" stock *(Fig. 1)*.

RABBETS. Next, the ends of the sides (E, F) are rabbeted to accept the fronts and backs. All the rabbets are $\frac{1}{4}$" deep, but since the fronts and backs are different thicknesses, make sure the widths of the rabbets match these pieces *(Fig. 1)*.

GROOVE. With the rabbets complete, cut $\frac{1}{8}$"-deep grooves on the inside faces of the fronts, backs, and sides to hold the $\frac{1}{8}$" hardboard bottoms *(Fig. 1a)*.

To determine the size of the bottom (G), dry-assemble a tray. Then measure the inside length and width and add $\frac{1}{4}$" to each dimension. Next, cut two bottoms to this size and glue up the five pieces for each tray *(Fig. 1)*.

TOP COVER & BASE

After you've glued up the trays, work can begin on the top cover (H) and base (I). These pieces are wider than the trays. This extra width is used to mount the caddy to the drill press column.

Start by edge-gluing enough $\frac{3}{4}$"-thick stock to form two blanks *(Fig. 2)*.

The length of the top cover and base is the same as the length of the trays (11"). But to allow the caddy to fit around the drill press column, the top cover and base are cut $4\frac{1}{2}$" wider than the trays ($10\frac{1}{2}$") *(Fig. 2)*.

NOTCHES. A section of the top cover becomes the clamp used to hold the caddy to the drill press column. To make this clamp, first lay out a circle on both blanks. Then rip the top cover and base through the center of the circle (to a width of 8") *(Fig. 2a)*.

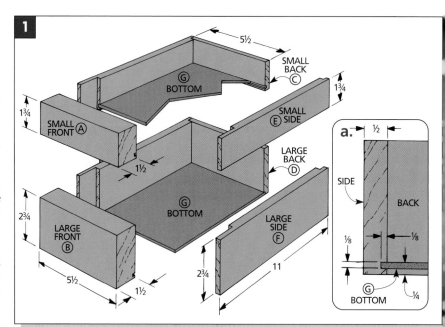

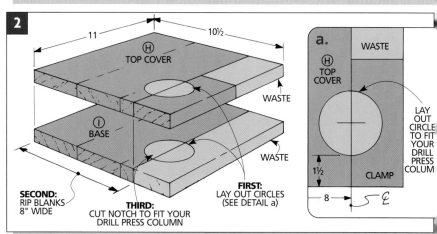

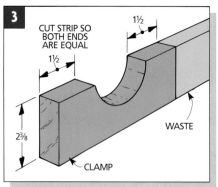

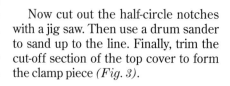

Now cut out the half-circle notches with a jig saw. Then use a drum sander to sand up to the line. Finally, trim the cut-off section of the top cover to form the clamp piece *(Fig. 3)*.

MOUNTING HOLES

The only thing left is to drill holes for the lag screws that attach the clamp to the top cover. To make sure that these holes are aligned, lay out the hole locations on both the top cover and clamp at the same time *(Fig. 4)*.

When drilling the holes, an auxiliary fence on the drill press table helps support the workpiece. With the fence in place, drill two $\frac{1}{4}$" shank holes through the clamp *(Fig. 5)*. Then, drill two $\frac{3}{16}$" pilot holes in the top cover *(Fig. 5a)*.

The top cover, trays, and base are joined with a long carriage bolt. This bolt serves as a pivot pin that allows the trays to swing out.

PIVOT HOLES. To make sure all the holes for the carriage bolt align in all the pieces, I used a simple positioning jig. It's just a pair of cleats clamped to the drill press table *(Figs. 6 and 7)*.

To position the cleats, first mark the location of the hole on one of the trays *(Fig. 6a)*. Then position a drill bit directly over the mark and clamp the cleats along the front and side of the tray *(Fig. 6)*.

Next, drill a hole in each tray. Then without moving the positioning cleats, drill holes through the top cover and the base *(Fig. 7)*.

STOP BLOCK. To keep the trays aligned when they're closed and to tie the top cover and base together, I added a stop block (J).

This block is cut from $1\frac{1}{2}$"-thick stock, and its length is the same as the combined height of the trays ($4\frac{1}{2}$") *(Fig. 8)*. To determine the width of the block, subtract the width of the trays from the width of the top cover (in my case, this was 2").

CHAMFERS. Before assembly, I eased the sharp edges by routing $\frac{1}{8}$" chamfers on all the parts. Then I wiped on two coats of tung oil finish.

ASSEMBLY. Once the finish is dry, bolt the top cover, trays, and base together with a $\frac{3}{8}$" carriage bolt and a lock nut *(Fig. 8)*. Then position the stop (J) and screw it in place *(Fig. 8)*.

MOUNTING. All that's left is to mount the caddy to your drill press column. To do this, simply attach the clamp to the top cover (H) with a pair of 4"-long lag screws *(Fig. 9)*.

Note: If your drill press has a toothed rack along its column for raising and lowering the table, you will need to mount the clamp *above* the retaining ring *(Fig. 9)*.

Position the caddy at a comfortable and convenient height, and then tighten up the lag screws. ∎

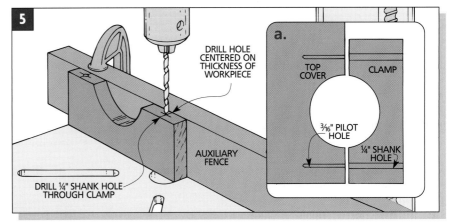

5

DRILL HOLE CENTERED ON THICKNESS OF WORKPIECE

AUXILIARY FENCE

DRILL $\frac{1}{4}$" SHANK HOLE THROUGH CLAMP

a. TOP COVER — CLAMP

$\frac{3}{16}$" PILOT HOLE

$\frac{1}{4}$" SHANK HOLE

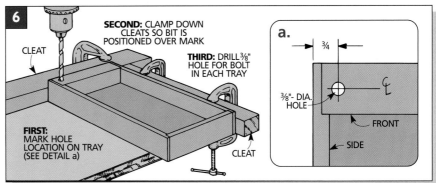

6

CLEAT

SECOND: CLAMP DOWN CLEATS SO BIT IS POSITIONED OVER MARK

THIRD: DRILL $\frac{3}{8}$" HOLE FOR BOLT IN EACH TRAY

FIRST: MARK HOLE LOCATION ON TRAY (SEE DETAIL a)

CLEAT

a. $\frac{3}{4}$

$\frac{3}{8}$"- DIA. HOLE

FRONT

SIDE

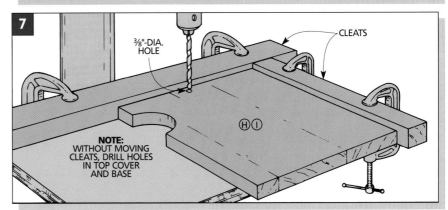

7

$\frac{3}{8}$"-DIA. HOLE

CLEATS

NOTE: WITHOUT MOVING CLEATS, DRILL HOLES IN TOP COVER AND BASE

(H)(I)

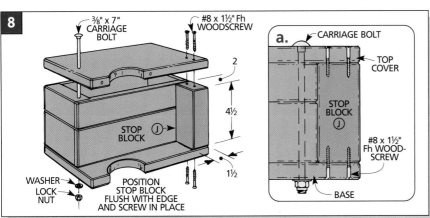

8

$\frac{3}{8}$" x 7" CARRIAGE BOLT

#8 x $1\frac{1}{2}$" Fh WOODSCREW

2

$4\frac{1}{2}$

$1\frac{1}{2}$

STOP BLOCK (J)

WASHER
LOCK NUT

POSITION STOP BLOCK FLUSH WITH EDGE AND SCREW IN PLACE

a. CARRIAGE BOLT

TOP COVER

STOP BLOCK (J)

#8 x $1\frac{1}{2}$" Fh WOOD-SCREW

BASE

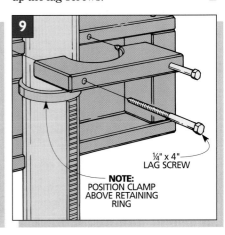

9

$\frac{1}{4}$" x 4" LAG SCREW

NOTE: POSITION CLAMP ABOVE RETAINING RING

Fitting a full complement of power tools into a small shop can be like packing a dozen sardines into a small tin. But it doesn't have to be that way. If the tools are selected and organized properly, you can have the tools and still have room to work. (For tips on how to arrange your tools once you've got them, see the Shop Info article about Shop Layout and Storage on page 12.)

SELECTING TOOLS

The key to selecting a power tool is to determine first how much use it'll get. If it's used a lot, go with a full-size stationary tool. If it'll only be used now and then, you can save space by choosing a benchtop tool that can be stored out of the way when not in use.

Shown here are the power tools I'd buy (in order) if I were outfitting a small shop today, starting from scratch.

Note: For those working in a really tight space, you might consider multipurpose or combination tools (see the bottom of the next page).

TABLE SAW

If I could only have one power tool in my shop, it would be a good quality contractor's table saw.

I use my table saw all the time to rip, crosscut, and miter workpieces. It's great for cutting rabbets and dadoes.

The large table top makes it easy and safe to cut sheet goods. And the flat table top can even be used when you're assembling the smaller parts of projects, such as doors and drawers.

Note: From time to time, you may need to move the saw around to make certain cuts. So it's also a good idea to invest in a set of casters or a mobile base. And check out the Saw Cabinet on pages 102-105 for a project that lets you store your saw's accessories conveniently.

DUST COLLECTOR

When working in a small, enclosed shop, you should be concerned about protecting your lungs from sawdust. (Refer to the Dust Control article on pages 50-51.) Since a table saw kicks up a lot of dust, your next purchase should be a two-stage dust collector to hook up to the saw.

Most small model two-stage dust collectors come with a quick-

disconnect hose that makes it easy for you to connect to other tools with the same mated connector. And many dust collectors also come with casters so you can roll them out of the way easily when they're not being used.

There are a number of reasonably priced dust collectors available. But if your budget is tight, a shop vacuum can also be used. It should do an adequate job of reducing dust in the air.

ROUTER TABLE

I never realized how much of a necessity a router table was until I started using one. The router table in my shop gets used on practically every project I build.

Not only is it used for routing decorative profiles, but it's also great for routing rabbets, dadoes, and box joints. And with special router bits, you can even rout raised panels.

Although in many cases a hand-held router could also get the job done, I'm more comfortable with the control the router table offers with its larger table top, adjustable fence, and miter gauge. (Plans for a portable Benchtop Router Table begin on page 70.)

DRILL PRESS

Depending on how small your home workshop is, you may not be able to go much further than the table saw, some sort of dust collection system and a router table.

But if you're going use your shop quite a bit and build a lot of different furniture projects, you'll be glad in the long run if you add more tools for extra versatility. The next tool I'd buy for a small shop would be a drill press. There are a couple of ways you can go here.

If you're only going to use a drill press for drilling holes, you might consider a small, benchtop model (see the photo on the opposite page). When it's not in use, you'll be able to lift it and store it out of the way in a corner or down under a workbench.

But if you're going to drill a lot of holes, mortises, or use the drill press to do sanding, you might consider a larger, full-size model. It only takes a bit more space, plus you'll get a larger table top, a bigger motor, and a broader range of speeds to handle the work.

Whichever style you choose, the Drill Press Caddy on page 18 provides handy storage for bits and accessories.

THICKNESS PLANER

Having a thickness planer in the shop gives you more freedom and control. It means you won't always be limited to only the lumber thicknesses available at your local lumberyard. And there are times when you can actually save some money by buying your rough stock directly from a sawmill and then planing it to final thickness yourself.

A thickness planer used to be found only in a professional cabinet shop. But the introduction of portable benchtop models made them affordable to most woodworkers.

You can choose from a number of quality 10" and 12" benchtop thickness planers that should handle most of your planing needs.

COMPOUND-MITER SAW

A radial arm saw is a great tool for crosscutting and mitering. But they take up a lot of space. And they're not portable.

Compound-miter saws, on the other hand, are both compact and easy to move. Miter saws have been used primarily by trim and finish carpenters because of their portability and accuracy. But they're starting to find their way into many workshops — for the same reasons. Although smaller, you'll find that a good compound-miter saw will cost about the same as a radial arm saw. (You'll find a great way to improve the performance of any 10" miter

saw with the portable Miter Saw Station that begins on page 52.)

BAND SAW

My final tool of choice for the small shop is the band saw. A band saw is great to have around if you're going to cut a lot of curves and circles. Or if you plan to resaw lumber — which can save you money when you need thin stock.

Again, like the other tools, determine how much use a band saw will get and how much room you have available.

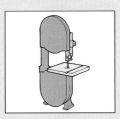

If you think you'll use a band saw a lot, choose a full-size model and add a mobile base. If it's only going to be used occasionally, a benchtop model will work just fine, and it will cost a lot less than a full-size saw.

MULTI-PURPOSE TOOLS

Another space-saving measure when you're working in a small shop is to select a power tool that can do more than one job.

A multi-purpose machine combines five tools or more into one (see photo below). This particular version combines a table saw, lathe, drill press, disc sander and shaper. Accessories allow for a jointer, band saw, planer and other tools to be added.

Features vary from one manufacturer to another, as does price. But they all provide a lot of woodworking in a small space. One trade-off is that setting up different operations isn't as efficient as it is with individual tools. For example, you may not be able to leave the table saw set up when you need to switch to the drill press.

You'll pay more initially for this type of machine, but it may be less than the total price of a shop full of stand-alone tools. Multi-purpose machine manufacturers are listed on page 126.

Another small shop option that's worth considering is a combination tool (see photo at right). With this type of

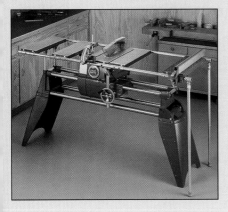

machine, you'll typically find a jointer combined with a planer or a disk sander combined with a belt sander. A combination tool like this has a smaller "footprint" than the two separate tools and can even be stored out of the way when it's not being used.

Revolving Parts Bin

Here's how to get thirty-two compartments in just over a square foot of bench space, and still have quick and easy access to everything. A lazy Susan lets you spin the bin to get to the parts you need.

One of the things that fascinated me as a kid was the circular nail bin at the local hardware store. I couldn't resist spinning the metal shelves and watching the piles of nails go by like a merry-go-round.

That same basic idea is what's behind this Revolving Parts Bin. Four separate tiers (with eight compartments each) help organize small parts and pieces of hardware. There are three different sizes of compartments to hold pieces of various sizes.

LAZY SUSAN. The bin rotates on a lazy Susan bearing. This lets you put the bin close to the wall and still have access to everything in it. If you've never installed a lazy Susan before, don't worry. A few screws are all it takes to fasten it to the bin.

PLYWOOD. Although a bin with this many compartments might seem a bit complicated to build, that's not the case. A 1/2"-thick plywood frame (I used Baltic birch) serves as a "backbone" that runs all the way through the parts bin. Then hardboard bottom pieces are added to establish the individual compartments. And to keep the contents from spilling out, thin hardwood strips are attached to the fronts.

ANGLES. The triangular compartments on the corners introduce some additional angles. Cutting the angles accurately on the pieces that form the bottoms of the compartments is automatic with a simple jig.

Then when it's time to miter the facing strips that wrap around the bin, a few test cuts (and some patience) will pay off with a nice, tight fit.

LABELS. With all those storage spaces, it would be easy to forget exactly what is stored where. To help keep things straight, I added a label holder in front of each compartment. If the contents of a bin change, the label can be changed easily as well.

EXPLODED VIEW

OVERALL DIMENSIONS:
12½W x 13D x 17³⁄₁₆H

A SIDE PANEL
EDGING
I
C WING
D
CENTER
BOTTOM
PIECE
B
CENTER
DIVIDER
EDGING
I
C
WING
J
BASE
E
SIDE
BOTTOM
PIECE
12"-DIA.
LAZY SUSAN
F
CORNER BOTTOM
PIECES
H
SHORT FACING STRIP
G
LONG FACING
STRIP

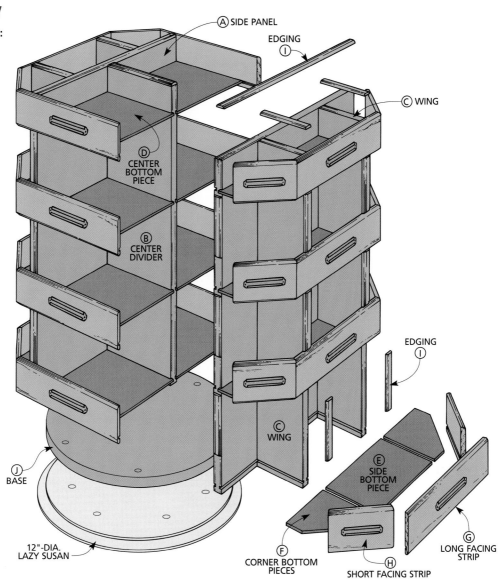

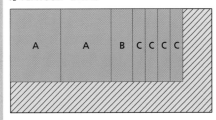

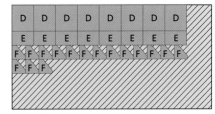

MATERIALS LIST

WOOD

A	Side Panel (2)	¾ ply - 16⅞ x 12
B	Center Divider (1)	¾ ply - 16⅞ x 5
C	Wings (4)	¾ ply - 16⅞ x 3
D	Ctr. Btm. Pieces (8)	⅛ hdbd. - 5¼ x 6
E	Side Btm. Pieces (8)	⅛ hdbd. - 3¼ x 5¼
F	Crnr. Btm. Pcs. (16)	⅛ hdbd. - 3¼ x 3¼
G	Lg. Fcng. Strips (16)	¼ x 2 - 7⅞ rough
H	Sh. Fcng. Strips (16)	¼ x 2 - 3½ rough
I	Edging	⅛ x ¾ - 9 ft. rough
J	Base (1)	½ ply - 11¼ dia.

HARDWARE SUPPLIES

(4) No. 10 x ⅝" Rh sheet-metal screws
(8) No. 6 x 1" Fh woodscrews
(42) 1" wire brads
(1) 12"-dia. lazy Susan
(32) 2½"-long label holders w/ tacks

CUTTING DIAGRAM

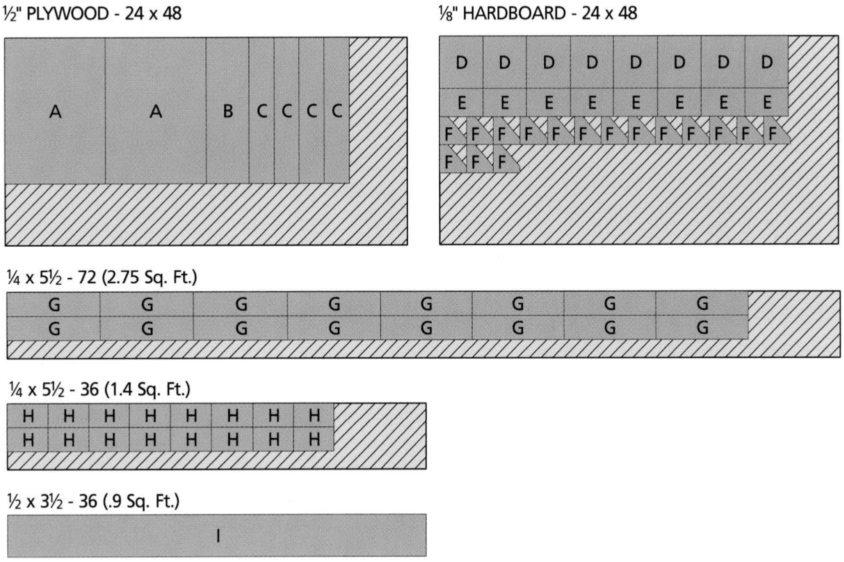

½" PLYWOOD - 24 x 48
A A B C C C C
⅛" HARDBOARD - 24 x 48
D D D D D D D D
E E E E E E E E
F F F F F F F F F F F F F
F F F
¼ x 5½ - 72 (2.75 Sq. Ft.)
G G G G G G G G
G G G G G G G G
¼ x 5½ - 36 (1.4 Sq. Ft.)
H H H H H H H H
H H H H H H H H
½ x 3½ - 36 (.9 Sq. Ft.)
I

FRAME

The core of the frame is an H-shaped assembly with two "wings" sticking out on each side *(Fig. 1b)*. This frame defines eight columns. To divide each of these columns into four compartments, grooves are cut in each side of the frame pieces to accept hardboard bottom pieces (refer to *Fig. 3*).

GROOVES. To get these grooves to align, it's best to cut them before cutting the individual frame pieces to size. Start with a piece of plywood the same width (height) as the frame ($16^7/8''$) *(Fig. 2)*. And to allow "extra" for the saw kerfs when cutting the frame pieces to size, I cut it to a rough length of 43''.

Now it's simply a matter of forming the grooves on both sides of the plywood *(Fig. 1a)*. The grooves are just shallow kerfs cut with the table saw.

Note: In most cases, $1/8''$ hardboard will fit the width of a saw kerf. But before cutting the grooves in the plywood blank, make a cut in a scrap piece to test the fit.

To make sure the grooves line up on opposite faces, position the rip fence to cut the first groove. After making the cut on one face of the panel, flip the panel end-for-end and cut a matching groove on the opposite face. Then you can adjust the fence for the next groove and repeat the process.

CUT PIECES. Once the grooves are complete, cut the two side panels (A), a center divider (B), and the four wings (C) to final length *(Fig. 2)*.

Note: The length is the measurement running *with* the grain. So all the frame pieces are wider ($16^7/8''$) than they are long.

ASSEMBLY

At this point, the frame is ready to be assembled. To make it easy to fit wood fronts on the bin later, the idea is to make one side of the frame a mirror image of the other.

To do this, I started by gluing and nailing two wings (C) to each side panel (A). The Shop Tip at right shows a trick that will make sure the wings are positioned properly. It's also important that the wings are square to the face of the side panels.

Once the wings are fastened to the side panels, glue and nail these two assemblies to the center divider (B).

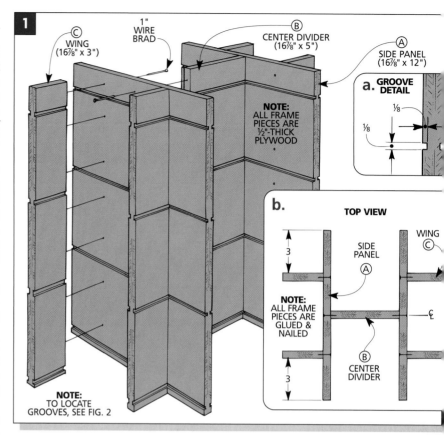

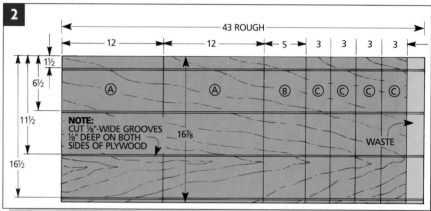

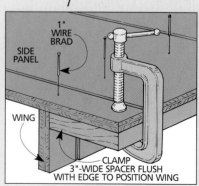

SHOP TIP . . . . *Spacer Block*

You could use a ruler to measure and mark the location of each wing, but that introduces several chances for errors.

Using a spacer solves that problem. Simply clamp it flush with the edge of the side panel, then press the wing against it.

A piece of scrap under the opposite end of the side panel will provide a stable and level surface while driving the nails.

The center divider should be centered exactly along the lengths of the side panels *(Fig. 1b)*.

BOTTOM PIECES. With the frame complete, you're ready to add the bottom pieces *(Figs. 3 and 3a)*. Each tier has three different size bottoms made from $1/8$"-thick hardboard: two large center bottoms (D), two smaller side bottoms (E), and four corner bottom pieces (F) *(Fig. 3)*.

Cutting the rectangular bottom pieces (D and E) is fairly straightforward *(Fig. 3a)*. They're cut to fit between the grooves and allow a $1/8$" overhang at the front. (This overhang fits into a groove in the facing strips that are added later.)

ANGLED CUTS. But making the angled cuts on the small corner pieces (F) is a bit trickier. To do this safely, I used a simple sled that carries the pieces through the saw blade at a 45° angle (see the Shop Jig below).

After cutting all the bottom pieces, it's simply a matter of gluing them tightly into the grooves cut in the frame. I glued in all of the side and center pieces first, then finished up with the corner pieces.

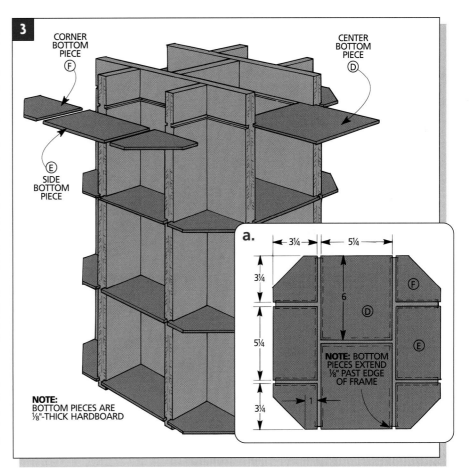

SHOP JIG .... *Corner Sled*

Cutting 16 identical corner pieces for the Revolving Parts Bin would be next to impossible without a jig to help you. This simple sled carries the piece past the blade, making it easy to form the 45° angle on one corner.

BASE. The base is just a 6"-wide piece of hardboard with two narrow strips attached to form a 90° corner. Start by cutting the base to size. Then rip a couple of 1"-wide hardboard strips that will be used to form the "cradle."

LAYOUT. Next, use a combination square to draw a layout line on the base at a 45° angle to one edge (see drawing). Glue one of the hardboard strips to the base, aligned with this mark. This is the first side of the cradle.

Once the glue is dry, use a square to position the second strip at a 90° angle to the first (see drawing).

CUT BLANKS. To make the corner pieces, cut 16 square blanks ($3^1/4$" x $3^1/4$"). You can check their size by dry-assembling the center and side bottom pieces (D, E) in the frame. The edges of the corner bottoms (F) should align with the edges of the side and center pieces (refer to *Fig. 3a* above).

CUT THE ANGLES. To use the jig, one side of the sled rides against the rip fence as the jig carries the corner piece past the saw blade (see drawing).

Setting the corner pieces in the sled automatically positions them so they're 45° to the saw blade. But you still need to adjust the rip fence to end up with two 1"-wide "ears" (see detail 'a').

What works well here is to start by taking an extra-wide cut. Then reposition the fence closer to the blade and sneak up on the final width of cut. (You'll be trimming the sled at the same time, but don't worry about this.) Once the fence is set, cut the corner pieces.

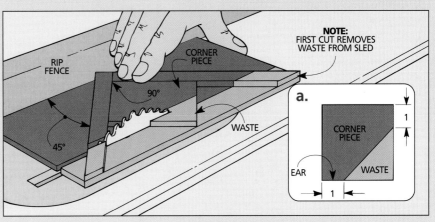

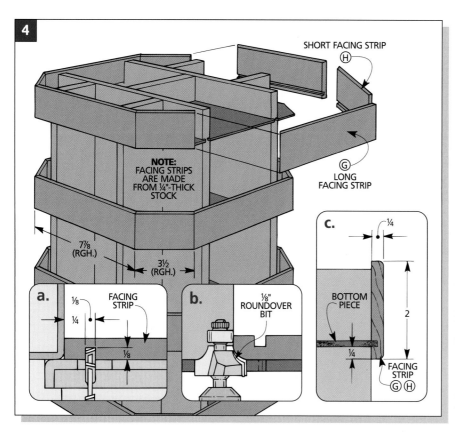

4

SHORT FACING STRIP
(H)

NOTE:
FACING STRIPS
ARE MADE
FROM ¼"-THICK
STOCK

LONG
FACING STRIP
(G)

7⅞
(RGH.)

3½
(RGH.)

a.
⅛
¼
FACING
STRIP
⅛

b.
⅛"
ROUNDOVER
BIT

c.
¼
BOTTOM
PIECE
2
¼
FACING
STRIP
(G) (H)

SHOP TIP
Hide Glue

There are a lot of facing strips to glue on to the parts bin. To provide more working time when positioning them, I used slow-setting liquid hide glue.

FACING STRIPS

At this point, the compartments have taken shape. But to keep hardware from spilling out of the front of them, each tier is "wrapped" with wood facing strips *(Fig. 4)*.

These strips are ¼"-thick pieces of hard maple that are mitered on the ends where they come together. To fit over the bottom pieces, there's a groove on the inside face of each strip.

Here again, it's easiest to cut these grooves before making the individual strips. So start by ripping about 18 linear feet of ¼"-thick stock to width. This provides enough material for all the facing strips and a bit extra for making a couple of test pieces.

Now just cut the grooves to fit the bottoms *(Figs. 4a and 4c)*. Before cutting the strips to length, I softened the sharp corners on the outside by routing roundovers on the top and bottom edges *(Fig. 4b)*.

MITERS. At this point, you're ready to

cut the miters on the ends of the facing strips. There are two things that affect the fit of these miters: the angle of the blade and the length of the strips.

ANGLE. Since there are eight strips on each tier, you'll need to tilt the saw blade to make a $22^1/_2°$ cut *(Fig. 5a)*. An easy way to check this angle is to cut miters on the ends of two test pieces. If they fit together tightly when held against the frame, you can concentrate on cutting the facing strips to length.

LENGTH. Each tier has four long facing strips (G) and four short strips (H) *(Fig. 4)*. Determining the length of these pieces to get a good fit all the way around each tier is a trial and error process. But it's easier than it sounds.

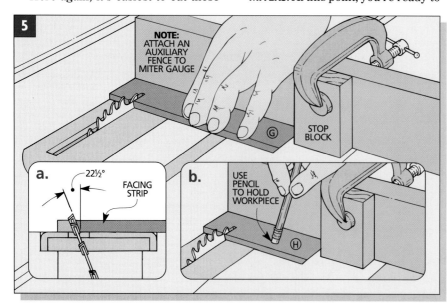

5

NOTE:
ATTACH AN
AUXILIARY
FENCE TO
MITER GAUGE

STOP
BLOCK

(G)

a. 22½°
FACING
STRIP

b. USE
PENCIL
TO HOLD
WORKPIECE
(H)

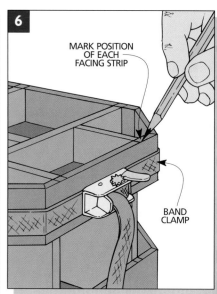

6

MARK POSITION
OF EACH
FACING STRIP

BAND
CLAMP

Rather than fitting them one by one, the idea here is to get all eight strips to fit together at the same time. To make this work, each long (or short) piece needs to be the exact same length.

To sneak up on the final length, I started by cutting all the strips 1/8" longer than needed *(Fig. 4)*. Clamping a stop block to an auxiliary fence attached to the miter gauge ensures accuracy *(Fig. 5)*. And a pencil makes a handy hold-down *(Fig. 5b)*.

After test-fitting the strips (I used a band clamp to help hold them in place) you may need to trim off a bit. Just be sure you cut all the long (or short) pieces to the same length. Since you'll be trimming four pieces, make the adjustments very small.

Once you're satisfied with the fit, it's a good idea to mark the location of each strip *(Fig. 6)*. This makes it easy to reposition them during glue-up.

EDGING. With the facing strips in place, I covered the exposed plywood edges of the frame with thin strips of hardwood edging (maple) *(Fig. 7)*.

But cutting these strips safely on the table saw can be a challenge. So I started by planing a wide workpiece to the same thickness as the plywood. Then after rounding over the edges *(Fig. 8a)*, I ripped a 1/8"-wide strip so it falls to the waste side of the blade *(Figs. 8 and 8b)*. Then simply repeat the process until you have about ten linear feet of edging.

Now it's just a matter of cutting short pieces of edging (I) to fit and gluing them in place. Since it's difficult to clamp these pieces, I used masking tape to secure them while the glue dried.

HARDWARE

There are just two things left to do to complete the parts bin. Add a lazy Susan bearing so you can spin it around. And attach label holders to tell you what's inside each compartment.

LAZY SUSAN. To provide a mounting platform for the lazy Susan, an 11¼"-dia. plywood base (J) is screwed to the bottom of the frame *(Fig. 9)*. Then the bearing is screwed in place.

LABEL HOLDERS. Finally, label holders are tacked to the front of each compartment, centered on the compartment's width. But because you're going into hardwood, be sure to drill pilot holes first.

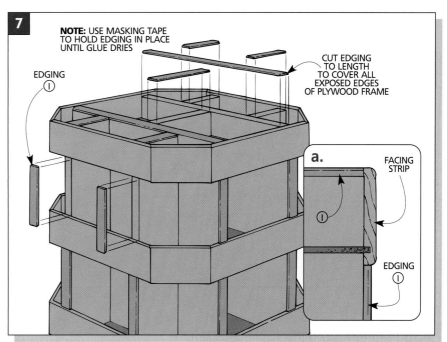

7

NOTE: USE MASKING TAPE TO HOLD EDGING IN PLACE UNTIL GLUE DRIES

CUT EDGING TO LENGTH TO COVER ALL EXPOSED EDGES OF PLYWOOD FRAME

EDGING (I)

a.

FACING STRIP

EDGING (I)

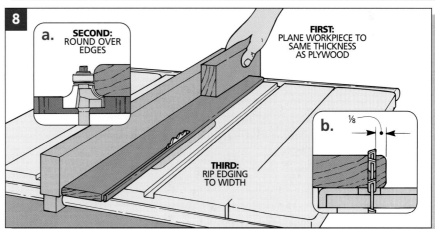

8

a. SECOND: ROUND OVER EDGES

FIRST: PLANE WORKPIECE TO SAME THICKNESS AS PLYWOOD

b. 1/8

THIRD: RIP EDGING TO WIDTH

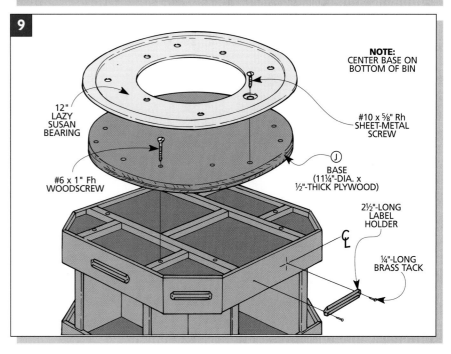

9

NOTE: CENTER BASE ON BOTTOM OF BIN

12" LAZY SUSAN BEARING

#10 x 5/8" Rh SHEET-METAL SCREW

#6 x 1" Fh WOODSCREW

BASE (11¼"-DIA. x 1/2"-THICK PLYWOOD) (J)

2½"-LONG LABEL HOLDER

¼"-LONG BRASS TACK

Sandpaper Storage

With this storage box that can be built from scrap, your sander and a supply of sandpaper are always ready to go. There's also a simple jig that lets you size sandpaper quickly to fit your sander.

Whenever I use a finish sander I'm amazed at what a great timesaver it is. However, the time I save using the sander is usually lost trying to dig it out of a drawer, and then trying to locate the right grade of sandpaper and cut it to size.

Not any more. I designed a very simple system of flip-open sleeves to store pre-cut sheets of sandpaper. Each sleeve holds a separate grit of paper. And to hold the sleeves, I made a storage bin that also holds the sander. Now everything I need to start sanding is ready to go, right at my fingertips.

SLEEVES. The sleeve design is simple. It's a 3/4" plywood cover piece and a base of 1/4" hardboard, connected by a fabric "hinge." The sandpaper sits between the base and cover, like the meat in a sandwich. A half-circle cut in the cover provides an easy grip to pull out the sleeve you need.

SHEET SIZE. I made the sleeves to hold sandpaper for a quarter-sheet finish sander. However, by changing the size of the sleeves, they could be made to hold third sheets, half sheets, or even full sheets of sandpaper.

STORAGE BIN. Once I finished making the sleeves, I decided to make a bin to keep them in. The bin is sized to hold four sleeves, with plenty of room left over to hold my palm sander. By putting the sander on top of the bin, the weight helps keep the sandpaper flat. And four sleeves is enough to keep coarse through very-fine grades of paper at the ready.

CUTTING JIG. To save even more time, I made a simple jig to help me cut full sheets of sandpaper quickly down to the right size for my sander. It doesn't take long to make, and can probably be built from scrap. Plus you can alter the jig easily so it cuts paper to fit your sander. Details on this jig can be found on page 33.

EXPLODED VIEW

OVERALL DIMENSIONS:
6⅝W x 7D x 6H

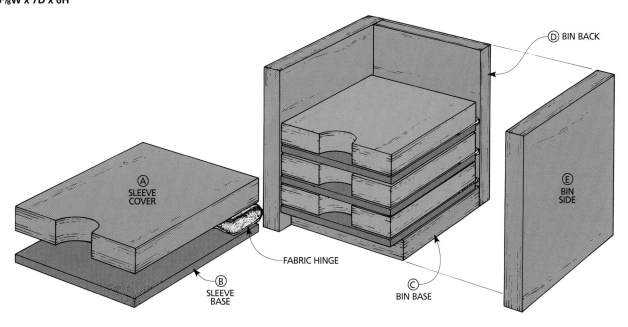

Ⓓ BIN BACK

Ⓐ SLEEVE COVER

Ⓔ BIN SIDE

FABRIC HINGE

Ⓑ SLEEVE BASE

Ⓒ BIN BASE

MATERIALS LIST

WOOD
A	Sleeve Covers (4)	¾ ply - 5 x 6
B	Sleeve Bases (4)	¼ hdbd. - 5 x 6
C	Bin Base (1)	¾ ply - 5⅛ x 5½
D	Bin Back (1)	¾ ply - 6 x 5⅛
E	Bin Sides (2)	¾ ply - 6 x 7

HARDWARE SUPPLIES
(1 piece) Canvas, 6" x 12" rough

CUTTING DIAGRAM

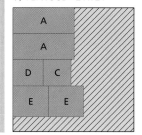

¾" PLYWOOD - 24 x 24

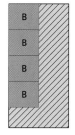

¼" HARDBOARD - 12 x 24

SHOP TIP .... *Curling Sandpaper*

The Sandpaper Storage unit is designed to keep your sandpaper flat. While this keeps things nice and neat, it can be a problem when it's time to load sandpaper onto the sander. This simple trick makes the job easier.

After pulling a sheet from the bin, lay the paper abrasive side down. Then lay a pencil on one of the edges that will be clamped in the sander and roll the edge of the sandpaper tightly around the pencil (see drawing).

When the paper is released, it will spring back with a nice semi-circular curve on the edge. Then curl the opposite end of the sandpaper.

After clamping one end in the sander, the other curled edge will be pointed right at the clamp (see drawing). Just smooth the paper across the pad, slide it under the clamp and you're ready to go.

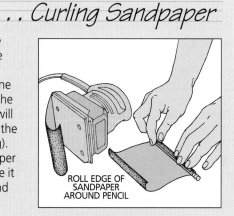

ROLL EDGE OF SANDPAPER AROUND PENCIL

To make the sleeves, first determine the size of sandpaper sheet you need. In my case, this is $4^1/_2$" x $5^1/_2$" (a quarter of a 9" x 11" sheet). Then add $^1/_2$" to both dimensions to get the finished sleeve size (5" x 6").

COVERS. After you've determined the size of the sleeve, you can cut out the $^3/_4$" plywood covers (A). To do this, cut a plywood blank 5" wide by $12^1/_8$" long. This is enough for two covers plus $^1/_8$" for the saw kerf. (Two blanks will make four sleeves.)

CUTOUTS. To make it easy to pull the sleeves out of the bin, each cover has a semi-circular cutout on the front edge. To make the cutouts, drill or cut a $1^1/_2$"-diameter hole in the center of the blank. (I used a Forstner bit.) Then cut the blank in half (*Fig. 1*).

BASES. Once the covers are cut to size, cut the bases (B) out of $^1/_4$" hardboard to match the covers (5" x 6") (*Fig. 2*). The only difference is that there are no cutouts in the bases.

FABRIC HINGE. With the bases cut, the next step is to glue on a fabric hinge that ties the base and cover together. (I used canvas for the hinge.)

Start by placing a $^1/_2$"-thick scrap block under the base (B) to keep it level with the cover (A) (*Fig. 3*). Then, align the bottom edges $^1/_2$" apart. This allows room for the sleeve to "expand" as sandpaper is placed in it.

Now apply glue to the bottom inside 1" of both pieces. Then place a $2^1/_2$"-wide piece of fabric over the glue so it's flush to the outside edges of the cover and base.

Note: If the canvas slides out of place slightly, it can be trimmed easily with a razor knife after the glue dries.

Finally, fold the sleeve so the edges of the cover and base are flush, and clamp the bottom edge until the glue dries (*Fig. 4*).

Note: There may be some glue squeeze-out as you clamp the pieces. To prevent the base and cover from being glued together, put a piece of wax paper between them.

STORAGE BIN

The sleeves provide a way to organize my sandpaper by grit. But I still needed a way to keep the sleeves themselves in order. So I made a simple storage bin

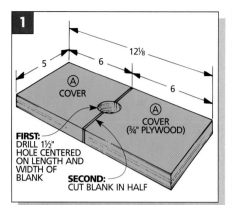

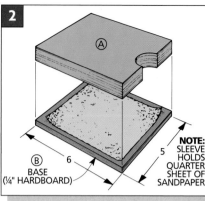

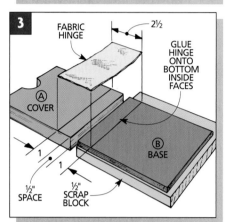

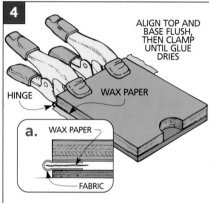

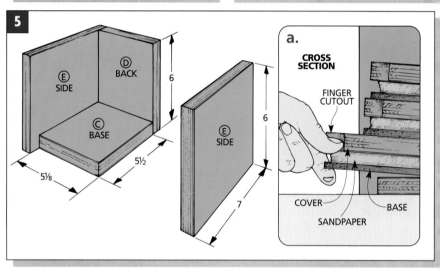

out of scrap plywood. And I sized it so there was room on top of the sleeves to set my palm sander.

BASE AND BACK. To make the storage bin, begin by cutting a $^3/_4$" plywood base (C) and back (D) slightly wider than the sleeves ($5^1/_8$"). Then trim the base (C) $^1/_2$" less than the length of the sleeve ($5^1/_2$"). (This allows room to get your finger under the bottom sleeve as shown in *Fig. 5a*.)

Now cut the back (D) 6" high. This height allows room for four sleeves plus some remaining height to "corral" the

sander. If you'll be making more than four sleeves, adjust the height of the back and sides accordingly.

SIDES. To complete the bin, cut two sides (E) to match the height of the back and 7" long (*Fig. 5*).

Finally, assemble the bin by gluing the back piece (D) behind the base (C) (*Fig. 5*). Then glue the sides (E) to the base (C) and back (D) (*Fig. 5*).

All that's left is to cut some sandpaper to size to fill the sleeves. The Shop Jig on the opposite page provides an easy and quick way to do this. ∎

SHOP JIG . . . . *Sandpaper Cutter*

Storing sandpaper is one thing; cutting it to size is another. I've sliced up my bench top cutting sandpaper with a utility knife. And trying to rip it seldom gives an even edge, or a piece that's the right size.

So it was frustration that led me to build this jig. The jig acts as a gauge to measure and cut quarter sheets of sandpaper to fit my finish sander. That helps me keep the Sandpaper Storage bin on the previous pages stocked, so I always have sandpaper ready to go when it's needed. (You can adjust the dimensions of the jig to fit your sander if it uses a different size sheet.)

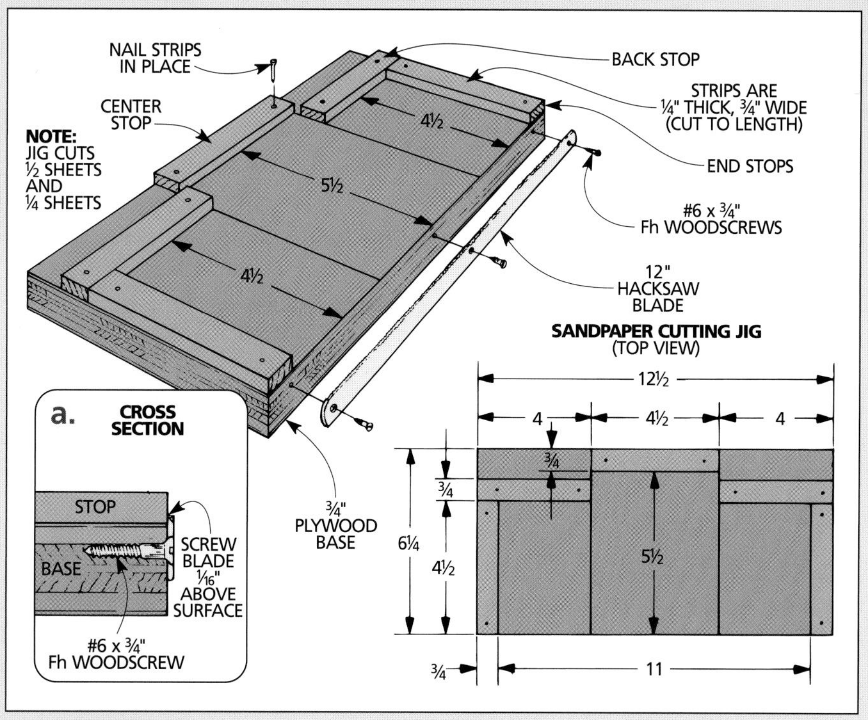

HOW IT WORKS. Using the jig is a two-step operation. First, a full (9" x 11") sheet of sandpaper is put into the jig and cut in half. Then the half sheets are turned 90° in the jig and cut in half again. So you end up with quarter-sheet (4½" x 5½") pieces of sandpaper with nice, neat edges.

MATERIALS. All that's needed for the jig is a piece of ¾" plywood for a base, five ¼"-thick stops, and a hacksaw blade (see drawing). You'll also need some screws to hold the blade, and a few small nails.

Start by ripping a 24" length of ¼"-thick stock to a width of ¾". Then from this blank, cut three 4½" lengths (for the end and center stops) and two 4" lengths (for the back stops).

To make the base, cut the plywood to a finished size of 6¼" x 12½".

ATTACH THE STOPS. The next step is to nail an end stop flush with one end and the front edge of the base (see drawing). Then use a square to help position the two back stops 4½" from the front edge of the base. Make sure you leave a 4½" gap between these pieces (see drawing).

Now, nail down the other end stop 11" from the first. These four stops are used to position a full sheet to tear it lengthwise (see *Step 2* below).

Once the paper is torn lengthwise, it needs to be torn in half again. That's why the center stop is positioned 5½" from the edge of the jig.

CUTTING EDGE. After the stops are nailed down, all that's needed to complete the jig is a cutting edge. This is a simple 12"-long hacksaw blade. Before fastening the blade to the jig, drill a hole centered on the blade's length to accept a screw. Countersink this hole and the existing holes at the ends of the blade (see detail 'a' in drawing and *Step 1* below).

Next, drill pilot holes and countersinks into the edge of the plywood base. Then secure the blade to the jig so it extends ¹⁄₁₆" above the edge (see detail 'a' in drawing).

USING THE JIG. Using the jig is easy. Refer to *Steps 2 and 3* below.

Drawing labels:

NAIL STRIPS IN PLACE

CENTER STOP

BACK STOP

STRIPS ARE ¼" THICK, ¾" WIDE (CUT TO LENGTH)

END STOPS

#6 x ¾" Fh WOODSCREWS

12" HACKSAW BLADE

NOTE: JIG CUTS ½ SHEETS AND ¼ SHEETS

4½   5½   4½

SANDPAPER CUTTING JIG
(TOP VIEW)

12½ — 4 — 4½ — 4
¾
6¼   4½   5½
¾   11

a. CROSS SECTION

STOP
BASE
SCREW
BLADE ¹⁄₁₆" ABOVE SURFACE
#6 x ¾" Fh WOODSCREW
¾" PLYWOOD BASE

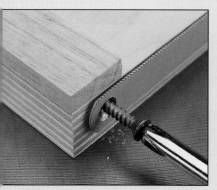

1 Before screwing the hacksaw blade to the front of the jig, countersink three mounting holes. Then position the blade's teeth slightly above the plywood base and screw it in place.

2 To make the first cut, place the sheet lengthwise between the two L-shaped stops. Hold the sheet in the jig with one hand while pulling down across the hacksaw blade with the other.

3 To cut the sandpaper to finished size, place the narrow end of the piece against the center stop. Hold it in place and tear the free end of the paper down across the hacksaw blade.

Overhead Racks

Take an afternoon to turn unused space above your head into storage for your lumber supply.
With these three easy racks, you'll be able to store even your longest stock out of the way.

About once a month or so, I have to take a day to clean up and organize my shop. It's usually the day after I've had trouble finding a particular tool (like my table saw) because it's buried under piles of lumber and cutoffs.

In a small shop, one of the reasons a mess starts to accumulate is because there is so little storage space — particularly for lumber. Most of my wall and floor space is already spoken for. As I mulled over the problem, I realized that just like a crowded city, sometimes the only way to go is up.

OVERHEAD RACKS. When you think about it, it's amazing how much storage space is available right above your head. This collection of simple racks is designed to hold your lumber in the space you aren't using above tools, your bench or anywhere else. And you can probably have all three built in an afternoon or evening.

LUMBER RACK. The first rack I built consisted of two pieces that looked like a couple of upside-down "Fs" (lower portion of photo). This rack is designed to hold longer lengths of lumber. (It's where I store my rough stock until I start a project.)

All the parts are cut from 2x6 lumber. The only hardware you'll need is a few screws, plus some lag screws or bolts to hang it. You'll need at least two arms to start (as shown above). If you need to store longer stock, add a third or even a fourth rack.

DOWEL RACK. The next storage rack I came up with was for my dowels (middle left in photo). It's just some sections of PVC pipe cut to length. You should be able to cut and mount this rack in a matter of minutes.

CUTOFF STORAGE. My last rack turned the space between the exposed joists into a place to keep my cutoffs and narrow lumber (top of photo). By spanning several joists with a few cleats, I created a series of compartments, perfect for sorting and storing cutoffs.

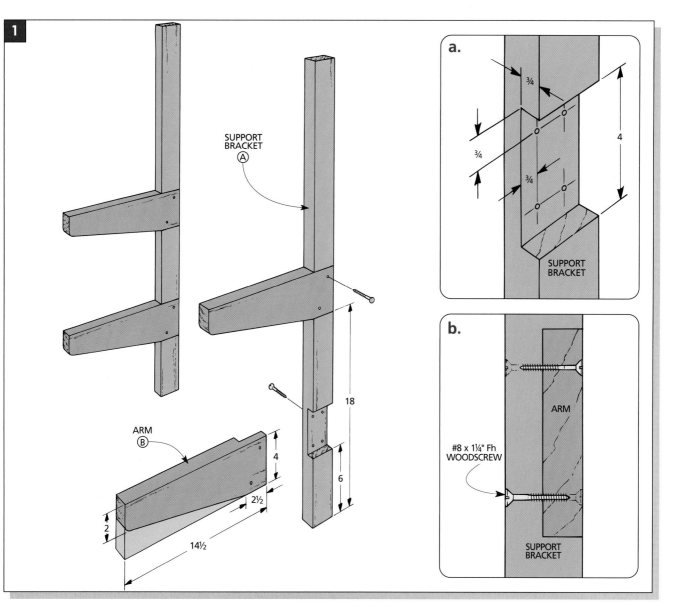

1

SUPPORT
BRACKET
Ⓐ

a.

¾
¾
¾
4

SUPPORT
BRACKET

ARM
Ⓑ

4

18

6

2½

2

14½

b.

ARM

#8 x 1¼" Fh
WOODSCREW

SUPPORT
BRACKET

LUMBER RACK

The lumber rack consists of three parts: a support bracket (A) and two identical arms (B) — all cut from "two-by" material *(Fig. 1)*.

The arms attach to the brackets with simple half-lap joints *(Fig. 1a)*. To cut this joint, I set up a ¾"-wide dado blade in my table saw. Set the height to exactly half of the thickness of the support bracket. Then, using the miter gauge to help guide the piece, make a pass to define the outside edge of each half-lap. Finally, make several more passes to remove the waste.

Once all the half-laps are cut, the arms are cut to final shape and then glued and screwed in place *(Fig. 1)*.

Note: I drove in a pair of screws from each side *(Fig. 1b)*.

CUTTING DIAGRAM

1½ x 5½ - 48 (2.75 Bd. Ft.)

A
A

NOTE: CLEATS (C) USED
FOR CUTOFF STORAGE RACK.
SEE PAGE 36.

1½ x 5½ - 72 (4.1 Bd. Ft.)

B   B   B   B

MATERIALS LIST

WOOD
A Support Brackets (2) 1½ x 2½ - 40
B Arms (4)   1½ x 4 - 14½
C Cleats (3)   ¾ x 5½ - cut to fit

HARDWARE SUPPLIES
(6) No. 8 x 1" Rh woodscrews
(16) No. 8 x 1¼" Fh woodscrews

(*) No. 8 x 1½" Fh woodscrews
*(4) ⁵⁄₁₆" x 5½" lag screws
*(4 or 8) ⁵⁄₁₆" washers
*(4) ⁵⁄₁₆" x 4½" hex bolts
*(4) ⁵⁄₁₆" nuts
(1) 6"-dia. PVC pipe, 12" long
*Depends on mounting configuration.
See page 36 for details.

Secured to the wall or to the ceiling, the Lumber Rack will keep your stock out from underfoot.

RACK MOUNTING OPTIONS

The lumber rack can be wall-mounted or fastened to exposed ceiling joists.

WALL. If you're mounting the rack to a finished wall, the first thing you need to do is locate the studs. Then drill pilot holes through the arms, and screw each rack to a stud with lag screws and washers *(Fig. 1)*.

If you're mounting the rack to a concrete or block wall, be sure to use the appropriate anchors and bolts to support the weight.

CEILING. The rack can also be hung from the ceiling *(Fig. 2)*. For this, all you have to do is drill holes through the joists and the rack for bolts.

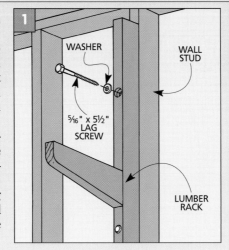

WASHER

WALL STUD

$\frac{5}{16}$" x $5\frac{1}{2}$" LAG SCREW

LUMBER RACK

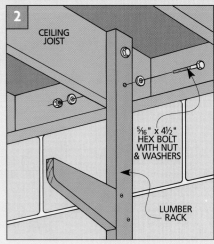

CEILING JOIST

$\frac{5}{16}$" x $4\frac{1}{2}$" HEX BOLT WITH NUT & WASHERS

LUMBER RACK

DOWEL RACK

One way to keep dowels organized and out of the way is with this joist-mounted dowel rack *(Fig. 2)*.

The dowel rack is nothing more than three 4"-long rings of 6"-dia. PVC pipe. After cutting the PVC with a hacksaw, lightly sand the sharp edges.

Finally, drill a couple of holes in each ring and then screw them in line to a ceiling joist *(Fig. 2a)*.

Note: To help me find the right size dowel, I use a marker to write the diameter on the end of the dowel.

CUTOFF STORAGE

The third overhead rack takes advantage of the space between exposed joists to store and organize cutoffs.

The organizer is just several rows of cleats screwed to the joists to form a lattice *(Fig. 3)*. (I used 1x6s.)

To make it easy to slide pieces in, rout $\frac{3}{8}$" roundovers on the long edges of the cleats *(Fig. 3a)*.

When you're positioning the cleats, make sure to leave enough room at one end to get the cutoffs in and out. ∎

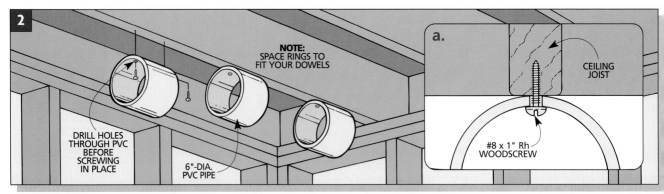

NOTE: SPACE RINGS TO FIT YOUR DOWELS

DRILL HOLES THROUGH PVC BEFORE SCREWING IN PLACE

6"-DIA. PVC PIPE

a. CEILING JOIST

#8 x 1" Rh WOODSCREW

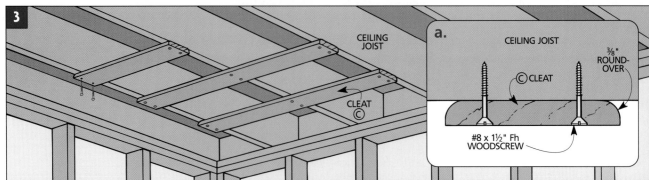

CEILING JOIST

CLEAT Ⓒ

a. CEILING JOIST

Ⓒ CLEAT

$\frac{3}{8}$" ROUND-OVER

#8 x $1\frac{1}{2}$" Fh WOODSCREW

Wall-Mounted Bins

This shop storage system features removable bins so you can take them wherever you need them. Options include a handy tote so you can carry several bins at once, and even a tape dispenser.

Storage that moves — that's the idea behind this system. Take a bin, hook it into strips mounted to the wall, or carry it right to your worksite. It couldn't be easier. But how do those bins stay in place?

RAILS. The hanging system may fool you at first glance. The bins don't actually hang from the wall. They sit on the rail below them. The rail above the bin simply traps the bin's back to keep it from falling forward. To remove a bin, just lift it slightly, then pivot the bottom out (see inset photo).

BINS. After seeing how many bins this system holds, your first question

may be how to cut all those pieces. The secret is to set up an "assembly line" to cut all of the same-size parts one after another. To keep the total parts to a minimum, I limited myself to two bin sizes.

BUILD TO FIT. In addition to the organized storage, another benefit of the Wall-Mounted Bins is that you can size it to fit the space you have available.

ACCESSORIES. I designed this system so I could add accessories. The first one I built was a portable carrier to hold several bins. Then by modifying the design of one of the larger bins, I added a tool bin to the carrier. (These items are on the bottom row in the main photo

above.) Another option is to convert bins for specialized uses, such as holding rolls of tape. (My tape dispenser is on the left end of the second row in the main photo). The Designer's Notebook on pages 42 and 43 has more about building these accessories.

EXPLODED VIEW

OVERALL DIMENSIONS:
48W x 8D x 26H

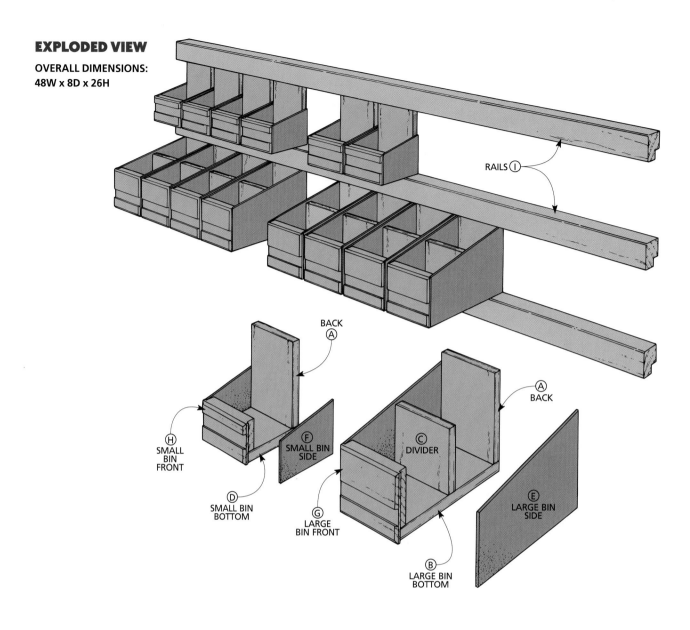

RAILS ⓘ

BACK
Ⓐ

Ⓐ
BACK

Ⓗ
SMALL
BIN
FRONT

Ⓕ
SMALL BIN
SIDE

Ⓒ
DIVIDER

Ⓓ
SMALL BIN
BOTTOM

Ⓖ
LARGE
BIN FRONT

Ⓔ
LARGE BIN
SIDE

Ⓑ
LARGE BIN
BOTTOM

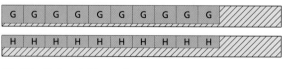

MATERIALS LIST

WOOD*

A	Backs	½ ply - 3½ x 4⅜
B	Large Bin Bottoms	½ ply - 3½ x 7¾
C	Dividers	½ ply - 3½ x 3
D	Small Bin Bottoms	½ ply - 3½ x 3¾
E	Large Bin Sides	⅛ hdbd. - 4⁵⁄₁₆ x 7¾
F	Small Bin Sides	⅛ hdbd. - 2⅝ x 3¾
G	Large Bin Fronts	¾ x 3 - 3¾
H	Small Bin Fronts	¾ x 2 - 3¾
I	Rails	1½ x 1½ - cut to fit

HARDWARE SUPPLIES*

No. 8 x 3½" Fh woodscrews
⅝"-long No. 18 brads (18 per large bin
with divider, 14 per large bin without
divider, 12 per small bin)

* Quantities depend on number of bins to
be built.

CUTTING DIAGRAM

⅛" HARDBOARD - 24 x 48

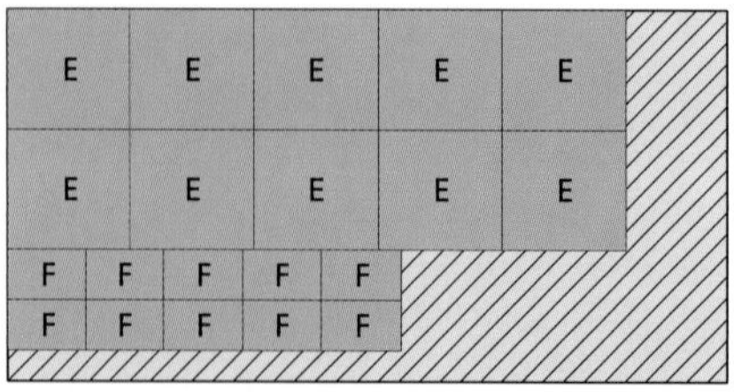

½" PLYWOOD - 24 x 48

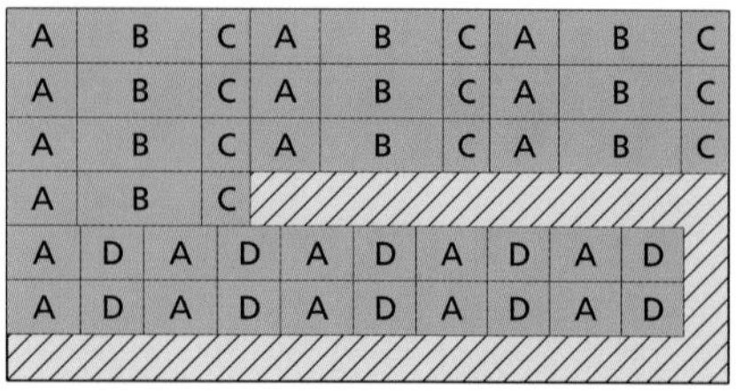

¾ x 3½ - 48

1½ x 5½ - 48 (Length May Vary)

NOTE: CUTTING DIAGRAM
ALLOWS FOR CONSTRUCTION
OF 10 SMALL BINS
AND 10 LARGE BINS

BOTTOMS & BACKS

Before making the bins, you have to determine how many of each size you want. To help you figure your needs, each bin takes about 4" of lineal wall space and each pair of rails is 7⅝" from top to bottom. Once you know how many bins you'll need, a plywood blank is cut for each bin.

PLYWOOD PIECES. For every large bin, it takes a strip of plywood about 16" long, and for every small bin a strip about 9" long (refer to the Cutting Diagram on the opposite page). Each strip is 3½" wide.

Here's your first chance to take advantage of a machine setup to cut a number of pieces. First, set up the table saw to rip the strips to finished width. Then cut them all to rough length.

Note: If you won't be using a divider in a long bin, the strip for that bin only needs to be about 13" long.

After cutting all the strips you need for the bins, each long strip is cut into a back (A), bottom (B), and the optional divider (C), while each short strip is cut into a back (A) and bottom (D) (see the Cutting Diagram on the opposite page). Here again, once I was set up to make a cut, I cut that piece for each bin. Then I set up for the next piece.

SIDES

Once all the plywood pieces were cut to size, I stacked them up and moved on to the sides (E, F). The sides are cut from blanks of ⅛"-thick hardboard *(Fig. 1)*.

BLANKS. First, cut enough blanks to size. (You'll need one blank for each bin.) Then the blanks are cut into two pieces to form the tapered sides.

The tricky part is cutting each side to exactly the same size while keeping your fingers away from the saw blade.

STOP BLOCK. To solve this problem, I made a combination stop block and hold-down (see the Shop Tip at right). The stop block/hold-down is clamped to an auxiliary fence that's screwed to the miter gauge *(Fig. 2)*.

CUT THE SIDES. To cut the tapered sides, first set the miter gauge to make a 10° cut. (This angle isn't critical. Just get it close.)

Then position the stop to cut the correct width (3" for the large bins, 2" for the small bins) at the short end of the side piece *(Figs. 2 and 2a)*. An easy way to do this is to make a cut through the auxiliary fence first. You can then measure from the kerf in the fence to the shoulder of the rabbet in the stop block.

Now you can cut one side piece off the blank, then rotate the blank and cut

SHOP TIP
Stop Block

To make a combination stop block and hold-down, cut a shallow rabbet in a scrap of 2x4 (see drawing). So the block presses down firmly on the stock, the rabbet's depth should be just a hair less than the thickness of the hardboard you'll use for the bin sides.

Then, for an even better grip, glue a strip of medium grade (100 grit) sandpaper into the rabbet.

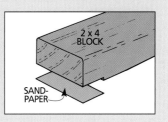

the mating side piece *(Fig. 2b)*.

To help me orient each blank properly for the second cut, I marked an "X" in the opposite corner *(Fig. 2)*.

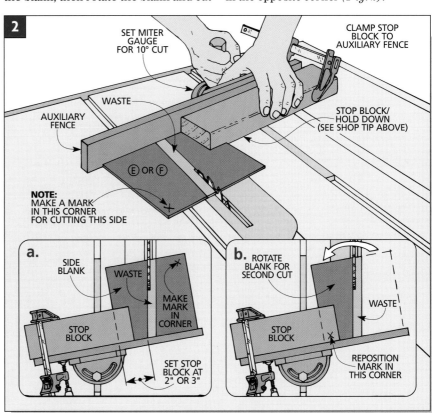

1

LARGE BIN BLANK

3

SIDE E | SIDE E

WASTE

7¾

8¼

10°

SMALL BIN BLANK

WASTE

2

SIDE F | SIDE F

3¾

10°

5¼

NOTE: CUT SIDES FROM ⅛" HARDBOARD

2

SET MITER GAUGE FOR 10° CUT

CLAMP STOP BLOCK TO AUXILIARY FENCE

WASTE

AUXILIARY FENCE

STOP BLOCK/ HOLD DOWN (SEE SHOP TIP ABOVE)

Ⓔ OR Ⓕ

NOTE: MAKE A MARK IN THIS CORNER FOR CUTTING THIS SIDE

a. SIDE BLANK

WASTE

MAKE MARK IN CORNER

STOP BLOCK

SET STOP BLOCK AT 2" OR 3"

b. ROTATE BLANK FOR SECOND CUT

WASTE

STOP BLOCK

REPOSITION MARK IN THIS CORNER

The only other pieces needed for the bins are the fronts (G, H). (I used pine, but any $3/4$"-thick stock will do.)

CUT STRIPS. The fronts are cut from strips that are 2" wide for the small bins or 3" wide for the large bins *(Fig. 3)*.

DETERMINE LENGTH. After the strips are ripped to width, cut the fronts to finished length. To determine the length of the fronts, measure the width of a bin bottom ($3^1/2$"). Then add the combined thicknesses of both side pieces ($1/4$"). (In my case, the fronts are $3^3/4$" long.)

CUT TO LENGTH. To cut all the fronts to the same length, I clamped an L-shaped stop block to the table saw rip fence *(Fig. 4)*. This provides clearance so the cutoff won't bind between the rip fence and the saw blade.

RABBETING. After the fronts are cut to length, they're rabbeted to accept the sides and the bin bottom *(Fig. 3)*. To do this, attach an auxiliary fence to the table saw rip fence. Then set a dado blade to cut a rabbet $1/2$" deep and wide enough to match the thickness of the sides ($1/8$") *(Fig. 5a)*.

Note: To support the pieces while cutting the rabbets, I use a large push block *(Fig. 5)*.

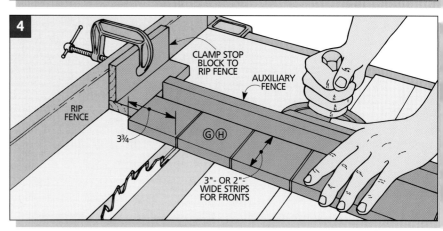

Next, reposition the fence and cut another rabbet wide enough to fit over the bottom *(Fig. 5b)*.

CHAMFERING. I cut small chamfers on the four outside edges of the bin fronts. I also chamfered the top inside edge *(Fig. 3)*.

CARD HOLDER. Finally, I routed a slot across the front of the bin to hold a cardboard label (see the Shop Tip below).

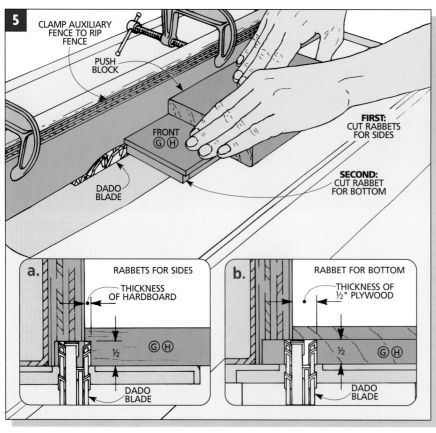

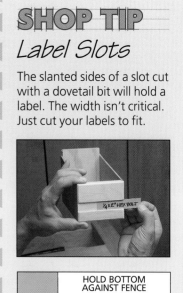

SHOP TIP
Label Slots

The slanted sides of a slot cut with a dovetail bit will hold a label. The width isn't critical. Just cut your labels to fit.

Assembling a large number of bins can be tedious work. It's easier and faster if you have a jig to hold the front, bottom, and back of the bin in place while you glue and nail on one of the sides (see photo).

To make the jig, start by cutting a scrap piece of 3/4"-thick plywood to size *(Fig. 1)*. Then, cut a 3/8"-deep groove to hold the bin's bottom. Next, cut two 3/8"-deep dadoes to position the backs of a

large and small bin *(Fig. 1)*. Finally, cut a 1/2"-deep dado to hold the bin's front. (The extra depth accounts for the lip on the outside edge of the bin front.)

To use the jig, insert a front, back, and bottom. Then glue and nail on one of the sides so it's flush with the bottom of the bin *(Fig. 2)*.

To complete the bin, simply remove it from the jig, flip it over and glue and nail on the remaining side.

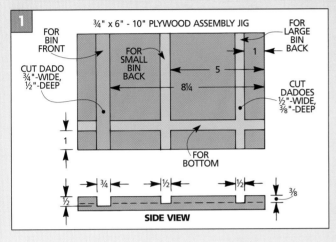

1

3/4" x 6" - 10" PLYWOOD ASSEMBLY JIG

FOR BIN FRONT
FOR SMALL BIN BACK
FOR LARGE BIN BACK
CUT DADO 3/4"-WIDE, 1/2"-DEEP
5
8 1/4
1
CUT DADOES 1/2"-WIDE, 3/8"-DEEP
FOR BOTTOM
1
1
3/4
1/2
1/2
1/2
3/8
SIDE VIEW

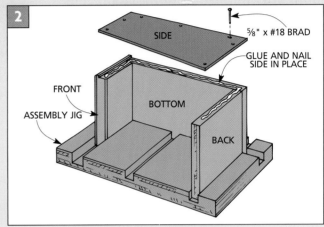

2

SIDE
5/8" x #18 BRAD
GLUE AND NAIL SIDE IN PLACE
FRONT
BOTTOM
ASSEMBLY JIG
BACK

ASSEMBLY

Now that you've got dozens of parts stacked up in the shop, you're ready to assemble them to make the bins.

Assembly is really very easy — the pieces are just glued and nailed together. The only thing you might want to do is to make a couple of spacer blocks to help center the dividers in the large bins *(Fig. 6)*.

Note: If you're assembling quite a few bins, the assembly jig shown above is a real timesaver.

RAILS

The bins are mounted to rails made from lengths of 2x6 stock, ripped 1 1/2" wide. The length of the rails is determined by the number of bins you want. (The rails shown in the photo on page 37 are 48" long.)

To form the retaining lip for the bins, cut a rabbet in the bottom back edge of each rail *(Fig. 7a)*. After the rabbets are cut, screw the rails to the wall, spacing them 4 5/8" apart. It's important that the rails are parallel, so here again, a spacer block is handy *(Fig. 7)*.

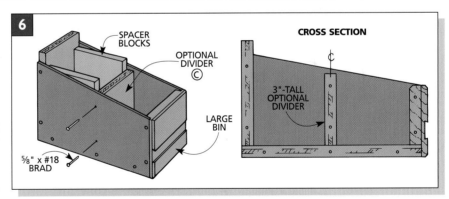

6

SPACER BLOCKS
OPTIONAL DIVIDER ©
LARGE BIN
5/8" x #18 BRAD

CROSS SECTION
3"-TALL OPTIONAL DIVIDER

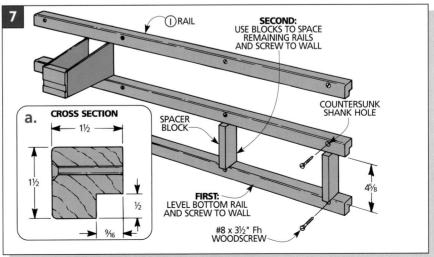

7

① RAIL
SECOND: USE BLOCKS TO SPACE REMAINING RAILS AND SCREW TO WALL
COUNTERSUNK SHANK HOLE
SPACER BLOCK
4 5/8
FIRST: LEVEL BOTTOM RAIL AND SCREW TO WALL
#8 x 3 1/2" Fh WOODSCREW

a. CROSS SECTION
1 1/2
1 1/2
1/2
9/16

DESIGNER'S NOTEBOOK

A few simple modifications to a bin turns it into a handy Tape Dispenser. And by building the optional Bin Carrier and Tool Bin, you'll be able to take hardware and even a few tools to your work.

TAPE DISPENSER

■ Start by cutting a plywood back piece (J), two hardboard side pieces (E), and the solid wood front (G) to size *(Fig. 1)*. (There is no bottom in the bin.)

■ When rabbeting the front piece, you only need rabbets for the sides.

■ Now cut a slot in each side for a dowel that holds the tape in place *(Fig. 1)*. Then glue and nail the bin together.

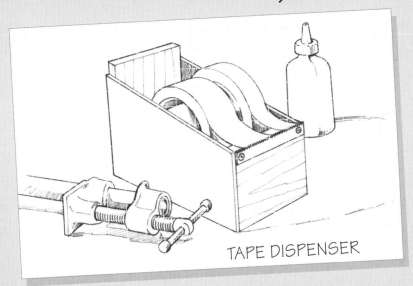

TAPE DISPENSER

MATERIALS LIST

TAPE DISPENSER
J Dispenser Back ½ ply - 3½ x 4⅞
K Center Block 1½ x 2¼ - 2¼
Note: Also need two parts E, one part G.

HARDWARE SUPPLIES
(2) No. 6 x ½" Rh woodscrews
(8) ⅝"-long No. 18 brads
(1) ½"-dia. dowel, 3¾" long
(1) Hacksaw blade

■ The dowel's length is the same as the outside width of the dispenser (3¾").

■ Cut a tenon on each end of the dowel that fits in the angled slots. To do this, clamp an auxiliary fence and a support jig to the table saw rip fence *(Fig. 2)*.

■ Next, cut a center block (K) from a square piece of stock *(Fig. 3)*. Chamfer the corners until it fits tight inside a roll of tape, then drill a hole for the dowel.

■ Finally, screw a short hacksaw blade to the front of the dispenser *(Fig. 3)*.

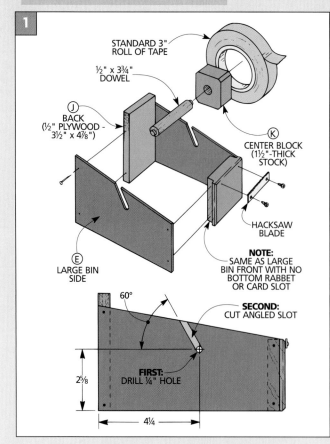

1

STANDARD 3" ROLL OF TAPE

½" x 3¾" DOWEL

J BACK (½" PLYWOOD - 3½" x 4⅞")

K CENTER BLOCK (1½"-THICK STOCK)

HACKSAW BLADE

E LARGE BIN SIDE

NOTE: SAME AS LARGE BIN FRONT WITH NO BOTTOM RABBET OR CARD SLOT

60°

SECOND: CUT ANGLED SLOT

FIRST: DRILL ¼" HOLE

2⅝

4¼

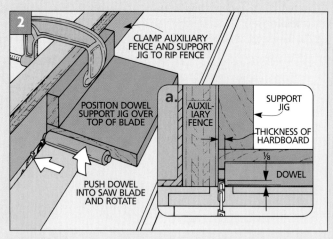

2

CLAMP AUXILIARY FENCE AND SUPPORT JIG TO RIP FENCE

POSITION DOWEL SUPPORT JIG OVER TOP OF BLADE

PUSH DOWEL INTO SAW BLADE AND ROTATE

a.

SUPPORT JIG

AUXILIARY FENCE

THICKNESS OF HARDBOARD

⅛

DOWEL

3

FILE CHAMFERS ON CORNERS UNTIL BLOCK FITS TIGHT

DRILL ½" HOLE FOR DOWEL

SCREW BLADE IN PLACE

#6 x ½" Rh SCREW

a. CENTER BLOCK (1½"-THICK STOCK)

2¼

½"-HOLE

2¼

K

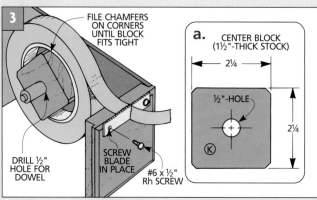

BIN CARRIER/TOOL BIN

This carrier provides a convenient way to hold up to eight bins at once. An extra-long tool bin fits on one side (see drawing at right).

The carrier consists of three main parts: a center divider (L), a base (M), and the rails (N) *(Fig. 4)*.

The first step is to make the divider (L) from ½" plywood. The length of the divider determines the number of bins you can carry. I made mine long enough to hold up to four bins on each side (15¾") *(Fig. 5)*.

After determining the length, cut the divider to shape *(Fig. 5)*.

Next, drill ⅜"-dia. holes in each corner of the handle and cut out the handle opening *(Fig. 5)*. Ease the sharp edges with a light sanding.

After the divider is complete, you can make the base (M). This is a piece of ½" plywood cut to the same length as the divider (15¾") *(Fig. 4)*. Then rip the base to a finished width of 4⅞".

After the base is cut to size, cut a ⅛"-deep groove down the center to hold the divider (L) *(Fig. 4)*.

Before assembling the carrier, a rail (N) is cut to fit on each side. These rails are identical to the rails for the Wall-Mounted Bins, except that their length matches the length of the divider. Rout a rabbet on the inside edge of each rail to hold the bins (refer to *Fig. 7a* on page 41). Then glue them in place on the divider *(Fig. 4)*.

Now, assemble the carrier, and glue and nail on a couple of end caps (O) made from ⅛" hardboard *(Fig. 4)*.

Another option is to make a long bin to hold hand tools. This bin is built to fit on one side of the carrier. (It can also hang on the wall strips.)

The tool bin is made just like a large storage bin, except it has a longer back (P), front (Q), and bottom (R) *(Fig. 6)*. Two large bin sides (E) are also used.

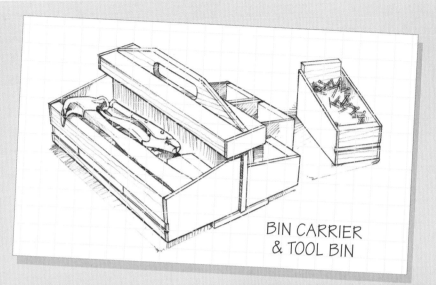

BIN CARRIER & TOOL BIN

MATERIALS LIST

BIN CARRIER & TOOL BIN

L	Divider (1)	½ ply - 8 x 15¾
M	Base (1)	½ ply - 4⅞ x 15¾
N	Rails (2)	1½ x 1½ - 15¾
O	End Caps (2)	⅛ hdbd. - 1½ x 3½
P	Tool Bin Back (1)	½ x 15½ - 4⅜
Q	Tool Bin Front (1)	¾ x 15¾ - 3
R	Tool Bin Btm. (1)	½ ply - 15½ x 7¾

Note: Also need two parts E.

HARDWARE SUPPLIES
(4) No. 8 x 1" Fh woodscrews
(4) No. 3 finish nails
(14) ⅝"-long No. 18 brads

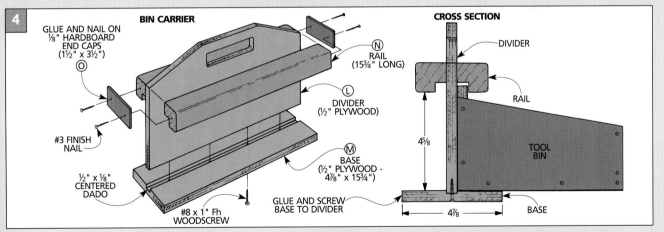

4 BIN CARRIER

GLUE AND NAIL ON ⅛" HARDBOARD END CAPS (1½" x 3½")
O

N RAIL (15¾" LONG)

L DIVIDER (½" PLYWOOD)

#3 FINISH NAIL

½" x ⅛" CENTERED DADO

M BASE (½" PLYWOOD - 4⅞" x 15¾")

GLUE AND SCREW BASE TO DIVIDER

#8 x 1" Fh WOODSCREW

CROSS SECTION

DIVIDER

RAIL

4⅝

TOOL BIN

4⅞

BASE

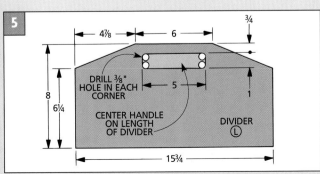

5

4⅞   6   ¾

DRILL ⅜" HOLE IN EACH CORNER

5

1

8

6¼

CENTER HANDLE ON LENGTH OF DIVIDER

DIVIDER **L**

15¾

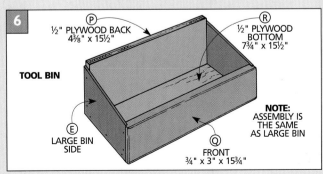

6

P ½" PLYWOOD BACK 4⅜" x 15½"

R ½" PLYWOOD BOTTOM 7¾" x 15½"

TOOL BIN

E LARGE BIN SIDE

Q FRONT ¾" x 3" x 15¾"

NOTE: ASSEMBLY IS THE SAME AS LARGE BIN

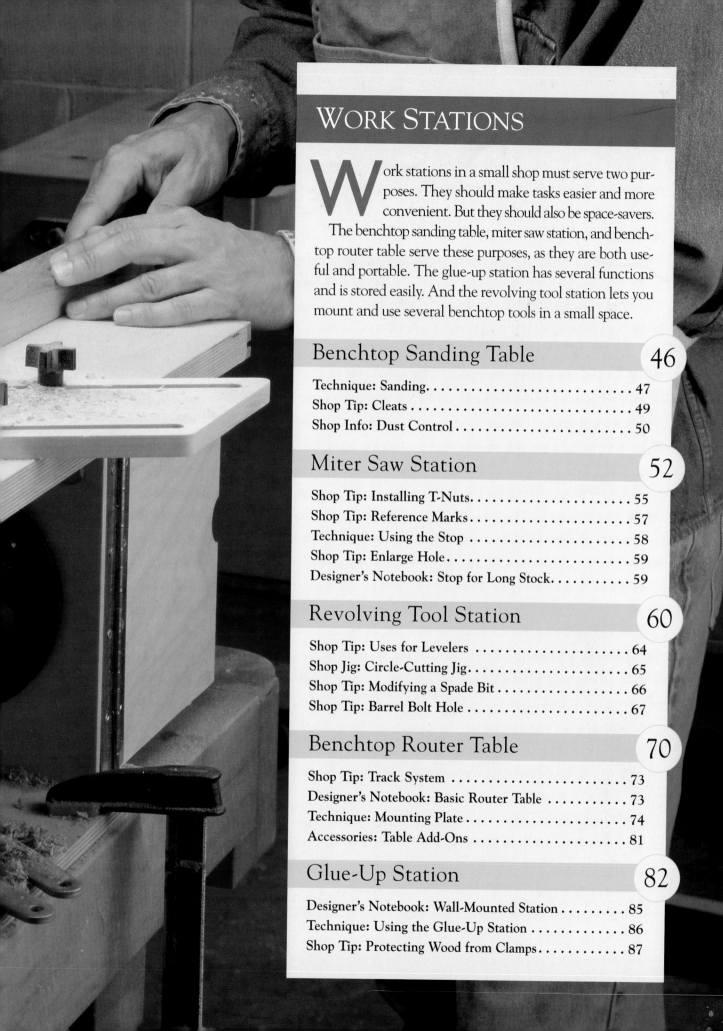

WORK STATIONS

Work stations in a small shop must serve two purposes. They should make tasks easier and more convenient. But they should also be space-savers. The benchtop sanding table, miter saw station, and benchtop router table serve these purposes, as they are both useful and portable. The glue-up station has several functions and is stored easily. And the revolving tool station lets you mount and use several benchtop tools in a small space.

Benchtop Sanding Table

The fine dust kicked into the air by sanding not only coats your shop with an annoying film, but it can cause respiratory problems. This shop-built table connects to your dust collector for dust-free sanding.

Most dust collectors do a great job of keeping the dust down, especially when it comes to the big chips produced by large, stationary tools. But dealing with the fine dust that's generated by a power sander is a different story.

These sanders kick up a cloud of dust that hangs in the air and fills my nose and lungs. And when it finally settles, there's a thin layer of dust that coats everything in the shop.

To capture this dust before it drifts into the air, I built a benchtop sanding table that hooks up to my dust collector (see photo above). It provides a conve-

nient sanding surface that pulls dust down through a perforated top and into the dust collector.

CONSTRUCTION. The design of the Benchtop Sanding Table is very simple. In essence, it's just a box with an angled baffle inside, a hole at one end, and a pegboard top panel.

But as simple as this sanding table is to build, keep in mind that it's important that all the pieces fit together correctly. Only then will all the fine sanding dust go exactly where it's supposed to.

MATERIALS. The only wood you'll need to build this table is some $3/4''$ hardwood stock, a $3/4''$ plywood panel,

and a $1/4''$ pegboard panel.

You don't need any specialty hardware for the sanding table, either — just a series of woodscrews and a handful of rubber bumpers.

CLEATS. When building your table, you may want to consider adding one or more small cleats that will hold the workpiece in place securely. For more on this, see the Shop Tip on page 49.

SANDING TIPS. Whenever I design or build a new project to help in sanding, I like to take a moment to remind myself of some quick but helpful sanding tips. Some of these are explained in the Technique box on the opposite page.

EXPLODED VIEW

OVERALL DIMENSIONS:
24W x 18D x 5H

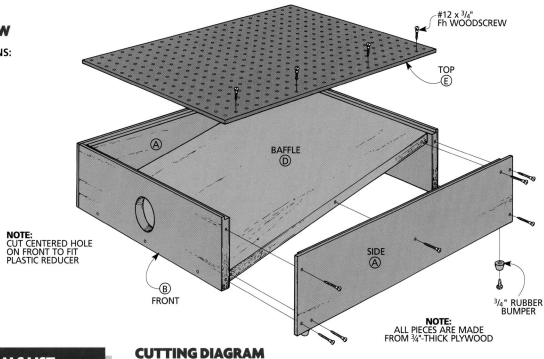

#12 x ³/₄"
Fh WOODSCREW

TOP
E

(A)

BAFFLE
D

SIDE
(A)

NOTE:
CUT CENTERED HOLE
ON FRONT TO FIT
PLASTIC REDUCER

(B)
FRONT

³/₄" RUBBER
BUMPER

NOTE:
ALL PIECES ARE MADE
FROM ³/₄"-THICK PLYWOOD

MATERIALS LIST

WOOD

A	Sides (2)	³/₄ ply - 5 x 23¹/₂
B	Front (1)	³/₄ ply - 5 x 17¹/₂
C	Back (1)	³/₄ ply - 5 x 17¹/₂
D	Baffle (1)	³/₄ ply - 19 rgh. x 24 rgh.
E	Top (1)	¹/₄ pgbd. - 17¹/₂ x 23

HARDWARE SUPPLIES

(16) No. 12 x ³/₄" Fh woodscrews
(22) No. 8 x 1¹/₂" Fh woodscrews
(4) ³/₄" rubber bumpers w/ screws

CUTTING DIAGRAM

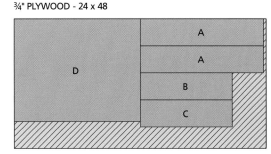

³/₄" PLYWOOD - 24 x 48

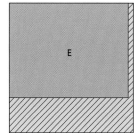

¹/₄" PEGBOARD - 24 x 24

TECHNIQUE .... Sanding

When sanding a project, sometimes what you *don't* do is just as important as what you do.

First, don't sand wood like you scrub the floor. Use long, even strokes. This way, you'll be sanding in a straight line with the grain, not going sideways across the grain.

Also, you should sand glued-up panels (and large pieces) before cutting them to size. This keeps the thickness more consistent around the edges, which otherwise tend to end up a little thinner.

Avoid sanding up to the edges of a board with a power sander (unless you

want to round them slightly). Instead, use a sanding block.

If you're sanding with 150-grit sandpaper and you find a deep scratch, stop and switch to a coarser grit to remove the scratch. Then work back up to 150 and continue.

End grain tends to "drink up" more stain, making it darker than the face grain. To get the end grain to accept a stain the same as the face grain, sand the end grain a couple grits finer.

If you've stained a project, be careful when sanding between coats of finish. And avoid the edges if possible. (Stay about ¹/₈" away.) It's

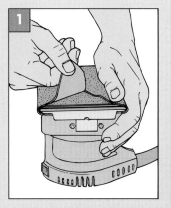

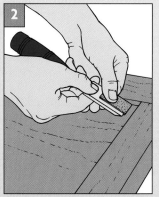

too easy to cut through the finish and remove the stain.

When using regular sandpaper, put four layers on a sander at the same time. Then rip off the top layer

when it's worn *(Fig. 1)*.

Finally, to sand "in tight" to a corner or up to an edge, just wrap some sandpaper around a dull chisel or a putty knife *(Fig. 2)*.

The heart of the Benchtop Sanding Table is a simple box. In addition to supporting the pegboard top, the box houses a baffle that controls the flow of air inside the table.

The sides (A), front (B), and back (C) of the box are all made from $3/4$"-thick plywood *(Fig. 1)*. A rabbet cut in the top edge of each piece accepts a $1/4$" pegboard top that's added later *(Fig. 1a)*. And the front and back pieces fit in rabbets cut in the ends of the side pieces *(Fig. 1b)*.

REDUCER. To hook the hose from your dust collector up to the sanding table, you'll need to cut a hole in the front (B) for a plastic reducer *(Fig. 1)*. Be sure to have your reducer in hand *before* cutting this hole. (You want an exact fit to prevent dust from escaping.)

Note: Reducers are available from many woodworking stores, home improvement centers, and tool catalogs. See page 126 for information on mail-order sources.

BAFFLE. Before assembling the box, the next step is to add the baffle (D). This is a piece of $3/4$"-thick plywood that fits inside the box at an angle *(Fig. 1)*.

The baffle is positioned on a slant for an important reason. By angling the baffle, the air flow is restricted at the back of the box. This evens out the suction across the table.

EXACT FIT. To produce a tight seal, it's important to cut the baffle for an exact fit. Since the baffle joins the front (B) and back (C) of the box at an angle, you'll need to bevel both ends. The trick to doing this is determining the *correct* angle for these bevels and then cutting them accurately.

What I found works best isn't a bunch of complicated measurements, but to start out with a workpiece that's longer and wider than the finished size of the baffle *(Fig. 2)*. (It will be beveled and ripped to fit the box later.)

Then position the baffle on one of the side pieces as shown in *Figs. 2a and 2b*. (It should be flush with the top rabbet toward the back and flush with the bottom edge near the front.)

Mark the two points on each face of the baffle where it meets the rabbets in the side. Then simply draw lines across the edge between the marks *(Fig. 2)*.

Now it's just a matter of tilting your table saw blade to match the lines and beveling the ends of the baffle at the marks as you cut it to length.

Next, assemble the plywood box with glue and screws and rip the baffle to width to fit inside.

Note: Even the snuggest fit will still leak a little air. So after screwing the baffle in place, I applied a few beads of silicone caulk around the top and bottom edges to help seal any gaps.

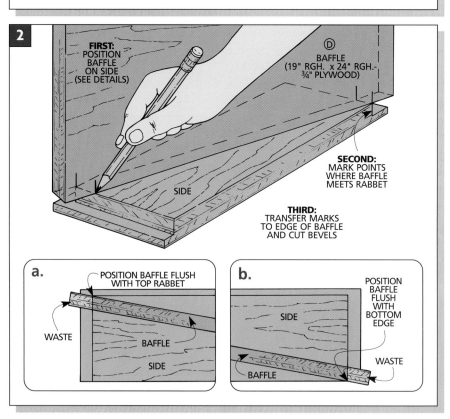

1

BACK (C)

BAFFLE (D)

SIDE (A)

(A)

5

17½

FRONT (B)

PLASTIC REDUCER

HOSE TO DUST COLLECTOR

NOTE: CUT CENTERED HOLE ON FRONT TO FIT PLASTIC REDUCER

5

23½

#8 x 1½" Fh WOODSCREW

NOTE: ALL PIECES ARE MADE FROM ¾"-THICK PLYWOOD

a. ½ ¼ (A)(B)(C)

b. ½ THICKNESS OF FRONT/BACK (A) SIDE

2

FIRST: POSITION BAFFLE ON SIDE (SEE DETAILS)

(D) BAFFLE (19" RGH. x 24" RGH.- ¾" PLYWOOD)

SECOND: MARK POINTS WHERE BAFFLE MEETS RABBET

SIDE

THIRD: TRANSFER MARKS TO EDGE OF BAFFLE AND CUT BEVELS

a. POSITION BAFFLE FLUSH WITH TOP RABBET

WASTE

BAFFLE

SIDE

b. POSITION BAFFLE FLUSH WITH BOTTOM EDGE

SIDE

WASTE

BAFFLE

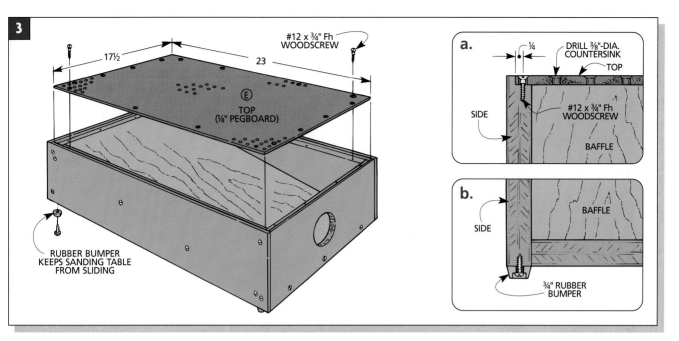

3

17½

23

#12 x ¾" Fh
WOODSCREW

ⓔ
TOP
(¼" PEGBOARD)

RUBBER BUMPER
KEEPS SANDING TABLE
FROM SLIDING

a.

¼

DRILL ⅜"-DIA.
COUNTERSINK

TOP

SIDE

#12 x ¾" Fh
WOODSCREW

BAFFLE

b.

BAFFLE

SIDE

¾" RUBBER
BUMPER

TOP

With the simple box complete, you're ready to add the top. This top acts as a flat sanding platform and helps funnel dust down into the box where it will be sucked into the dust collector.

What makes this work is a number of holes in the top. But rather than take the time to lay out and drill that many holes (refer to the photo on page 46), I decided to make the top (E) from a single piece of ¼"-thick pegboard.

This pegboard panel is cut to fit inside the rabbets cut earlier in the front, back, and sides *(Fig. 3)*.

Note: To make it easy to screw the top in place, cut the pegboard so the centerpoints of the holes around the perimeter are each ¼" in from the edges *(Fig. 3a)*.

COUNTERSINKS. At this point, you can hook up the sanding table and use it as it is. But a couple more improvements will help to increase the airflow into the box.

To begin with, I enlarged the existing holes in the pegboard with a straight drill bit. Then, to help "funnel" dust in, I chamfered the edges of these holes by drilling a shallow countersink on the top of each one *(Fig. 3a)*.

BUMPERS. All that's left to complete the sanding table is to screw four rubber bumpers to the bottom of the box *(Fig. 3b)*. These bumpers grip the surface of your bench and keep the sanding table from sliding around in use. They are screwed to the sides, near the corners.

CLEAT. Finally, to keep your workpiece from wandering across the table while you sand, you may want to add a simple shop-made cleat (see the Shop Tip below). ■

SHOP TIP .... Cleats

The enlarged holes in the pegboard top of the Benchtop Sanding Table can actually serve two different purposes.

First, they act as intake ports for the fine airborne dust particles that are produced when power sanding.

Second, these holes can also be used to anchor wood cleats to the top, making it possible to brace the workpiece. By holding the workpiece in place, you can achieve more consistent sanding (see the photo at left).

To make a cleat, just take a thin piece of scrap hardboard, hardwood or plywood and cut it down to a manageable size. Make sure the sides are straight and true so it will hold the edge of your workpiece securely (see drawing at right).

Then drill one hole through the scrap at each end to hold a small dowel. Make sure the holes are spaced so the dowels will fit into holes in the peg-board top panel without being bent or forced.

Once the cleat is in place, position the workpiece against it and sand *toward* the cleat so the piece stays put. (You might want to make more than one cleat, depending on the size and shape of the piece you're working on.)

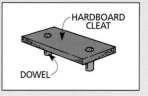

HARDBOARD
CLEAT

DOWEL

Every now and then, I receive a disheartening letter from an avid woodworker who had to hang up his or her tools because of a respiratory problem caused by sawdust.

Dealing with dust in the shop is one of the toughest problems facing a woodworker. And when the workshop is small, the problem is compounded. In just seconds, a power tool can kick up dust in the shop just like the snow that swirls around inside a glass paperweight. So protecting yourself and your tools is a constant problem that must be dealt with effectively and consistently.

TWO PROBLEMS. One thing that makes dealing with sawdust in the small home workshop such a challenge is that you're actually faced with two different problems.

First, you'll need to find a way to handle the mess that the tools create. From the large chips your jointer or planer produces to the dust a table saw or radial arm saw kicks up. And don't forget the fine dust generated by a power sander, which ultimately ends up coating everything in your shop.

Second, you'll need to develop a strategy for keeping harmful dust out of your lungs. Fortunately, there are a number of simple (and some surprisingly economical) ways to take care of both of these problems.

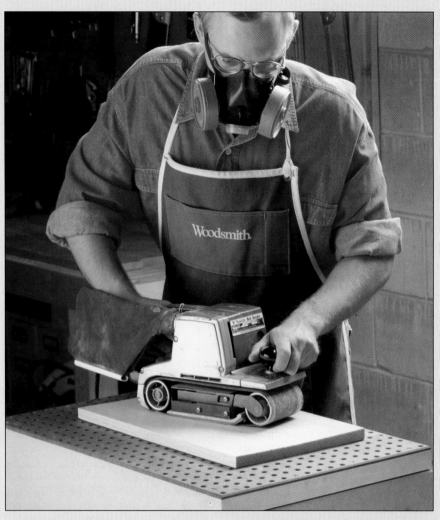

CONTAINING DUST

It's no surprise that the most common solution to containing dust is to use a small dust collection system. You can pick from a wide variety of quality single or two-stage collectors, like the one shown at right. With a little advance thought, it's often possible to pick a central location in the shop that can service the majority of your tools.

The disadvantage to these systems is that they take up a lot of valuable space. And they range in price from $300 to $800 or more (not including the hook-ups and pipe).

SHOP VACUUM. A more economical option is to purchase several small shop vacuums (approximately $50 to $100) and dedicate each one to a single machine (see far right photo). To make this setup even more convenient, you can purchase an automated switch from

Dust Collector. *If you have room, a dust collector is one of the most effective ways to contain dust in a small shop.*

Shop Vacuum. *Another solution is to dedicate an inexpensive shop vacuum to each sawdust-producing machine.*

many mail-order woodworking catalogs (see sources on page 126). This switch turns on the vacuum for you automatically whenever you power up the tool.

HOOK-UPS. Besides handling your stationary tools, there's another advantage to a shop vacuum or dust collector. You may be able to hook them up to one of the largest dust producers in the shop — power sanders.

Many sanders offer a vacuum hook-up (see photo at right). Or a dust bag (see top photo on opposite page). If your model doesn't have either, see if they're available separately. If not, you can upgrade to a sander with built-in vacuum assist (see photo at right). These sanders pull dust up through holes in the sandpaper. They're effective and highly portable.

FILTERING DUST

Even the best dust collection system won't filter out all the dust. And it's this fine dust that will coat both your shop and the inside of your lungs.

FAN AND FILTER. One of the simplest and most economical ways to capture airborne dust is to pull it into a fan with a pleated furnace filter strapped over the intake (see photo below). Just position the fan near the source of the dust.

Note: To further increase the efficiency of your dust filtering, try using two separate fans — one to blow the dust into the other.

FILTER UNIT. Another option is to purchase (or build) a filter unit to clean the air whenever you're working in the shop. Here again, one of the simplest methods is to use an inexpensive fan with a pleated filter.

The more sophisticated filter units can be moved around the shop where the dust is being produced. Or you can hang them from the ceiling over a particularly bothersome dust source (see photo below).

Note: To help control the fine dust that's produced while sanding, you can build a sanding table that hooks up to your dust collector. See page 46 for plans for a convenient benchtop model that is easy to build and doesn't take up much space.

DUST MASKS. Whether or not you decide to live with a layer of sawdust in your shop, you can still protect your lungs by always using a good quality dust mask (see photo at bottom right and sources on page 126). When buying one of these, it's a good idea to pay a little more for a system that has replaceable canisters that can filter both sawdust and chemical fumes (around $50). These normally offer better protection than an average disposable mask.

DUST HELMET. A dust mask will keep the dust out of your lungs but not out of your eyes. For complete protection from dust, you may want to consider a dust helmet.

Recent advances in technology have allowed many manufacturers to produce lightweight self-contained units that are surprisingly comfortable (see photo at right). Although they cost considerably more than a dust mask (around $300), they do an excellent job of keeping airborne dust out of your face and lungs.

Safety Note: Although it's tempting, don't avoid the dust problem. Invest in your lungs now. You'll breathe easier, and your shop will be cleaner, too.

Power Sanders. *A built-in vacuum (left) or an attachment (right) are two ways to control sanding dust.*

Dust Helmet. *If you're really concerned about that fine sawdust and the health problems it can cause, don't be afraid to protect yourself. A good way to keep dust out of your lungs and face is to use a self-contained dust helmet.*

Fan Filter. *One way to reduce airborne dust in the shop is to attach a pleated filter to a household fan (or use two fans for even greater control). This is an ideal solution if you have a limited budget.*

Suspended Filter. *If floor or bench space is at a premium in your small shop, you might consider a simple filter unit that can be suspended overhead where it's out of the way.*

Dust Mask. *An economical and convenient way to keep dust out of your lungs is to use a dust mask with replaceable filters. This style tends to produce a tighter seal than disposable masks.*

Miter Saw Station

Just because your power miter saw is portable doesn't mean it shouldn't have its own work station. This design combines extension wings for long stock with a stop system for accurate repeat cuts.

Every time I looked at my power miter saw, I'd think about building a work station for it — something to support long stock, with a system for making repeat cuts accurately.

The challenge was to incorporate all those ideas without sacrificing portability. My answer was this Miter Saw Station (see photo above).

EXTENSION WINGS. To support long workpieces, I designed a pair of extension wings that attach to the ends of the station. For portability, these wings can be "tucked" away inside the case (see left photo below). And when stored, the wings provide built-in handles to make it easy to lift and move the miter saw (see photo below).

FENCE SYSTEM. One problem with most miter saws is that they have short fences. This makes it difficult to position a long workpiece for an accurate cut. To solve this, I added a pair of rails to extend the fences. And for accurate repeat cuts, there's even a stop system that slides in slots cut in the fence rails (see photo below).

EXPLODED VIEW

OVERALL DIMENSIONS:
84W x 16D x 6³/₄H

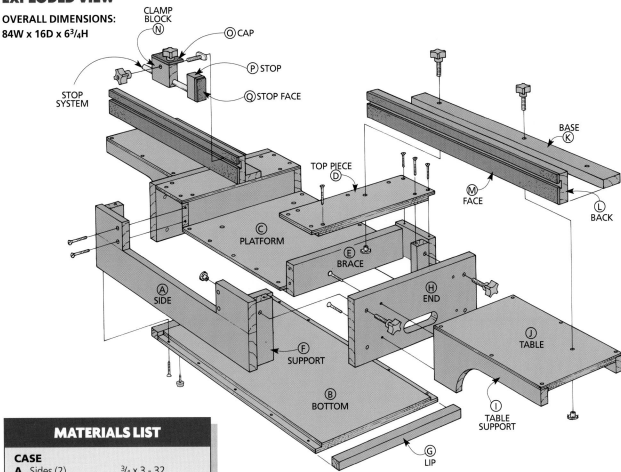

CLAMP BLOCK Ⓝ

Ⓞ CAP

Ⓟ STOP

Ⓠ STOP FACE

STOP SYSTEM

TOP PIECE Ⓓ

BASE Ⓚ

Ⓜ FACE

Ⓛ BACK

Ⓒ PLATFORM

Ⓔ BRACE

Ⓐ SIDE

Ⓗ END

Ⓙ TABLE

Ⓕ SUPPORT

Ⓘ TABLE SUPPORT

Ⓑ BOTTOM

Ⓖ LIP

MATERIALS LIST

CASE
A	Sides (2)	³/₄ x 3 - 32
B	Bottom (1)	³/₄ ply - 16 x 32
C	Platform (1)	³/₄ ply - 16 x 20
D	Top Pieces (2)	³/₄ ply - 6 x 16
E	Braces (2)	³/₄ x 3³/₈ - 14¹/₂
F	Supports (4)	³/₄ x 1³/₄ - 5¹/₄
G	Lips (2)	³/₄ x ³/₄ - 16
H	Ends (2)	³/₄ x 6 - 16
I	Table Supports (4)	³/₄ x 4¹/₈ - 15⁷/₈
J	Tables (2)	³/₄ ply - 10⁷/₈ x 15⁷/₈

FENCE & STOP SYSTEM
K	Bases (2)	³/₄ x 2 - 32
L	Backs (2)	³/₄ x 3 - 32
M	Faces (2)	¹/₄ hdbd. - 3 x 32
N	Clamp Block (1)	³/₄ x 3 - 3
O	Cap (1)	¹/₄ hdbd. - 1³/₄ x 3
P	Stop (1)	³/₄ x 1 - 3
Q	Stop Face (1)	¹/₄ hdbd. - ³/₄ x 3

HARDWARE SUPPLIES
(1) ⁵/₁₆" toilet bolt, 1³/₄" long
(1) ⁵/₁₆" plastic knob
(12) ⁵/₁₆" T-nuts
(8) ⁵/₁₆" x 1¹/₂" threaded knobs
(1) ⁵/₁₆" threaded insert
(1) ⁵/₁₆" x 2¹/₄" threaded knob
(1) ³/₈"-dia. x 36"-long steel rod
(4) Rubber feet ⁵/₁₆" x ³/₄"
(4) Bolts and T-nuts to mount miter saw
(46) No. 8 x 1" Fh woodscrews
(24) No. 8 x 1³/₄" Fh woodscrews

CUTTING DIAGRAM

³/₄ x 7¹/₄ - 72 (3.6 Bd. Ft.)

| A | A |

³/₄ x 7¹/₄ - 72 (3.6 Bd. Ft.)

| H | H | E / E | F F F F / N P G |

³/₄ x 5¹/₂ - 72 (2.75 Bd. Ft.)

| K | K |
| L | L |

³/₄ x 5¹/₂ - 72 (2.75 Bd. Ft.)

| I | I | I | I |

¹/₄" HARDBOARD - 12 x 48

| M | O |
| M | Q |

NOTE: ALSO NEED ONE 48 x 48 SHEET ³/₄" PLYWOOD

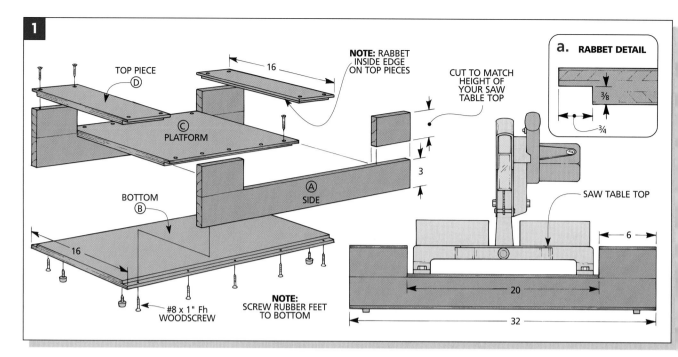

1

TOP PIECE (D)

NOTE: RABBET INSIDE EDGE ON TOP PIECES

16

CUT TO MATCH HEIGHT OF YOUR SAW TABLE TOP

a. RABBET DETAIL

3/8

3/4

(C) PLATFORM

BOTTOM (B)

(A) SIDE

3

SAW TABLE TOP

16

6

#8 x 1" Fh WOODSCREW

NOTE: SCREW RUBBER FEET TO BOTTOM

20

32

CASE

I started work on the Miter Saw Station by making the case. It's a simple open-ended box with U-shaped sides *(Fig. 1)*.

SIDES. The U-shape forms a recess for the miter saw to sit in *(Fig. 1)*. At the same time, it creates a work support surface on either side of the saw.

To fit most 10" miter saws, the recess in each side (A) is 20" wide.

Note: For a sliding compound or large miter saw, you may need to adjust the case dimensions. Have your saw on hand before you cut any pieces.

The important thing is that the top of the case end up flush with the table of your saw. For this to happen, the height (width) of the short pieces that form the sides of the "U" must match the height of the saw table top *(Fig. 1)*.

BOTTOM, PLATFORM, AND TOP. The bottom (B), platform (C), and top pieces (D) are all the same width (16"). But the lengths of these pieces vary *(Fig. 1)*. To keep the pieces aligned, I cut rabbets on the edges *(Fig. 1a)*. Then I glued and screwed the case together.

BRACES. Next, to strengthen the case and to help prevent it from racking during use, I added two 3/4"-thick hardwood braces (E) *(Fig. 2)*. They fit between the sides and under the top pieces (D).

MOUNT SAW. At this point the saw can be attached to the case. To do this, center the saw on the platform between the sides. And slide it as close to the front edge of the platform as possible. Then drill holes and secure the saw with T-nuts and hex bolts *(Fig. 2a)*.

SUPPORTS. Next, two supports (F) are cut and glued in each end of the case *(Fig. 3)*. These supports are used later to mount the wings.

Note: I found it was easiest to drill holes in the supports (for the wings) before gluing and screwing them in place *(Fig. 3)*.

To complete the station's case, I screwed four rubber feet to the bottom (refer to *Fig. 1*). These keep the station from sliding around during use.

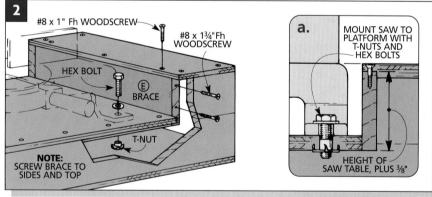

2

#8 x 1" Fh WOODSCREW

#8 x 1¾"Fh WOODSCREW

HEX BOLT

(E) BRACE

T-NUT

NOTE: SCREW BRACE TO SIDES AND TOP

a.

MOUNT SAW TO PLATFORM WITH T-NUTS AND HEX BOLTS

HEIGHT OF SAW TABLE, PLUS 3/8"

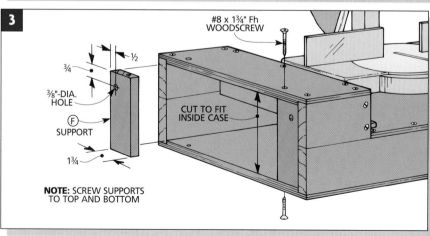

3

#8 x 1¾" Fh WOODSCREW

1/2

3/4

3/8"-DIA. HOLE

(F) SUPPORT

1¾

CUT TO FIT INSIDE CASE

NOTE: SCREW SUPPORTS TO TOP AND BOTTOM

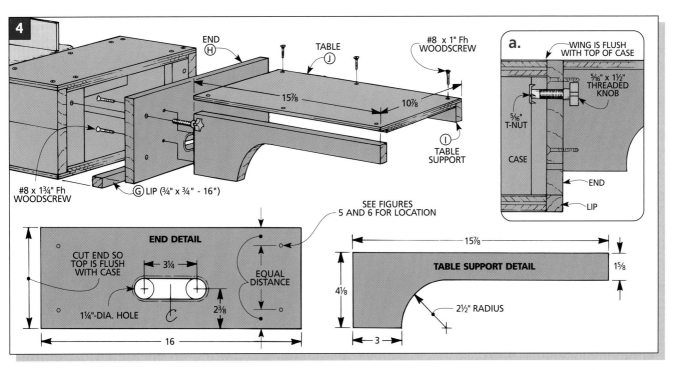

4

END (H) · TABLE (J) · #8 x 1" Fh WOODSCREW

15⅞ · 10⅞

#8 x 1¾" Fh WOODSCREW · G LIP (¾" x ¾" - 16")

TABLE SUPPORT (I)

a. WING IS FLUSH WITH TOP OF CASE · ⁵⁄₁₆" x 1½" THREADED KNOB · ⁵⁄₁₆" T-NUT · CASE · END · LIP

END DETAIL
CUT END SO TOP IS FLUSH WITH CASE · 3¼ · EQUAL DISTANCE · 2⅜ · 1¼"-DIA. HOLE · 16

SEE FIGURES 5 AND 6 FOR LOCATION

TABLE SUPPORT DETAIL
15⅞ · 1⅝ · 4⅛ · 2½" RADIUS · 3

WINGS

After completing the case, I started on a pair of wings to support long work-pieces *(Fig. 4)*.

LIP. But before work can begin on these wings, you'll need to glue a hard-wood lip (G) across each end of the case *(Fig. 4)*. This lip covers the edge of the plywood bottom (B) and helps to support the wings.

WINGS. With the lips glued in place, you can make the wings. Each wing consists of an end (H), two supports (I), and a table (J) *(Fig. 4)*.

The first step is to make the ends. To prevent a work-piece from catching on the wings, it's important that the ends (H) be flush with the top of the case. The height of the ends (H) is the distance from the top of the lip to the top of the case (for me, this distance was 6").

To complete the ends (H), I cut a handle hole in each to make it easy to move the saw *(Fig. 4)*.

SUPPORTS AND TABLE. Attached to each end (H) are two table supports (I) and a table (J) *(Fig. 4)*. To size the table so the wings will fit inside the case, measure between the supports (F)

and subtract ⅛" for clearance (10⅞"). Then rabbet the edges and glue and screw the wings together.

ATTACH THE WINGS. In order to knock down and set up the wings quickly, they're held in place with threaded knobs (or thumbscrews) and T-nuts. (For mail-order hardware sources, see page 126.) The threaded knobs pass through the holes you drilled earlier in the supports (F) and thread into T-nuts *(Fig. 4a)*.

Two sets of holes in each wing allow you to use the same knobs to secure the wing in either the open or stored position. The tricky part is aligning these holes with the ones you drilled in the supports (F). To do this, I used dowel centers *(Figs. 5 and 6)*.

Next install the T-nuts. Finally, position the wings and thread in the knobs.

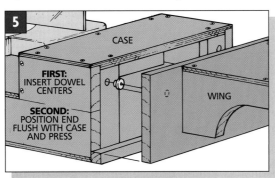

5 CASE · WING
FIRST: INSERT DOWEL CENTERS
SECOND: POSITION END FLUSH WITH CASE AND PRESS

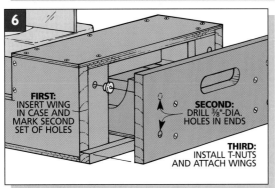

6
FIRST: INSERT WING IN CASE AND MARK SECOND SET OF HOLES
SECOND: DRILL ⅜"-DIA. HOLES IN ENDS
THIRD: INSTALL T-NUTS AND ATTACH WINGS

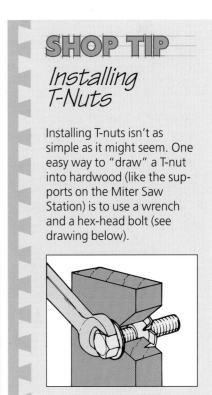

SHOP TIP

Installing T-Nuts

Installing T-nuts isn't as simple as it might seem. One easy way to "draw" a T-nut into hardwood (like the supports on the Miter Saw Station) is to use a wrench and a hex-head bolt (see drawing below).

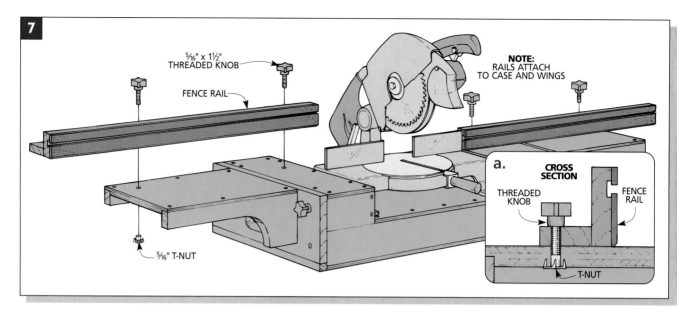

7

5/16" x 1½" THREADED KNOB

FENCE RAIL

NOTE: RAILS ATTACH TO CASE AND WINGS

5/16" T-NUT

a. **CROSS SECTION**

THREADED KNOB

FENCE RAIL

T-NUT

FENCE RAILS

Once the wings are complete, the Miter Saw Station is ready to use. But I've never been satisfied with the short fences on my miter saw. It's awkward to position and hold a long workpiece. And for repeat cuts, there's nothing to clamp a stop block to.

To solve both of these problems, I decided to add a pair of shop-built fence rails *(Fig. 7)*. They feature a built-in T-slot for a stop system added later (refer to page 58).

And just like the wings, the rails attach to the case with threaded knobs. This way they can be removed easily and stored *(Fig. 11 on the opposite page)*.

THREE PARTS. Each fence rail is made up of three parts: a base, back, and face *(Fig. 8)*. The base (K) provides a foundation for the back. And two mounting holes drilled in each base allow you to attach the rails to the case later *(Figs. 7 and 8)*.

Each back (L) supports the workpiece and is grooved for the stop system added later *(Fig. 8)*. After each groove is cut, a back is glued to a base to form an "L" *(Fig. 8)*.

For accurate cuts, it's important that the back is 90° to the base. So before you glue these pieces up, dry clamp them and check for square.

Note: Make sure to glue on each base (K) to create a right and a left fence rail. The end of each base with the mounting hole should face in toward the saw *(Figs. 7 and 8)*.

FACE. The next step is to add the face pieces. Each face (M) is cut from 1/4"-thick hardboard and is glued on top of the groove in each back *(Fig. 8)*.

Note: After gluing on the faces, sand or rout a chamfer on the bottom front edge for sawdust relief *(Fig. 8)*.

T-SLOT. Finally, to create the "T" (and provide a rock-solid way to lock the stop system in place), a slot is cut in each face *(Figs. 9 and 9a)*.

MOUNTING THE RAILS

After the fence rails have been completed, they can be attached to the station's case. Just like the wings you made earlier (refer to page 55), the rails will be held in place with threaded knobs and T-nuts *(Fig. 10)*.

8

PRE-DRILL TWO 3/8" MOUNTING HOLES IN EACH RAIL

3

16½

BASE (K)

(M) FACE

3/16

½

5/8

32

NOTE: BASE AND BACK ARE MADE FROM ¾"-THICK STOCK

RAIL DETAIL

2

5/8

3

(L) BACK

NOTE: CHAMFER BOTTOM EDGE OF FACE FOR SAWDUST RELIEF

9

RIP FENCE

CUT GROOVE IN FACE TO CREATE T-SLOT

BASE

BACK

a.

CUT 3/8"-WIDE GROOVE CENTERED ON GROOVE IN BACK

BACK

FACE

The tricky part is mounting the rails so they're in line with the miter saw fence. To do this, I use a long straightedge (in my case, a four-foot level) to position the rails *(Fig. 10)*.

MOUNTING HOLES. To locate the holes for the T-nuts, clamp the straightedge to the saw fence, and the fence rail to the wing *(Fig. 10)*.

Holding the other end of the rail in place, drill through the holes in the base and into the case and wings *(Fig. 10a)*.

Note: Making the rails removable means more convenience and versatility for you, but it could make for more problems if you have to follow the same procedure to position them every time. To make it easy to realign the rails whenever they're removed, see the Shop Tip below right.

T-NUTS. All that's left is to add T-nuts and threaded knobs, then screw the rails in place *(Fig. 7a)*.

STORING THE FENCE RAILS

I wanted the Miter Saw Station to be not only useful, but also portable.

To make it as convenient as possible to lift and move the station, the fence rails can be mounted out of the way on the rear of the case *(Fig. 11)*. They're held in place there with the same plastic knobs used to mount them on top of the case *(Fig. 11)*.

THIRD HOLE. To bolt both rail ends to the case, you'll need to drill a third $^3/_8$"-dia. mounting hole 3" in from the end of each fence rail *(Fig. 11)*.

Then, to locate the matching holes in the case for the T-nuts, just hold each rail up against the case. And drill through the hole in each end of the rail and into the side *(Figs. 11 and 11a)*.

MOUNT RAILS. Finally, to secure the fence rails, insert the T-nuts and screw the rails to the case with the threaded knobs *(Fig. 11)*.

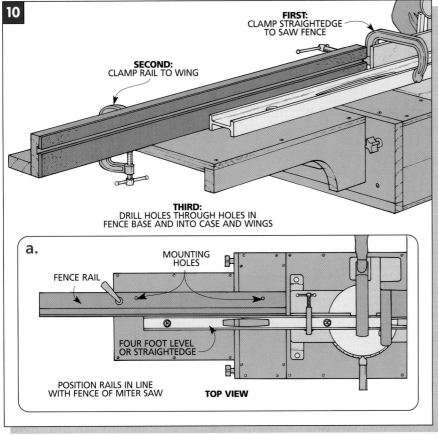

10

FIRST:
CLAMP STRAIGHTEDGE
TO SAW FENCE

SECOND:
CLAMP RAIL TO WING

THIRD:
DRILL HOLES THROUGH HOLES IN
FENCE BASE AND INTO CASE AND WINGS

a.

MOUNTING
HOLES

FENCE RAIL

FOUR FOOT LEVEL
OR STRAIGHTEDGE

POSITION RAILS IN LINE
WITH FENCE OF MITER SAW   **TOP VIEW**

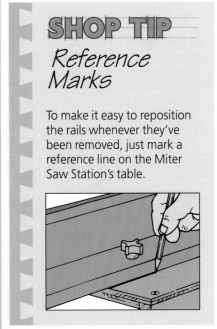

SHOP TIP

Reference Marks

To make it easy to reposition the rails whenever they've been removed, just mark a reference line on the Miter Saw Station's table.

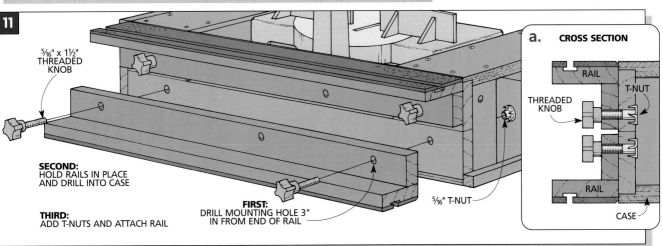

11

$^5/_{16}$" x 1½"
THREADED
KNOB

SECOND:
HOLD RAILS IN PLACE
AND DRILL INTO CASE

THIRD:
ADD T-NUTS AND ATTACH RAIL

FIRST:
DRILL MOUNTING HOLE 3"
IN FROM END OF RAIL

$^5/_{16}$" T-NUT

a.   CROSS SECTION

RAIL

T-NUT

THREADED
KNOB

RAIL

CASE

STOP SYSTEM

With the fence rails mounted, work can begin on the stop system. To help you make quick and accurate repeat cuts, the easily adjustable stop system slides in the T-slot in the fence rails *(Fig. 12)*.

THREE PARTS. The only problem is there isn't a T-slot in the miter saw fence. In order to use the stop close to the saw blade, the stop is made up of three parts: a clamp block, a length of steel rod, and a sliding stop. This way you can extend the stop out over the table of the miter saw (see photo above).

CLAMP BLOCK. I started work by making the clamp block (N) *(Fig. 13)*. The clamping action is provided by a toilet bolt (available at most hardware stores and home centers). It passes through the block and fits in the T-slot

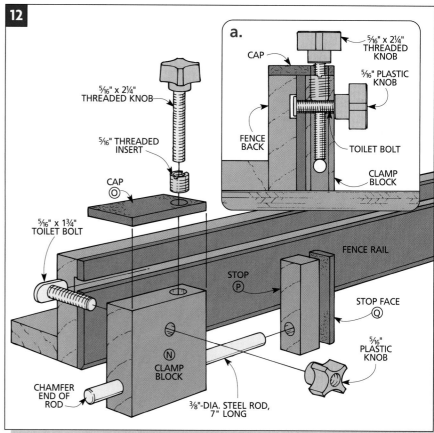

in the fence rail *(Fig. 12a)*. Tightening a plastic knob (or wing nut) on the end of the bolt pinches the bolt in the slot and locks the stop in place.

Next, a hole is drilled through the length of the block to accept a steel rod *(Figs. 12 and 13* and the Shop Tip on the opposite page).

TECHNIQUE .... *Using the Stop*

CLOSED

For the majority of cuts I make, I butt the stop (P) up against the clamp block (N) and lock it in place (see drawing at right).

To set up the stop for making accurate repeat cuts, start by loosening the plastic knob that secures the clamp block to the fence. Then position the entire stop block assembly for the desired cut and lock it in place.

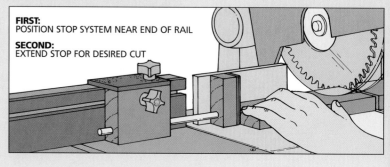

EXTENDED

To cut shorter workpieces, slide the stop assembly near the end of the rail and lock it in place (see drawing at right). Then loosen the threaded knob on top of the clamp block and extend the stop (P) out for the desired cut.

Safety Note: To allow room for you to hold the workpiece, the stop should always be at least 6" away from the blade.

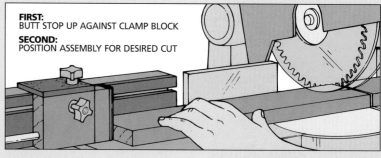

SHOP TIP

Enlarge Hole

To prevent the steel rod from binding in the clamp block, just use a dowel wrapped with sandpaper to enlarge the hole first.

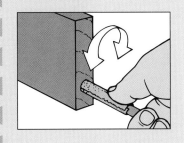

To help prevent the clamp block from twisting and binding as it slides back and forth, I glued a $1/4$"-thick hardboard cap (O) to the top of the clamp block *(Fig. 13)*.

THREADED INSERT. In use, the steel rod is locked in place with a threaded knob (or a thumbscrew). It runs through a $5/16$" threaded insert in the clamp body to pinch the rod in the hole *(Figs. 13 and 13a)*.

13

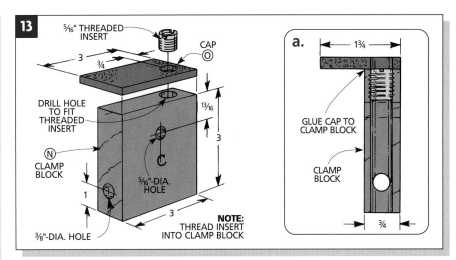

5/16" THREADED INSERT
CAP (O)
3
3/4
DRILL HOLE TO FIT THREADED INSERT
(N)
CLAMP BLOCK
13/16
3
5/16"-DIA. HOLE
C
1
3
3/8"-DIA. HOLE
NOTE: THREAD INSERT INTO CLAMP BLOCK

a.
1 3/4
GLUE CAP TO CLAMP BLOCK
CLAMP BLOCK
3/4

STOP. Next, I added a stop (P) to the end of the rod *(Fig. 14)*.

To strengthen the stop, I cut and glued a hardboard face (Q) to one end *(Fig. 14)*. And for sawdust relief, I sanded a chamfer on all edges of the face.

Finally, epoxy the steel rod in the stop. When it's dry, slide it into the clamp body and attach the stop system to the fence rail.

Safety Note: So that you don't place your hand too close to the blade, the stop extends only to within 6" of it.

14

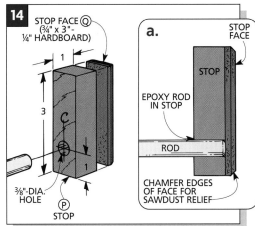

STOP FACE (Q) (3/4" x 3"-1/4" HARDBOARD)
1
3
C
3/8"-DIA. HOLE
1
(P) STOP

a.
STOP FACE
STOP
EPOXY ROD IN STOP
ROD
CHAMFER EDGES OF FACE FOR SAWDUST RELIEF

DESIGNER'S NOTEBOOK

Making repeat cuts on workpieces longer than the wings is simple when you add this optional stop.

STOP FOR LONG STOCK

■ To make repeat cuts on stock longer than the fence rails, I added an optional stop (see photo). It's similar to the station's fence system, except that it fits *under* the left wing.

■ The optional stop consists of a rod clamp (R) and a two-piece stop (see drawing). These two parts are connected with a $3/8$"-diameter steel rod.

Note: I wanted to be able to store the stop in the case and still get the maximum extension. So I cut the steel rod to a length of 22".

■ To mount the stop, position it under the wing so it butts up against the face of the fence rail. Then glue and screw the clamp block to the wing table (J).

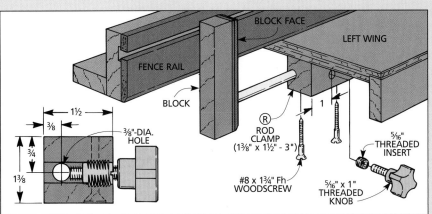

BLOCK FACE
LEFT WING
FENCE RAIL
BLOCK
1 1/2
3/8
3/4
1 3/8
3/8"-DIA. HOLE
(R) ROD CLAMP (1 3/8" x 1 1/2" - 3")
#8 x 1 3/4" Fh WOODSCREW
1
5/16" THREADED INSERT
5/16" x 1" THREADED KNOB

Revolving Tool Station

Giving the "carousel" on top of this station a spin or rotating the turntable underneath allows easy access to your power tools. Multiple drawers also provide convenient storage for accessories.

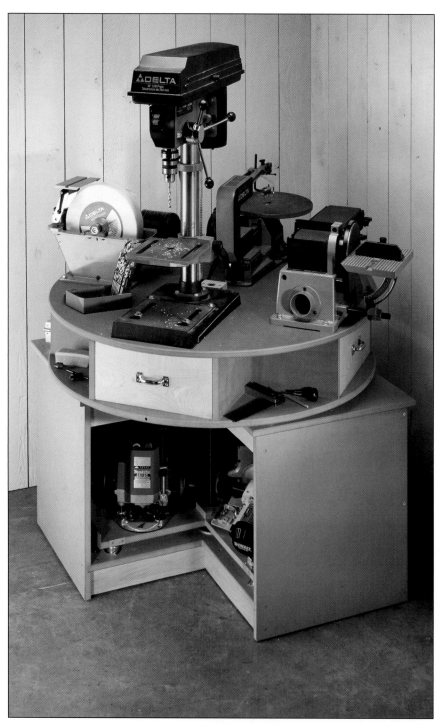

I've never met a home woodworker yet who had too much space in the workshop. Maybe that explains why they're always looking for ways to use the space that is available as efficiently as possible.

One of the most useful, space-saving ideas I've come up with is this Revolving Tool Station. Basically, it's a rotating tool stand that provides easy access to a number of benchtop tools in a small amount of space.

TOOL STATION. This station has a "footprint" that only takes up about eleven square feet of space. (I like to tuck mine in a corner of the shop.) Even so, it combines a work center and a convenient storage area that would normally take up much more room.

WORK CENTER. The heart of the work center is a large circular platform that spins around like a carousel. Mounting your benchtop tools to this platform provides quick access to each tool while keeping the others close at hand.

STORAGE AREAS. The carousel also features plenty of room for storage. Directly underneath each tool is a drawer that's perfect for storing accessories. Between the drawers are open shelves. And a large rotating turntable in the base provides storage for a number of your portable power tools.

MATERIALS. I decided to use $3/4"$ MDF (medium-density fiberboard) for the large parts of this station, not only because it's easy to work with, but also because its density will help damp the vibration of the tools mounted to it. If you prefer, you could also use plywood.

HARDWARE. There isn't much special hardware needed for this project. You will need an iron pipe with a flange, a couple of small pieces of aluminum angle, and several 1"-roller bearings. These bearings let the turntable and carousel spin smoothly. For mail-order sources of hardware, see page 126.

EXPLODED VIEW

OVERALL DIMENSIONS:
40W x 40D x 32¾H

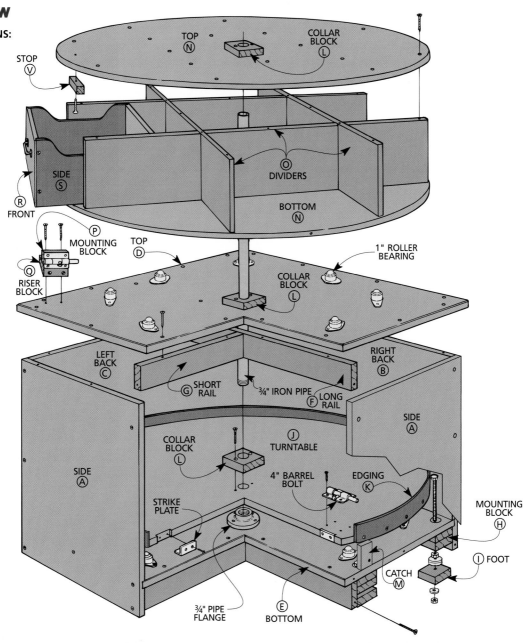

MATERIALS LIST

BASE

A	Sides (2)	¾ MDF - 22 x 19½
B	Right Back (1)	¾ MDF - 22 x 33¾
C	Left Back (1)	¾ MDF - 22 x 33
D	Top (1)	¾ MDF - 36 x 36
E	Bottom (1)	¾ MDF - 33¾ x 33¾
F	Long Rails (2)	¾ x 3 - 33
G	Short Rails (2)	¾ x 3 - 15
H	Mounting Blks. (10)	¾ x 3 - 3
I	Feet (5)	¾ x 3 - 3

TURNTABLE

J	Turntable (1)	¾ MDF - 30 x 30
K	Edging (1)	⅛ hdbd. - 1¾ x 72¼
L	Collar Blocks (3)	¾ x 3 - 3
M	Catch (1)	¾ x 1 - 3

CAROUSEL

N	Top/Bottom (2)	¾ MDF - 40 x 40
O	Dividers (4)	¾ MDF - 6 x 36½
P	Mounting Block (1)	¾ x 1 - 3
Q	Riser Block (1)	¾ x 2½ - 3

DRAWERS

R	Fronts/Backs (8)	¾ x 5⅞ - 14⅛
S	Sides (8)	¼ hdbd. - 5⅞ x 9⅞
T	Bottoms (4)	¼ hdbd. - 13⅝ x 9⅝
U	Cleats (8)	½ x ½ - 8⅞
V	Stops (4)	¾ x ½ - 2

HARDWARE SUPPLIES

(28) No. 8 x ⅜" Ph screws
(24) No. 6 x ½" Fh sheet-metal screws
(19) No. 6 x ¾" Fh sheet-metal screws
(36) No. 6 x 1¼" Fh sheet-metal screws
(15) No. 8 x 1¼" Fh sheet-metal screws
(91) No. 8 x 1½" Fh sheet-metal screws
(10) No. 8 x 2" Fh sheet-metal screws
(2) 4" barrel bolts w/ screws
(5) ⅜" x 4" full-thread hex bolts
(5) ⅜"-16 T-nuts
(10) ⅜" lock nuts
(10) ⅜" x 1½" fender washers
(5) ⅜" flat washers
(14) 1" roller bearings
(2) ¾" x ¾" aluminum angle, 2" long
(1) ¾" pipe flange w/ screws
(1) ¾" iron pipe, 28" long
(4) 4" sash handles

CUTTING DIAGRAM

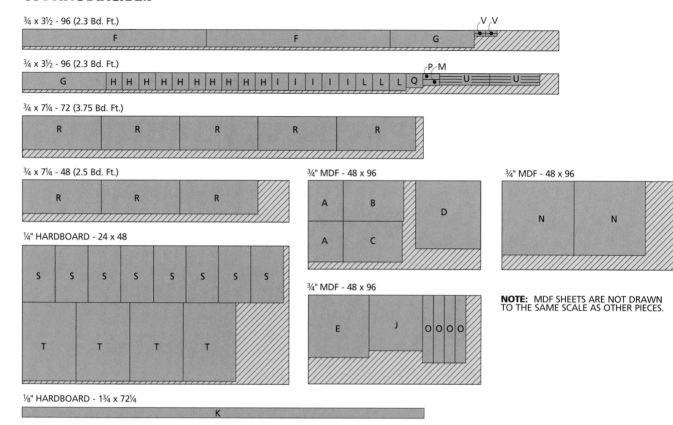

¾ x 3½ - 96 (2.3 Bd. Ft.)

| F | F | G | V V |

¾ x 3½ - 96 (2.3 Bd. Ft.)

| G | H H H H H H H H H H I I I I I L L L | Q | P M | U U |

¾ x 7¼ - 72 (3.75 Bd. Ft.)

| R | R | R | R | R |

¾ x 7¼ - 48 (2.5 Bd. Ft.)

| R | R | R |

¼" HARDBOARD - 24 x 48

| S | S | S | S | S | S | S | S |
| T | T | T | T |

¾" MDF - 48 x 96

| A | B | D |
| A | C | |

¾" MDF - 48 x 96

| E | J | O O O O |

¾" MDF - 48 x 96

| N | N |

NOTE: MDF SHEETS ARE NOT DRAWN TO THE SAME SCALE AS OTHER PIECES.

⅛" HARDBOARD - 1¾ x 72¼

| K |

BASE

I began work on the Revolving Tool Station by making an open, L-shaped base cabinet *(Fig. 1)*. The shape of the base will provide easy access to the turntable that's added later. And it will allow plenty of leg room when working at the tools on the carousel — while still fitting conveniently into a corner of your workshop.

SIDES AND BACKS. The base cabinet starts out as two sides (A) and a right (B) and left back (C) piece *(Fig. 1)*.

Note: I used ³/₄" MDF (medium-density fiberboard) for these pieces, but plywood would work just as well.

These four pieces are held together with simple butt joints. So to allow for the joinery in the back corner, the *right* back is a little wider (33³/₄") than the *left* back (33").

After cutting all the side and back pieces to size, there's one more thing to do before moving on to the top and bottom pieces. That's to cut a long dado in each piece for the bottom of the base cabinet *(Fig. 1a)*. This dado is ³/₈" deep and cut to width to match the thickness of the ³/₄" MDF.

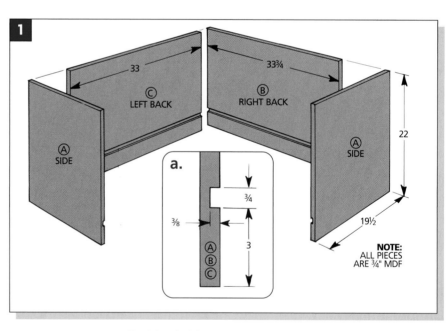

TOP AND BOTTOM. Besides holding the case together, the top and bottom provide a surface for mounting a number of roller bearings (see the photo on the opposite page). The roller bearings on the bottom make it easy to spin the turntable around, while those on the top allow you to rotate the carousel smoothly.

Both the top (D) and bottom (E) start out as a square piece of ³/₄" MDF *(Fig. 2)*. But to create an overhang, the top is larger than the bottom.

NOTCH. With the pieces cut to size, the next step is to cut a large notch in each one so they don't extend into the opening in front of the base. While you're at it, rout small (¹/₈") chamfers

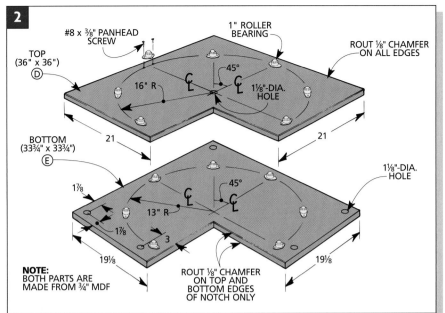

2

#8 x ⅜" PANHEAD SCREW

TOP (36" x 36") D

1" ROLLER BEARING

ROUT ⅛" CHAMFER ON ALL EDGES

45°

16" R

1⅛"-DIA. HOLE

21

21

BOTTOM (33¾" x 33¾") E

1⅞"

13" R

45°

1⅛"-DIA. HOLE

1⅞"

3

19⅛

19⅛

ROUT ⅛" CHAMFER ON TOP AND BOTTOM EDGES OF NOTCH ONLY

NOTE: BOTH PARTS ARE MADE FROM ¾" MDF

ROLLER BEARINGS. *Mounting a number of roller bearings to the top and bottom of the tool station in a circular pattern will allow both the carousel above and the turntable below to spin smoothly and easily. For sources of roller bearings like the one shown in the photo above, see page 126.*

on the top and bottom edges of the top and the top edge of the bottom *(Fig. 2)*.

ATTACH ROLLERS. Now you're ready to attach the rollers to the top and bottom. After spacing the rollers evenly around the perimeter of a large circle, they're screwed in place *(Fig. 2)*.

Note: To provide plenty of support near the edge of the carousel, the circle on top has a larger radius (16") than the one on the bottom (13").

Before assembling the base, it's best to drill several large holes. There's a hole in the top for an iron pipe that serves as a pivot point for the turntable and carousel *(Fig. 2)*. Also, five holes in the bottom will be used when levelers are added later.

ASSEMBLY. At this point, you can begin putting together the base cabinet. I started by gluing up a U-shaped assembly consisting of one side and the two back pieces.

Then I slipped the bottom in place and added the other side.

Note: Reinforcing each joint with screws during assembly will help strengthen the base.

RAILS. To add even more rigidity, I installed two hardwood rails under the top and bottom *(Figs. 3 and 4)*. A long rail (F) spans from one side to the left back. And a short rail (G) connects the long rail to the opposite side.

ATTACH TOP. All that's left to complete the base of the station is to attach the top. It's simply positioned, then glued and screwed to the rails, backs, and sides *(Fig. 4)*.

3

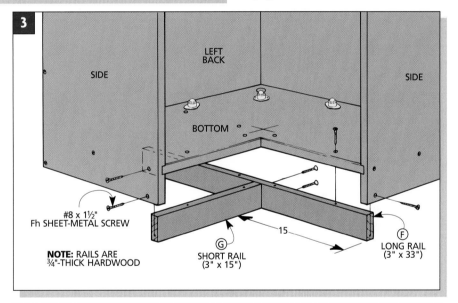

LEFT BACK

SIDE

SIDE

BOTTOM

#8 x 1½" Fh SHEET-METAL SCREW

NOTE: RAILS ARE ¾"-THICK HARDWOOD

SHORT RAIL (3" x 15") G

15

LONG RAIL (3" x 33") F

4

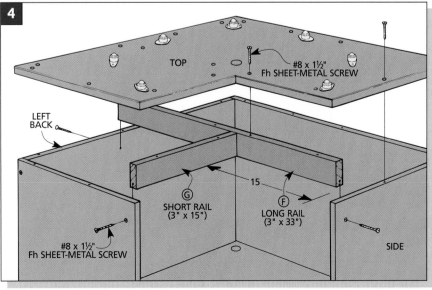

TOP

#8 x 1½" Fh SHEET-METAL SCREW

LEFT BACK

SHORT RAIL (3" x 15") G

15

LONG RAIL (3" x 33") F

#8 x 1½" Fh SHEET-METAL SCREW

SIDE

SHOP TIP . . . . . Uses for Levelers

The shop-made leveling system I used for the Revolving Tool Station can easily be adapted to other projects and fixtures.

For example, if your bench rocks on an uneven floor, you can add a leveler to one leg to compensate.

Bookcases that sit on a carpeted floor next to a wall tend to lean forward because of the tack bar under the carpet. If this is a problem for a cabinet in your house, levelers at the front of the case will keep the unit from tipping forward.

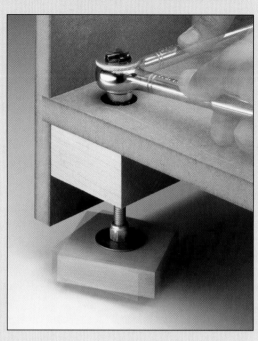

LEVELERS

To compensate for an uneven floor, I added five levelers. They allow each outside corner of the base to be leveled independently.

Basically, each leveler consists of two parts: a thick mounting block that attaches to the bottom of the base and an adjustable foot *(Fig. 5)*. By turning a bolt that passes through the center of each part, you can raise or lower the foot (see Shop Tip at left).

MOUNTING BLOCK. The weight of the MDF combined with a load of tools, means the completed project will be rather heavy. To provide plenty of strength for lifting this weight, each mounting block (H) is made by gluing up two pieces of $3/4$"-thick hardwood *(Fig. 5)*. (I used maple.)

Before gluing and screwing the mounting block to the bottom of the base, you'll need to drill a counterbored shank hole for a T-nut that accepts the adjustment bolt *(Fig. 5a)*. (See the Shop Tip on page 55 for an easy way to install T-nuts.)

FOOT. Once the block is in place, you can add the foot (I). It's a piece of $3/4$"-thick hardwood that's captured on the end of the bolt by a pair of lock nuts.

One nut rests in a counterbored shank hole drilled in the bottom of the foot. The other tightens against the top of the foot to lock it in place.

Note: When threading the bolt into the foot, make sure it doesn't extend past the bottom face of the foot.

TURNTABLE

The base of the tool carousel provides plenty of storage for portable power tools. To make it easy to remove a tool (or put one back) without having to reach deep inside the base, I added a turntable *(Fig. 6)*. This lets you bring to the front whatever you need.

The turntable is nothing more than a circular shelf that spins around on the roller bearings. An iron pipe acts as an axle that keeps the turntable centered in the base (refer to *Fig. 10* on page 67).

BLANK. The turntable starts out as a large, square blank of $3/4$"-thick MDF *(Fig. 6)*. Using a square blank provides straight reference edges for laying out and cutting a notch that matches the shape of the opening in the base. To cut this notch, I used a straightedge to

---

5

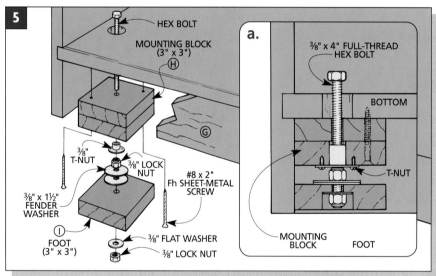

HEX BOLT

MOUNTING BLOCK (3" x 3")
(H)

(G)

$3/8$" T-NUT

$3/8$" LOCK NUT

$3/8$" x 1½" FENDER WASHER

#8 x 2" Fh SHEET-METAL SCREW

(I)

FOOT (3" x 3")

$3/8$" FLAT WASHER

$3/8$" LOCK NUT

a.

$3/8$" x 4" FULL-THREAD HEX BOLT

BOTTOM

T-NUT

MOUNTING BLOCK   FOOT

6

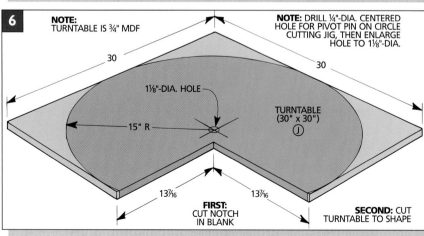

NOTE: TURNTABLE IS $3/4$" MDF

NOTE: DRILL ¼"-DIA. CENTERED HOLE FOR PIVOT PIN ON CIRCLE CUTTING JIG, THEN ENLARGE HOLE TO 1⅛"-DIA.

30

30

1⅛"-DIA. HOLE

15" R

TURNTABLE (30" x 30")
(J)

13⁷⁄₁₆   13⁷⁄₁₆

FIRST: CUT NOTCH IN BLANK

SECOND: CUT TURNTABLE TO SHAPE

---

guide my circular saw. Stop the cut just short of the inside corner, then finish up with a hand saw.

CUT TO SHAPE. Once the notch is done, you're ready to cut the turntable (J) to its final shape. An easy way to do this is to mount a router with a straight bit to a simple circle-cutting jig. (For details about making this jig, refer to the box below.)

To use the jig, you'll need to drill a small, centered hole in the turntable for a bolt that acts as a pivot pin. This hole needs to be enlarged so the iron pipe can stick through. But trying to center a bit in a hole can be difficult. So I plugged a short piece of dowel in the hole to give the bit something to "bite" into. I drilled this final hole slightly larger than the outside diameter of the pipe to prevent wear on the turntable.

STRIKE PLATES. Another place that could wear is along the edge of the

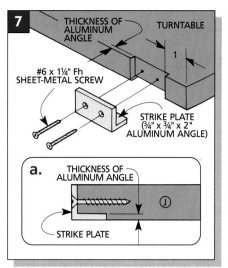

notch in the turntable where it rides up on the roller bearings. To prevent this, I added a metal strike plate to each notch.

These strike plates are simple — just short pieces of aluminum angle. They

TURNTABLE. *A spin of the turntable in the base of the Revolving Tool Station provides quick and easy access to your portable power tools.*

fit in shallow mortises cut in both the front edge and bottom of the turntable *(Fig. 7)*. After laying out the location of the mortises, just remove the waste material with a chisel.

SHOP JIG .... *Circle-Cutting Jig*

An easy way to cut the large circular workpieces on the Revolving Tool Station is to use a router that's mounted to a simple jig (see drawing).

BASE. The jig is just a hardboard base that pivots on a bolt. The length of the base isn't critical, but it needs to be long enough to hold your router and measure at least 20" from the bit to the pivot bolt. (The turntable has a 15" radius, but the carousel added later on top of the Tool Station has a radius of 20". Refer to *Fig. 12* on page 68).

PIVOT BOLT. A bolt passes through the base and into a centered hole drilled in the workpiece. To determine the location of the hole in the base, you'll need to know the radius of the workpiece. The hole is drilled that same distance away from the *inside* edge of a straight bit (see details 'a' and 'b'). To cut a different size circle, just drill a new hole in the base.

SET UP. Before routing the circle, it's a good idea to cut the workpiece to rough size first. (I used a jig saw and tried to stay within 1/16" of the line.) This way, there's not as much material to remove as you rout it to final size.

Then set the blank on a couple of pieces of scrap to raise it off the work surface. This will provide clearance for

the pivot bolt and the router bit (see details 'a' and 'b'.)

ROUT. As you rout, move the jig counter-clockwise around the work-

piece. Keep one hand firmly on the router. The other hand helps move the jig smoothly and keeps it pressed against the workpiece (see drawing).

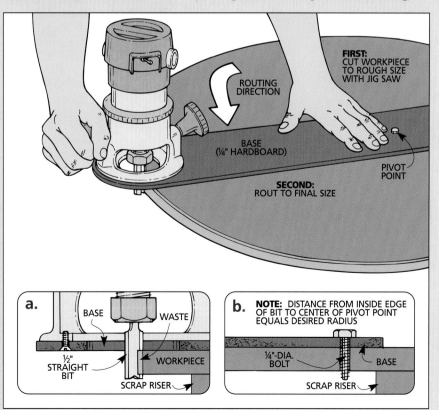

EDGING. Once the strike plates are screwed in place, the next step is to wrap a thin ($^1/_8$") strip of hardboard edging (K) around the curved part of the turntable.

This edging is a little taller (wider) than the thickness of the turntable. This way, it forms a lip that will keep tools and materials from falling off the turntable's edge.

One thing to notice about the edging is that it's actually cut $1^1/_2$" shorter than the distance around the curved part of the turntable *(Figs. 8 and 8a)*. This is done to provide enough clearance for a barrel bolt that's installed later. This barrel bolt will be used to lock the turntable in place so it won't spin around when you don't want it to (refer to *Figs. 10 and 11* on opposite page).

All it takes to attach the edging is to apply a little glue and hold the edging in place securely using a band clamp *(Fig. 8)*. After the glue dries and you have removed the band clamp, it's a good idea to secure the hardboard edging with screws *(Fig. 8a)*.

COLLAR BLOCK. At this point, you're almost ready to install the turntable. But first, to prevent it from rubbing against the pipe, I added a simple collar block *(Fig. 9)*.

The collar block (L) is a $^3/_4$"-thick piece of hardwood with a centered hole that's sized to fit the iron pipe.

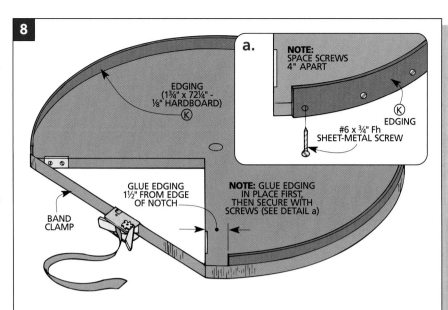

8

EDGING
($1^3/_4$" x $72^1/_4$" –
$^1/_8$" HARDBOARD)
(K)

a.

NOTE:
SPACE SCREWS
4" APART

(K)
EDGING

#6 x $^3/_4$" Fh
SHEET-METAL SCREW

GLUE EDGING
$1^1/_2$" FROM EDGE
OF NOTCH

NOTE: GLUE EDGING
IN PLACE FIRST,
THEN SECURE WITH
SCREWS (SEE DETAIL a)

BAND
CLAMP

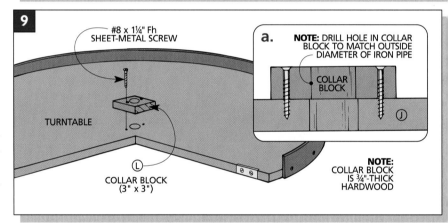

9

#8 x $1^1/_4$" Fh
SHEET-METAL SCREW

a.

NOTE: DRILL HOLE IN COLLAR
BLOCK TO MATCH OUTSIDE
DIAMETER OF IRON PIPE

COLLAR
BLOCK

(J)

TURNTABLE

(L)

COLLAR BLOCK
(3" x 3")

NOTE:
COLLAR BLOCK
IS $^3/_4$"-THICK
HARDWOOD

SHOP TIP . . . . *Modifying a Spade Bit*

The turntable (J), top (N), and bottom (N) each have a $1^1/_8$"-dia. hole in them to make it easy to slide the pipe through these pieces. However, I wanted the wood collar blocks (L) to fit closely around the pipe. But I ran into a snag when it came time to drill the holes in the collars. There wasn't a spade bit available that matched the $1^1/_{16}$" outside diameter of the pipe. So I modified a larger ($1^1/_8$"-dia.) spade bit by filing the sides until it was the correct size.

To ensure that the bit is balanced and cuts evenly,

it's important to remove the same amount of material from each side. A handy way to do this is to use a nail and a scrap block. Just clamp the spade bit to the scrap so that the edge of the bit extends $^1/_{32}$" above the

scrap's edge *(Fig. 1)*. Then drive a nail below the point of the bit to keep it from slipping down. (I marked the location of the nail, then removed the bit to drive the nail.)

Now file one side until it's even with the top of

the scrap block *(Fig. 2)*. (Don't file into the scrap.) Then flip the bit over and repeat the process on the other side.

Test the size of the modified bit on some scrap before boring holes in the collar blocks.

1

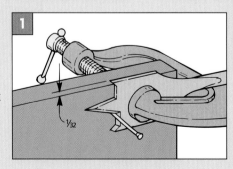

$^1/_{32}$

2

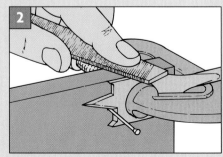

PIPE FLANGE. *A pre-threaded flange secured to the bottom of the Revolving Tool Station provides a solid foundation for the pipe that serves as a pivot for the turntable and carousel.*

Note: To drill this hole so the collar block fits snugly around the pipe, refer to the Shop Tip on the opposite page.

PIPE. After screwing the collar block in place, you can turn your attention to the pipe that serves as a pivot point for the turntable *(Fig. 10).* (I used a piece of $^3/_4$" iron pipe.) The pipe fits into a flange screwed to the bottom of the base *(Fig. 10a* and photo above).

Note: The pipe is extra long so it can double as a pivot point for the carousel that's added later.

Before installing the pipe, you'll need to set the turntable in place. Then slip the pipe through the top of the base and turntable and thread the end into the pipe flange.

Here again, to keep the pipe from rubbing, I screwed a second collar block (L) to the top of the base *(Fig. 10).*

BARREL BOLT. Finally, to lock the turntable in place, I added a barrel bolt

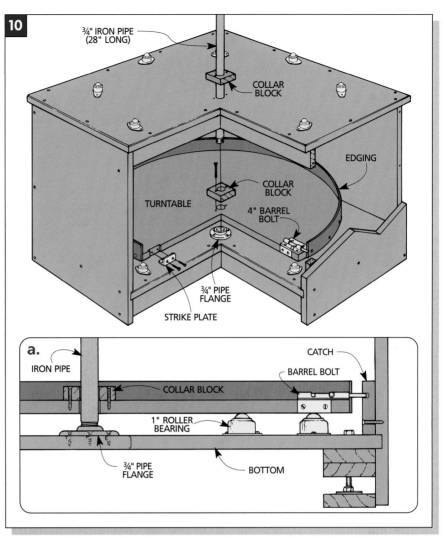

(Fig. 11). The bolt slides into a $^3/_4$"-thick hardwood catch (M) that's attached to the side of the base.

After gluing and screwing the catch in place, I located and drilled a hole in the catch to accept the end of the barrel bolt. For more on how to do this, see the Shop Tip at right.

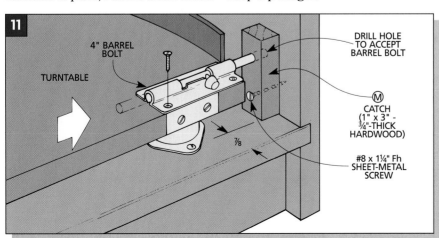

SHOP TIP
Barrel Bolt Hole

To locate the hole for the barrel bolt, slip a dowel center over the end of the bolt and press it against the catch. You may have to tap the back of the bolt with a hammer to leave a mark.

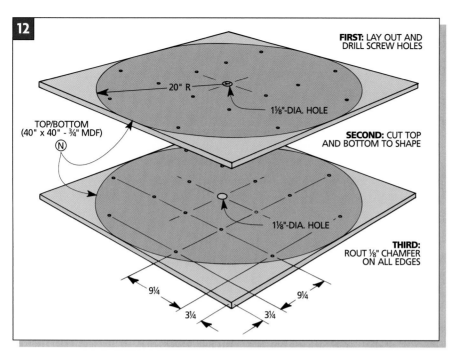

12

FIRST: LAY OUT AND DRILL SCREW HOLES

20" R

1⅛"-DIA. HOLE

TOP/BOTTOM (40" x 40" - ¾" MDF) Ⓝ

SECOND: CUT TOP AND BOTTOM TO SHAPE

1⅛"-DIA. HOLE

THIRD: ROUT ⅛" CHAMFER ON ALL EDGES

9¼

9¼

3¼

3¼

CAROUSEL. *Just spin the carousel until the tool you need is directly in front of you, then lock it in place.*

CAROUSEL

One of the handiest things about this tool station is a large revolving carousel that supports your benchtop tools. Spinning the carousel around provides quick access to the tool you need.

The carousel consists of a grid that's sandwiched between a circular top and bottom *(Fig. 12)*. The grid creates an opening under each tool for a drawer as well as small storage areas on the sides.

TOP AND BOTTOM. The top and bottom (N) of the carousel each start out as large square pieces of ¾" MDF *(Fig. 12)*. After laying out the locations of the screws used to fasten the top and

bottom to the grid, they can be cut to shape. Here again, a router and a circle jig make quick work of this (see the Shop Jig on page 65).

As with the turntable, you'll need to enlarge the pivot hole in each piece to provide clearance for the iron pipe. Also, it's a good idea to drill the pilot holes in the bottom face of the top now for the drawer stops that are added later (refer to *Figs. 17 and 17a* on the opposite page).

GRID. Now you can turn your attention to the grid that divides the carousel into separate compartments. The grid consists of four dividers (O) with interlocking slots in each one *(Fig. 13)*.

ASSEMBLY. Once the slots are cut, you can assemble the grid and attach the top and bottom with screws *(Fig. 14)*. After screwing one last collar block (L) in place on the top, just get a friend to help you lift the carousel onto the base.

BARREL BOLT. To lock the carousel in place when using a tool, another barrel bolt is attached to the base *(Fig. 15)*. This bolt slides into holes drilled in the bottom edge of the carousel.

To raise the barrel bolt off the base so it aligns with the carousel, I added an L-shaped mounting assembly *(Fig. 15)*. It's made up of two small pieces of ¾"-thick hardwood: a mounting block (P) that's screwed to the base and a riser block (Q) that positions the barrel bolt in line with the bottom edge of the carousel *(Fig. 15a)*.

MOUNT TOOLS. Before drilling the holes in the carousel's edge, you'll want to mount your individual power tools. (I

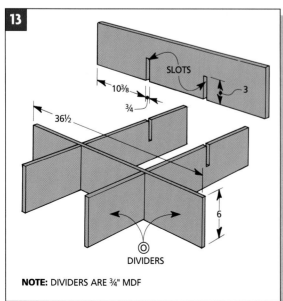

13

SLOTS

10⅜

¾

3

36½

6

6

Ⓞ DIVIDERS

NOTE: DIVIDERS ARE ¾" MDF

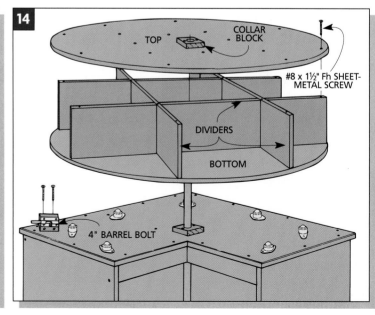

14

TOP

COLLAR BLOCK

#8 x 1½" Fh SHEET-METAL SCREW

DIVIDERS

BOTTOM

4" BARREL BOLT

used lag screws to mount them.) This way, you can rotate the carousel to the most comfortable working position for each specific tool. Then just drill each of the holes at the correct locations.

DRAWERS

With the carousel complete, I added a set of four drawers. These drawers fit into the openings directly below each tool to keep accessories right at hand where you need them.

FRONT AND BACK. To build the drawers, start by cutting a front and back (R) for each one. These are $3/4$"-thick pieces of hardwood that are sized to allow $1/8$" gaps along the sides and top of the opening.

Shallow rabbets in the ends of the front and back accept the sides of the drawer *(Figs. 16 and 16c)*. And there's a groove in each piece for the drawer bottom *(Fig. 16b)*.

SIDES. After completing the front and back, you can add the sides (S). These are pieces of $1/4$" hardboard with a notch at the top *(Fig. 16a)*. When the drawer stops are added later, this notch makes it possible to remove a drawer and put it back in.

BOTTOM AND CLEATS. There are just two things left to do to complete each drawer. A hardboard bottom (T) is cut to fit so the drawer can be glued and screwed together. Then two hardwood cleats (U) are glued to the bottom and sides to provide extra support.

STOP. Before installing the drawers, I attached four stops (V) under the top of the carousel *(Fig. 17)*. They keep the drawer from being pulled out too far and spilling what's inside. ■

DRAWERS. *With a drawer below each tool, there's plenty of storage for accessories and other items.*

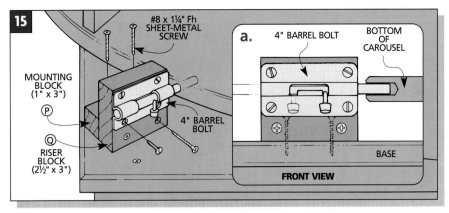

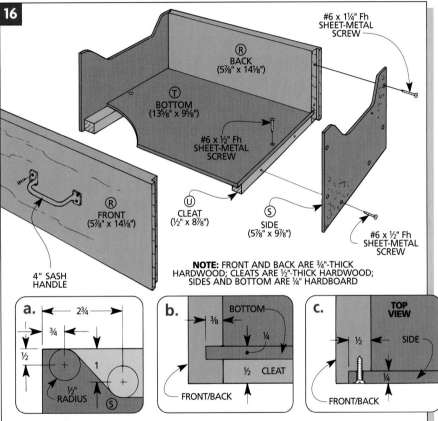

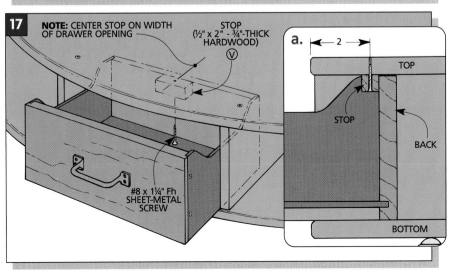

Benchtop Router Table

This table has many of the features of a full-size router table and cabinet. Its large top has wings which fold away, making it compact and easy to store. The multi-purpose fence doubles as a sturdy handle.

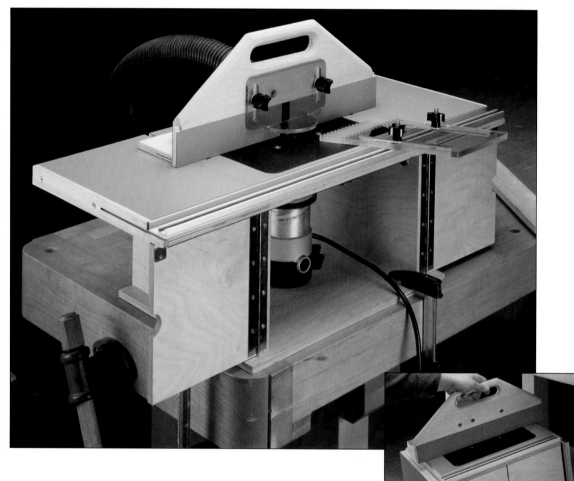

L et's face it. Not every shop has room for a large, stationary router table. That's the reason I like this Benchtop Router Table.

Instead of taking up valuable floor space, the router table simply clamps to a bench. And once a job is completed, it folds up into a compact box that's stored neatly out of the way (see inset photo).

With the router table folded up, it's only about as big as a picnic basket. But don't let its small size fool you.

LARGE TABLE. The "wings" on each side of the router table fold out to create a large, flat table. To provide support for the wings, just open the doors and swing them underneath. The doors "click" into a shop-made catch with a reassuring sound.

FENCE. As much as I like the table, it's the fence that impresses me the most. It adjusts easily and locks down tight. And a pair of sliding faces let you change the size of the opening around the bit. The fence even doubles as a handle to make it easy to carry the router table.

ALUMINUM TRACK. Another handy thing about this router table is that it has an aluminum track that runs along the front edge. Actually, it's *two* tracks in one. One part acts as a smooth, accurate slot for a miter gauge. The other

lets you attach a featherboard.

ANOTHER VERSION. If you want a less expensive version of this router table, take a look at the Designer's Notebook on page 73. It uses the same basic design as the deluxe version, but I left out the aluminum track system and a few other options to keep the cost down.

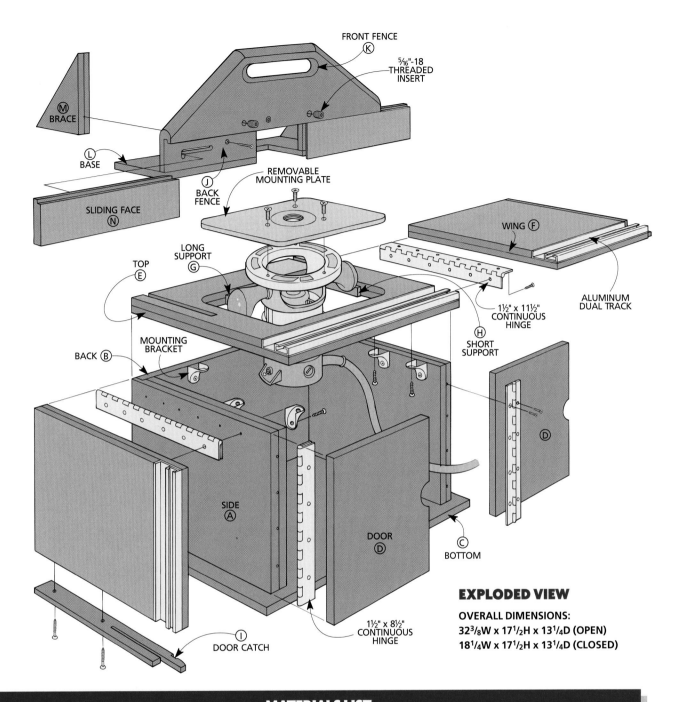

FRONT FENCE
Ⓚ

5/16"-18
THREADED
INSERT

Ⓜ
BRACE

Ⓛ
BASE

SLIDING FACE
Ⓝ

Ⓙ
BACK
FENCE

REMOVABLE
MOUNTING PLATE

WING Ⓕ

ALUMINUM
DUAL TRACK

LONG
SUPPORT
Ⓖ

TOP
Ⓔ

1½" x 11½"
CONTINUOUS
HINGE

Ⓗ
SHORT
SUPPORT

MOUNTING
BRACKET

BACK Ⓑ

Ⓓ

SIDE
Ⓐ

DOOR
Ⓓ

Ⓒ
BOTTOM

1½" x 8½"
CONTINUOUS
HINGE

Ⓘ
DOOR CATCH

EXPLODED VIEW

OVERALL DIMENSIONS:
32³⁄₈W x 17¹⁄₂H x 13¹⁄₄D (OPEN)
18¹⁄₄W x 17¹⁄₂H x 13¹⁄₄D (CLOSED)

MATERIALS LIST

CASE
A	Sides (2)	1 ply - 8³⁄₄ x 12¹⁄₂
B	Back (1)	¹⁄₂ ply - 8³⁄₄ x 15¹⁄₂
C	Bottom (1)	¹⁄₂ ply - 13¹⁄₄ x 18¹⁄₂
D	Doors (2)	¹⁄₂ ply - 8³⁄₄ x7¹⁵⁄₁₆
E	Top (1)	1 ply - 13¹⁄₄ x 16
F	Wings (2)	1 ply - 13¹⁄₄ x 7⁷⁄₈
G	Long Supports (2)	¹⁄₄ x ¹¹⁄₁₆ - 9
H	Short Supports (2)	¹⁄₄ x ¹¹⁄₁₆ - 6
I	Door Catches (2)	⁵⁄₁₆ x 1¹⁄₈ - 13¹⁄₄

FENCE
J	Back Fence (1)	¹⁄₂ ply - 6³⁄₄ x 18¹⁄₄
K	Front Fence (1)	¹⁄₂ ply - 5 x 18¹⁄₄
L	Base (1)	¹⁄₂ ply - 4 x 18¹⁄₄

M	Braces (2)	1 ply - 3¹⁄₂ x 5
N	Sliding Faces (2)	¹⁄₂ ply - 2¹⁄₂ x 9¹⁄₈

Note: All 1"-thick plywood is made by
face-gluing two pieces of ¹⁄₂"-thick stock.

HARDWARE SUPPLIES
(1) Router mounting plate
(1 pc.) 48" x 48" plastic laminate
(50) No. 4 x ¹⁄₂" Fh woodscrews
(16) No. 6 x ³⁄₄" Fh woodscrews
(16) No. 6 x 1¹⁄₂" Fh woodscrews
(4) 1" wire brads (18 gauge)
(6) Mounting brackets
(1) Magnetic catch

(2) 1¹⁄₂" x 8¹⁄₂" cont. hinges w/ screws
(2) 1¹⁄₂" x 11¹⁄₂" cont. hinges w/ screws
(2) ¹⁄₄"-20 threaded rods (1¹⁄₈" long)
(2) ⁵⁄₁₆"-18 x 1³⁄₄" toilet bolts
(2) ⁵⁄₁₆" flat washers
(2) ¹⁄₄" flat washers
(2) ¹⁄₄"-20 star knob (through-hole)
(2) ⁵⁄₁₆"-18 star knob (through-hole)
(3) ⁵⁄₁₆"-18 threaded inserts (³⁄₈" long)
(1) 32"-long aluminum dual track

CUTTING DIAGRAM

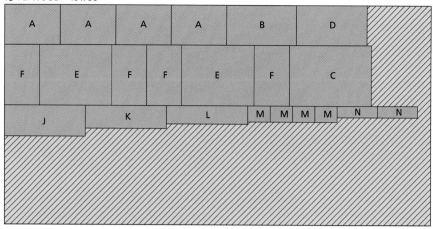

½" PLYWOOD - 48 x 96

¾ x 3½ - 96 (2.7 Bd. Ft.)

I began work on the router table by making the case. In addition to housing the router, the case provides a sturdy mounting platform for the table.

Note: Depending on your router, you may need to modify the height of the case. Just be sure it's tall enough that you can adjust the height of the bit without having the router contact the bottom of the case.

U-SHAPED ASSEMBLY. The case starts out as a U-shaped assembly that consists of two sides and a back *(Fig. 1)*. Each side is glued up from two oversize pieces of ¹/₂" plywood. (I used Baltic birch.)

After trimming the sides (A) to final size, you'll need to rabbet the back, inside edge of each one to accept the back (B) *(Fig. 1a)*. The back is a piece of ¹/₂" plywood that's glued and screwed to the sides.

BOTTOM. The next step is to add a plywood bottom (C) *(Fig. 1)*. The bottom is sized to extend an equal amount past the sides and front of the case. (It's flush at the back.) This provides several clamping surfaces that allow you to secure the router table to a workbench.

DOORS. After attaching the bottom with glue and screws, I added a pair of doors (D) *(Fig. 2)*. Besides enclosing the front of the case, the doors have another (more important) job. When you swing the doors open, they hold up the "wings" of the router table.

To create a continuous, flat surface, the wings work best when supported at the exact same height as the center part of the table. This center part rests on the sides (A) and back (B) of the case. So making the doors the same height (width) as these pieces will prevent the wings from sagging.

Of course, this means that the doors will fit quite tightly in the opening when the top is added later. But that's okay. In fact, the goal is to size the doors so they'll just barely scrape against the top and bottom.

To do this, I made both doors from a single blank of ¹/₂" plywood *(Fig. 2)*. As I mentioned, the plywood is ripped to width to match the height of the sides. And it's cut to length to match the distance of the case from one outside face to the other.

FINGER RECESSES. Before crosscutting the blank into two equal pieces to make the doors, it's best to drill a hole

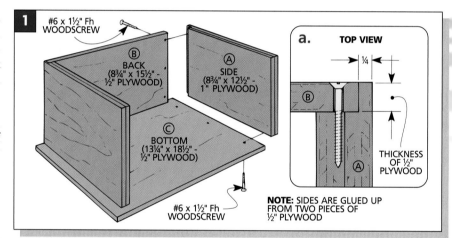

1 #6 x 1½" Fh WOODSCREW

BACK
(8¾" x 15½" - ½" PLYWOOD)

SIDE
(8¾" x 12½" - 1" PLYWOOD)

BOTTOM
(13¼" x 18½" - ½" PLYWOOD)

#6 x 1½" Fh WOODSCREW

a. TOP VIEW

¼

THICKNESS OF ½" PLYWOOD

NOTE: SIDES ARE GLUED UP FROM TWO PIECES OF ½" PLYWOOD

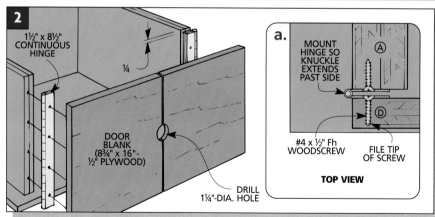

2 1½" x 8½" CONTINUOUS HINGE

¼

DOOR BLANK
(8¾" x 16" - ½" PLYWOOD)

DRILL 1¼"-DIA. HOLE

a. MOUNT HINGE SO KNUCKLE EXTENDS PAST SIDE

#4 x ½" Fh WOODSCREW

FILE TIP OF SCREW

TOP VIEW

for the finger recesses. This is just a matter of drilling a centered hole in the plywood blank before making the crosscut (the kerf from this cut leaves a ¹/₈" gap between the doors).

INSTALL DOORS. All that's left to complete the case is to install the doors.

They're held in place with a pair of continuous (piano) hinges *(Fig. 2a)*. One thing to be aware of here is that the hinges are located ¹/₄" *below* the top of the door and side. This provides clearance that keeps the wings from binding against the hinge.

Once the hinges are screwed in place, you can turn your attention to the table. Basically it consists of three parts: a top (E) and two wings (F) *(Fig. 4)*.

GLUE UP BLANK. Here again, it's easiest to make all three parts from one blank. I wanted to create a thick, sturdy table. To do this, I simply glued up two pieces of $1/2$" plywood *(Fig. 3)*.

PLASTIC LAMINATE. Regardless of its thickness, the surface of the table will still get worn from sliding workpieces across it. So to produce a durable surface, it's a good idea to glue a piece of plastic laminate to the top of the blank. And add another piece to the bottom of the blank. Laminating both sides helps keep the table from warping.

TRACK SYSTEM. After trimming the laminate flush, I added an aluminum track system. This system consists of two parts: a wide, L-shaped piece, and on top of it, a narrow mounting strip with a T-shaped slot *(Fig. 3)*.

Together, these parts form a slot for the miter gauge. And the mounting strip makes it easy to attach a featherboard. Just slip the head of a toilet bolt into the T-slot and secure the featherboard with a knob.

Note: This track system is available exclusively from *Woodsmith Project Supplies*. Refer to Sources on page 126.

Of course, you can build the router table without using the track at all. In that case, you may want to rout a slot in the blank for a miter gauge. Or just plan on using a squared-up block to push the workpiece past the bit.

INSTALL TRACK. There's nothing complicated about installing the track. The L-shaped piece fits in a rabbet that's cut in the edge of the blank *(Fig. 3a)*. Then, to position the narrow mounting strip, I used the bar on the miter gauge and a single layer of paper as a spacer. (See the Shop Tip above for the best way to do this.)

CROSSCUT BLANK. After attaching the narrow strip with screws, it's time to crosscut the blank to form the three table pieces *(Fig. 4)*. A table saw and a miter gauge with an auxiliary fence make quick work of the job of cutting the blank. And as long as you use a carbide-tipped saw blade, there's no need to worry about cutting through the aluminum track. Aluminum is quite soft, and it cuts easily.

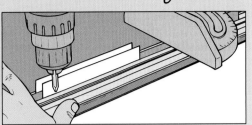

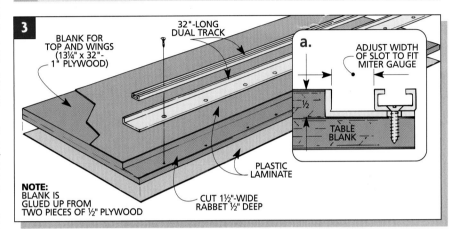

3

BLANK FOR TOP AND WINGS ($13\frac{1}{4}$" x 32"- 1" PLYWOOD)

32"-LONG DUAL TRACK

a. ADJUST WIDTH OF SLOT TO FIT MITER GAUGE

$\frac{1}{2}$

$\frac{1}{2}$

TABLE BLANK

PLASTIC LAMINATE

CUT $1\frac{1}{2}$"-WIDE RABBET $\frac{1}{2}$" DEEP

NOTE: BLANK IS GLUED UP FROM TWO PIECES OF $\frac{1}{2}$" PLYWOOD

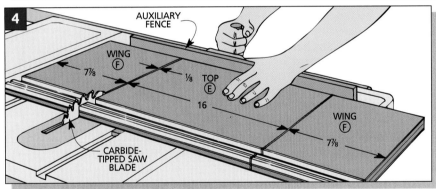

4

AUXILIARY FENCE

WING (F)

$7\frac{7}{8}$

$\frac{1}{8}$

TOP (E)

16

WING (F)

$7\frac{7}{8}$

CARBIDE-TIPPED SAW BLADE

DESIGNER'S NOTEBOOK

BASIC ROUTER TABLE

This router table uses the same basic design as the deluxe version. But in order to simplify construction and reduce the cost, there are a few minor changes.

First of all, the table and the sliding faces on the fence aren't covered with laminate.

The table also features a removable mounting plate. It's just a $1/4$"-thick phenolic plate, pre-drilled for the router bit and finger holes.

Finally, the aluminum track system was eliminated. The featherboard is attached with knobs into threaded inserts installed in the table.

Thanks to a mounting plate that fits into an opening in the router table, changing bits is a snap (see photo).

To provide easy access to the router, just lift the mounting plate out of the opening. Then change the bit and drop the mounting plate back in.

TEMPLATE. The challenge is cutting an opening that allows the mounting plate to fit nice and snug. To do this, I made a hardboard template *(Steps 1 through 3)*.

CUT OPENING. By using the template as a guide, you can cut an identical opening in the top (E) of the router table *(Steps 4 and 5)*.

SUPPORT STRIPS. Next add several hardwood strips to support the mounting plate *(Step 6)*. Then simply attach the router to the mounting plate *(Step 7)*.

1 To make the template, start by cutting a ¹/₄" hardboard blank to the same size as the top of the table. Then center the mounting plate on the blank and surround it with hardboard guide strips. The strips are simply butted against the plate and secured with carpet tape.

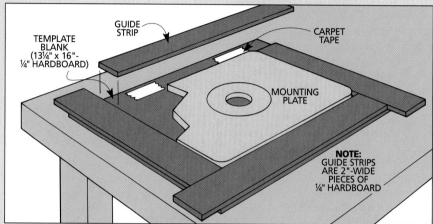

TEMPLATE BLANK (13¼" x 16"- ¼" HARDBOARD)

GUIDE STRIP

CARPET TAPE

MOUNTING PLATE

NOTE: GUIDE STRIPS ARE 2"-WIDE PIECES OF ¼" HARDBOARD

2 After removing the mounting plate, the next step is to cut a rough opening in the template. To do this, drill a hole in each corner that just grazes the edges of the guide strips (see detail 'a'). Then remove the bulk of the waste with a jig saw by cutting inside the strips.

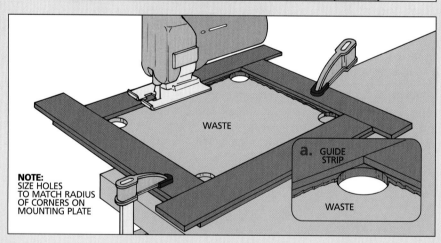

WASTE

NOTE: SIZE HOLES TO MATCH RADIUS OF CORNERS ON MOUNTING PLATE

a. GUIDE STRIP

WASTE

3 Now flip the template over so the guide strips are on the bottom and clean up the rest of the waste with a hand-held router and flush-trim bit. To avoid changing the radius of the corners, stop routing just short of the corner holes. This leaves a ridge that's easily sanded smooth.

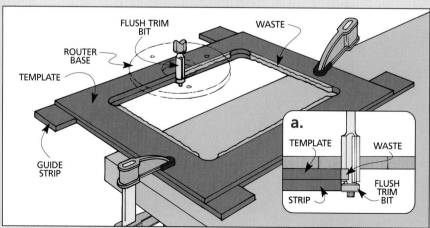

FLUSH TRIM BIT

WASTE

ROUTER BASE

TEMPLATE

GUIDE STRIP

a.

TEMPLATE

WASTE

FLUSH TRIM BIT

STRIP

4 Now you can use the template as a guide to cut the opening in the table top. After carpet-taping the template flush with the top, drill holes in the corners as before. Then cut the opening to rough size, staying about $1/8$" to the inside edge of the template (see detail 'a').

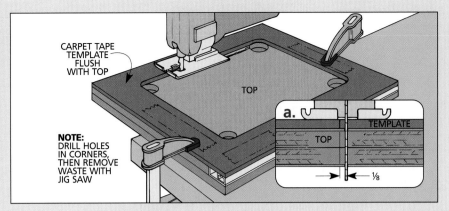

CARPET TAPE TEMPLATE FLUSH WITH TOP

TOP

NOTE: DRILL HOLES IN CORNERS, THEN REMOVE WASTE WITH JIG SAW

a. TEMPLATE

TOP

$1/8$

5 At this point, it's just a matter of trimming the edges of the opening flush with the template. Here again, a hand-held router and flush-trim bit make quick work of this. Just flip the top so the template is on the bottom. Then clean up the waste by routing in the direction shown.

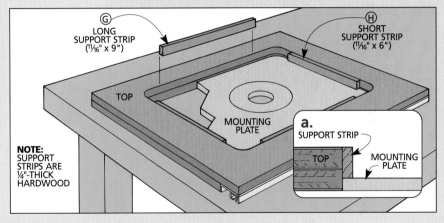

FLUSH TRIM BIT

WASTE

TEMPLATE

TOP

a.

TOP

FLUSH TRIM BIT

TEMPLATE

6 Once the opening is complete, you'll need to add thin, hardwood strips to provide support for the mounting plate. To ensure that the mounting plate is flush with the top, start by placing both parts face down on a flat surface. Then butt the strips against the plate and glue them to the top.

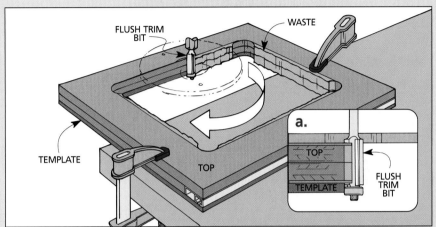

Ⓖ LONG SUPPORT STRIP ($^{11}/_{16}$" x 9")

Ⓗ SHORT SUPPORT STRIP ($^{11}/_{16}$" x 6")

TOP

MOUNTING PLATE

a. SUPPORT STRIP

TOP

MOUNTING PLATE

NOTE: SUPPORT STRIPS ARE $1/4$"-THICK HARDWOOD

7 All that's left to do is to attach the router to the mounting plate. This requires drilling holes for the machine screws that hold it in place. An easy way to locate the holes for the screws is to use the existing base on your router. (I used two-sided carpet tape to keep the base from shifting.)

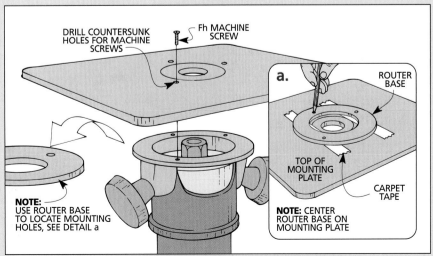

DRILL COUNTERSUNK HOLES FOR MACHINE SCREWS

Fh MACHINE SCREW

a. ROUTER BASE

TOP OF MOUNTING PLATE

CARPET TAPE

NOTE: USE ROUTER BASE TO LOCATE MOUNTING HOLES, SEE DETAIL a

NOTE: CENTER ROUTER BASE ON MOUNTING PLATE

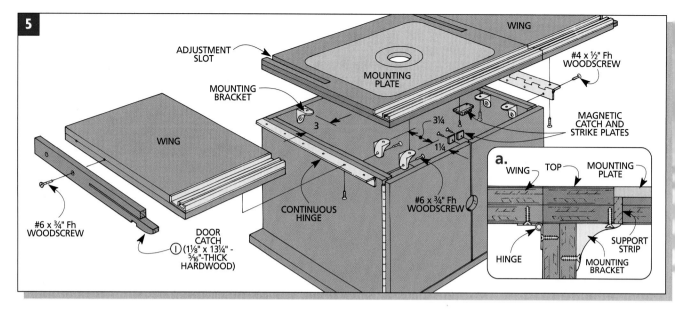

5

ADJUSTMENT SLOT

MOUNTING BRACKET

WING

MOUNTING PLATE

WING

#4 x ½" Fh WOODSCREW

MAGNETIC CATCH AND STRIKE PLATES

3

3¼

1¼

#6 x ¾" Fh WOODSCREW

CONTINUOUS HINGE

#6 x ¾" Fh WOODSCREW

DOOR CATCH (1⅛" x 13¼" - 5/16"-THICK HARDWOOD)

a. WING TOP MOUNTING PLATE

HINGE MOUNTING BRACKET SUPPORT STRIP

ASSEMBLY

Assembling the table is a fairly straightforward process. But getting all three parts to form a continuous, flat surface does require some care. Before you get started though, there's still some work to do on the top (center) of the table.

ADJUSTMENT SLOTS. To make the fence adjustable from front to back, cut two slots that extend about halfway across the top of the table *(Fig. 5)*.

Later, these adjustment slots will accept a pair of toilet bolts. So each one is shaped like an upside-down "T". The narrow part of each slot accepts the shank of the bolt. And the head of the bolt fits in a wide, shallow recess.

To cut the narrow part of each slot in a single pass, I mounted a $3/8$"-wide dado blade in the table saw *(Fig. 6a)*.

Note: This cut will leave an arc at the end of the slot. But that's okay, as long as it's on the bottom of the table. It won't show once the table is assembled.

This means you'll need to mark the end of the slot on the top of the workpiece and then cut up to the line *(Fig. 6)*. To reduce the chance of kickback, turn off the saw and let the blade stop spinning before sliding the top back across the saw table.

To cut the narrow part of the slot in the opposite end, you could flip the workpiece over and use the same setup. But then the arc would be cut in the top surface of the table. So I moved the fence to the opposite side of the blade to cut this slot.

RECESS. Now you're ready to cut the shallow recess for the head of the bolt. The procedure is the same, only here I used a $5/8$"-wide dado blade and set it for an $1/8$"-deep cut *(Fig. 7a)*.

Since the blade won't extend all the way through the top, it won't be visible. So add a reference mark to establish the end of the recess. A pencil mark on the rip fence that indicates the top (center) of the blade will work fine *(Fig. 7)*.

Now just turn on the saw and push the workpiece forward until the end of the slot aligns with the mark. As before, move the fence to the *opposite* side of the blade to cut the other recess.

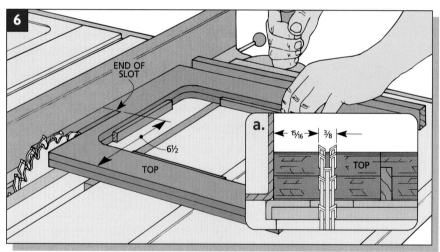

6

END OF SLOT

6½

TOP

a. 15/16 3/8 TOP

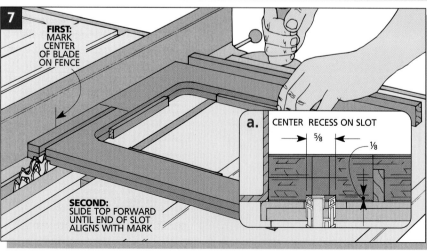

7

FIRST: MARK CENTER OF BLADE ON FENCE

SECOND: SLIDE TOP FORWARD UNTIL END OF SLOT ALIGNS WITH MARK

a. CENTER RECESS ON SLOT

5/8 1/8

MOUNT TOP. Once the adjustment slots are completed, you can mount the top. It's attached with six metal brackets to the case *(Fig. 5a)*.

After positioning the top flush with the sides and back, the brackets are just screwed in place. I also added a magnetic catch and two strike plates to keep the doors closed.

ATTACH WINGS. The next step is to attach the wings. As with the doors, they're hinged to the case. But first, you'll want to make sure the aluminum track in the wings aligns with the aluminum track in the top. Also, it's important that the top surface of all three pieces is perfectly flush.

The best way I found to accomplish both things is to cut a scrap to fit snugly in the track *(Fig. 8a)*. The scrap should be long enough to span all three pieces of the router table top. Then turn the case and wings upside down on a *flat* surface and clamp all three pieces together *(Fig. 8)*.

Now it's just a matter of marking the location of the pilot holes for the

mounting screws. To provide clearance for the doors as they are swung open, the hinges are set back 1" from the front edge of the sides.

Note: I used carpet tape to keep the continuous hinges from shifting.

After carefully marking the center-

points of the mounting holes, you can unclamp the wings and drill the pilot holes. Then just screw the hinges to the wings and sides.

CATCHES. To complete the table, I added a wood catch (I) to each wing *(Fig. 9)*. The catch is just a thin strip of hardwood that "locks" the door in the open position. This prevents the door from swinging out from under the wing if it accidentally becomes dislodged after being bumped.

FINGERS. To make this work, a kerf in each catch forms two "fingers" that flex like an old-fashioned clothespin. The lower edge of the finger tapers toward the end, and it has a small notch in the bottom edge *(Fig. 9a)*. This way, as you swing the door open, it contacts the tapered end of the catch and lifts up the lower finger. To secure the door, just open it a bit further. The lower finger of the catch drops down, and the notch will securely "capture" the door.

Before attaching the catches, you'll need to trim the end of the *upper* finger. This allows the miter gauge to slide in and out of the track. Now glue and screw the catches to the wings. Just make sure you don't apply glue to the lower finger.

ADJUSTMENT SCREWS. At this point it's a good idea to flip up the wings, open the doors, and check the table to make sure it's flat and level. If necessary, you can install an adjustment screw in the bottom of each wing *(Fig. 10)*. Pre-drill a countersunk hole for the screw. The adjustment screw allows you to "tweak" the wings to create a flat, level work surface *(Fig. 10a)*.

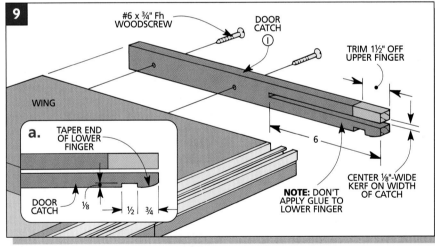

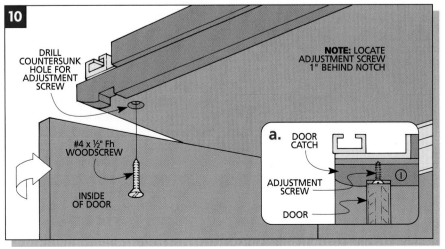

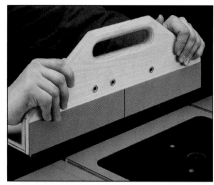

ADJUSTMENT SLOTS. *Two convenient adjustment slots will make it easy for you to slide the fence on and off the router table top.*

FENCE

The most unique thing about this router table is that the fence doubles as a handle. The top of the fence body has a long, wide slot for a handhold. And the inside edges of the slot are rounded for comfort. But there's more to it than that.

A simple clamping system is used to lock the fence in place quickly and accurately. There's also an adjustable opening in the fence to accommodate different sized router bits.

The fence consists of three main parts: a tall body with angled corners, a fence support for rigidity *(Fig. 11)*, and two sliding faces to adjust the size of the bit opening (refer to *Fig. 17*).

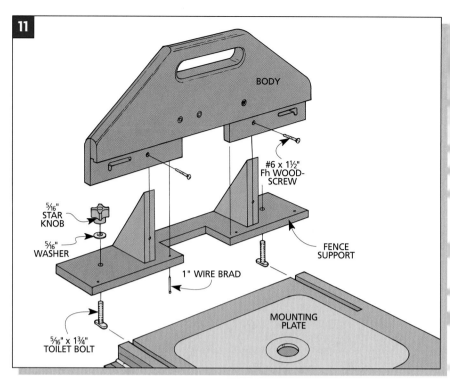

BODY

Besides acting as the handle, the body of the fence houses the sliding faces. To support the weight of the router table *and* the router, the body needs to be sturdy and strong. So it's made up of two pieces of $1/2$"-thick plywood. But I didn't glue these pieces together right away. Instead, I worked on one at a time. This made it easier to "build in" a recess for the two sliding faces.

BACK FENCE. I began by cutting the back fence (J) to final size *(Fig. 12)*. A wide notch in the bottom edge of this piece forms an opening that prevents the bit from chewing up the fence.

In addition to the notch, you also need to cut a pair of L-shaped slots *(Fig. 12a)*. The long part of each slot lets you adjust the sliding face. And later, the "leg" makes it possible to attach the sliding faces to the fence.

A quick way to cut these slots is to first drill a series of overlapping holes. Then just clean up the ridges with a chisel.

FRONT FENCE. Now you're ready to start on the front fence (K) *(Fig. 13)*. It's the same length as the back, but it's narrower. The difference in widths forms the recess for the sliding faces. Cutting a rabbet in the bottom edge of this piece creates a lip that holds the sliding faces in the recess *(Fig. 13a)*.

GLUE-UP. The next step is to glue up the front and back fence pieces. This

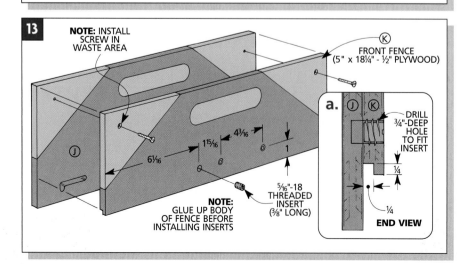

presents a bit of a problem. If the pieces slip out of alignment, the sliding faces will bind in the recess. To prevent this, I used a simple trick.

Start by first screwing the pieces together (no glue) so the top edges and ends are flush *(Fig. 13)*.

Note: Install the screws in the waste areas of the two upper corners.

Now separate the pieces, apply glue, and reinstall the screws. This keeps the pieces from shifting around as you clamp up the assembly.

INSERTS. All that's left to complete the body is to install three threaded inserts, for attaching accessories like a bit guard or featherboard *(Fig. 13a)*.

HANDHOLD. Now you can turn your attention to the handhold. It's a long, wide slot at the top of the body *(Fig. 14)*. The ends of the handhold are established by drilling two large holes, and a jig saw makes quick work of removing the rest of the waste. After smoothing the rough spots with a file, I routed roundovers on all the edges to provide a comfortable grip.

To "slim down" the profile of the fence (and reduce its overall weight), it's also a good idea to cut the upper corners of the body at an angle. Here again, sand the rough surfaces smooth and round over the edges.

FENCE SUPPORT

To provide accurate results, the fence needs to be square to the table. And since this fence is used to carry the router table around, I wanted to make sure it stayed square. So I added a sturdy fence support as a foundation. It's just a wide base and two triangular braces.

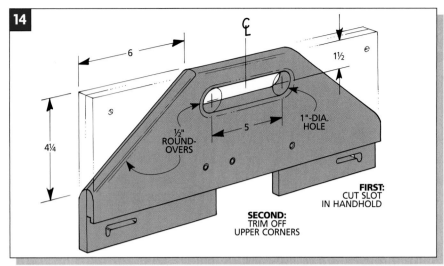

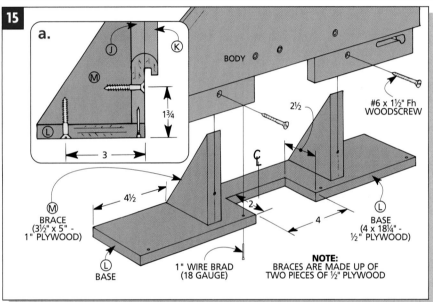

BASE. The base is cut from $1/2$" plywood (L) *(Fig. 15)*. As with the back fence, cutting a large notch in the base provides clearance for the router bit.

BRACES. Next, to hold the fence square to the base, I added two triangular braces (M). Each brace is made by gluing up two pieces of $1/2$" plywood. The braces are held in place with glue and screws. But to simplify the assembly, I first glued and nailed the back fence (J) flush with the front edge of the base *(Fig. 15a)*.

MOUNTING HOLES. There's one more thing to do and that's to drill two mounting holes for the toilet bolts that are used to secure the fence to the table *(Figs. 16 and 16a)*.

To locate these holes, position the fence flush with the back edge of the table. Then, after checking that there's an equal overhang on each side, center the holes on the T-slots in the table. Now it's just a matter of drilling the holes for the toilet bolts and installing the bolts and lock knobs.

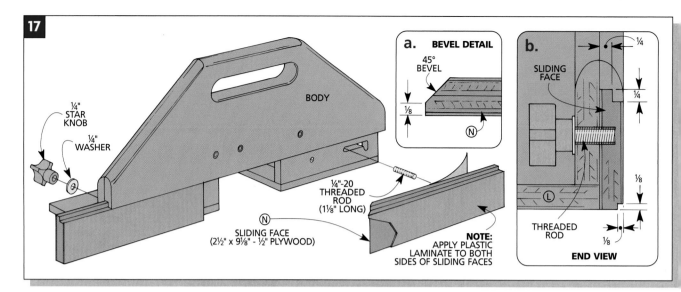

17

¼" STAR KNOB

¼" WASHER

BODY

a. BEVEL DETAIL

45° BEVEL

⅛"

N

b.

¼

SLIDING FACE

¼

⅛

THREADED ROD

⅛

L

END VIEW

¼"-20 THREADED ROD (1⅛" LONG)

N

SLIDING FACE (2½" x 9⅛" - ½" PLYWOOD)

NOTE: APPLY PLASTIC LAMINATE TO BOTH SIDES OF SLIDING FACES

SLIDING FACES

All that's left to complete the fence is to add two sliding faces. Including these makes it possible to quickly adjust the fence opening for different sized bits. The sliding faces can easily be moved in or out along the fence as needed. A threaded rod and knob hold the faces in place once they're properly adjusted.

Each of the sliding faces (N) starts out as a piece of ¹/₂" plywood *(Fig. 17)*. To create a durable surface on the faces, both sides are covered with plastic laminate. But don't apply the laminate yet. This would make the sliding faces thicker than the front fence piece. As a result there would be a slight "step" between the faces and body of the fence.

The solution, in this case, is simple. Just use two layers of laminate as a "gauge" and mark the amount of material to remove *(Fig. 18a)*. Then slice off the extra thickness from the plywood on the table saw *(Fig. 18)*.

BEVEL ENDS. After applying the laminate, you can cut a bevel on the *inside* end of each face *(Fig. 17a)*. The bevels provide clearance for large bits, so that the size of the fence opening can be reduced even more.

CUT RABBET. In addition to the bevels, you'll also need to rabbet the top edge of each sliding face *(Fig. 17b)*. This forms a lip that fits under the lip in the front fence (K). Together, they form an interlocking (sliding) joint that keeps the sliding faces nice and flat against the fence.

DUST RELIEF. The bottom edge of each sliding face is also rabbeted *(Fig. 17b)*. It's just a small rabbet that provides some dust relief at the bottom of the fence.

THREADED ROD. Now all that's left is to add a short, threaded rod to each sliding face. These rods pass through the L-shaped slots in the fence. Tightening a knob on the end of each rod locks the face in place.

It's easy to lay out the location of the rods. Just slide each face into the fence so the ends are flush *(Fig. 19)*. (It should also be snug along the top edge.) After marking around the slot, drill a hole in the end and glue in the rod with epoxy *(Fig. 19a)*.

To install the sliding face, insert the rod in the short "leg" of the slot. Then lift *up* on the face so the top edge engages the fence, slide it *over*, and thread on a knob. ∎

18

NOTE: RESAW SLIDING FACE TO THICKNESS AS MARKED IN DETAIL a

a.

SLIDING FACE

MARK AMOUNT OF MATERIAL TO BE REMOVED

PLASTIC LAMINATE (TWO LAYERS)

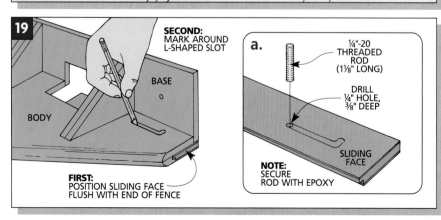

19

SECOND: MARK AROUND L-SHAPED SLOT

BASE

BODY

FIRST: POSITION SLIDING FACE FLUSH WITH END OF FENCE

a.

¼"-20 THREADED ROD (1⅛" LONG)

DRILL ¼" HOLE, ⅜" DEEP

SLIDING FACE

NOTE: SECURE ROD WITH EPOXY

ACCESSORIES ....Table Add-Ons

After completing the router table, one of the first improvements I made was to build three simple accessories for the router table and fence.

The featherboard, the router bit guard, and the vacuum attachment can all be made easily in a couple of hours (*Figs. 1, 2, and 3* and photos below).

Otherwise, durable plastic versions (see photo on page 70) are available as part of our *Woodsmith Project Supplies* hardware kit (see page 126).

FEATHERBOARD

One nice thing about the featherboard shown here is that it can be attached either to the router table fence or to the aluminum track. That gives you the kind of convenience and versatility that always comes in so handy in a small home workshop.

To keep a workpiece flat on the Benchtop Router Table, all you need to do is mount the featherboard to the fence with knobs that thread into the inserts. Or, if you prefer, secure the featherboard to the track with toilet bolts and knobs to hold the workpiece against the fence.

The featherboard is a piece of 1/2"-thick hardwood. It has mitered ends and a pair of adjustment slots cut parallel to its sides (*Fig. 1*). To cut the slots that form the fingers, I tilted the blade on the table saw and clamped the featherboard to an auxiliary fence on the miter gauge.

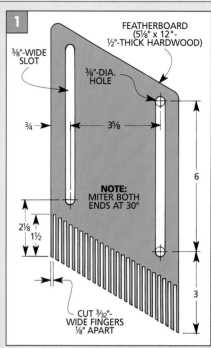

ROUTER BIT GUARD

For safety, you should include a bit guard on the router table. This guard attaches to the fence with knobs that thread into the two outer inserts.

Note: The middle insert is for the featherboard (see photo above).

The guard consists of a hardwood back and a shield made from 1/4" polycarbonate plastic (*Fig. 2*). After cutting two adjustment slots in the back, the shield is screwed in place.

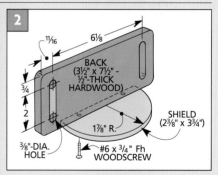

VACUUM ATTACHMENT

Finally, I decided to add a simple dust collection system that attaches to the back of the router table fence and connects to a shop vacuum.

It's made up of two triangular sides and a faceplate with a hole cut to fit the vacuum hose (*Fig. 3*). After beveling the faceplate to fit against the fence and table, it's simply glued to the sides. Gluing the attachment to the fence holds it securely in place.

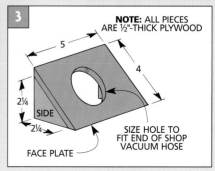

Glue-Up Station

This vertical work station not only makes gluing up solid wood panels easier, but it also doubles as a pipe clamp storage rack. When it's not being used, it conveniently folds together for compact storage.

Okay, I'll admit it. Gluing up a solid wood panel with pipe clamps standing on end looks a bit unorthodox. But it works great. And with this vertical Glue-Up Station to support the clamps, the whole glue-up process is simplified considerably.

CLAMP STORAGE. For example, there's no need to drag heavy pipe clamps around the shop. That's because the Glue-Up Station doubles as a storage rack.

WORK SURFACES. With a row of clamps on each side of the station, there are two flat work surfaces for gluing up panels. So in addition to the fact that you

don't have to clear off a work surface somewhere else in the shop, you can glue up several panels at a time.

SAVES SPACE. Finally, to save space, the Glue-Up Station hinges in the middle. When the glue dries, just remove the panels and fold the station for storage (see inset photo).

MATERIALS. All the wood parts for this project can be cut from four 2x4s and one 2x6 (see Cutting Diagram on opposite page). The only special hardware is a pair of light-duty chains and some broom clips for storing clamps.

Note: If floor space is limited, there's even a wall-mounted version. See the

Designer's Notebook on page 85 for more on this option.

PIPE CLAMP TIPS. There are a couple of minor problems that seem to get in my way when I work with pipe clamps. For some simple solutions that I've discovered, see the Shop Tip on page 87.

EXPLODED VIEW

OVERALL DIMENSIONS:
48W x 35D x 33½H

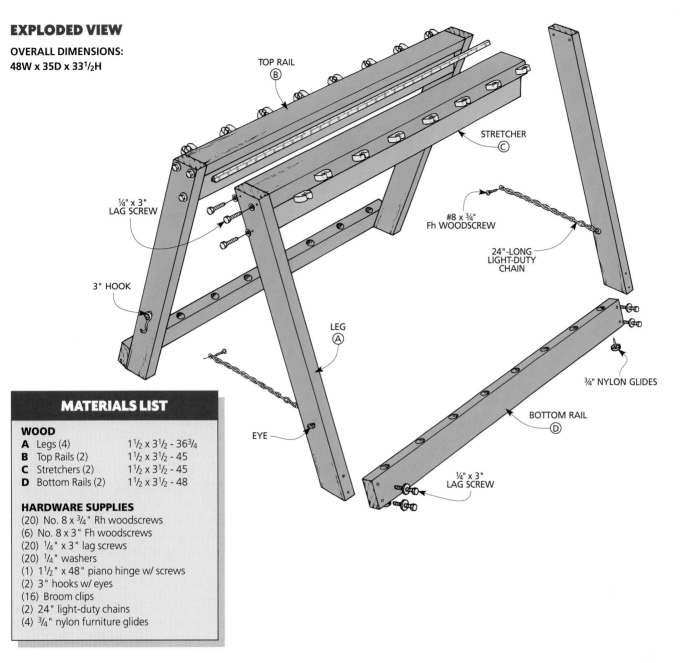

TOP RAIL
Ⓑ

STRETCHER
Ⓒ

¼" x 3"
LAG SCREW

#8 x ¾"
Fh WOODSCREW

24"-LONG
LIGHT-DUTY
CHAIN

3" HOOK

LEG
Ⓐ

¾" NYLON GLIDES

BOTTOM RAIL
Ⓓ

EYE

¼" x 3"
LAG SCREW

MATERIALS LIST

WOOD

A	Legs (4)	1½ x 3½ - 36¾
B	Top Rails (2)	1½ x 3½ - 45
C	Stretchers (2)	1½ x 3½ - 45
D	Bottom Rails (2)	1½ x 3½ - 48

HARDWARE SUPPLIES

(20) No. 8 x ¾" Rh woodscrews
(6) No. 8 x 3" Fh woodscrews
(20) ¼" x 3" lag screws
(20) ¼" washers
(1) 1½" x 48" piano hinge w/ screws
(2) 3" hooks w/ eyes
(16) Broom clips
(2) 24" light-duty chains
(4) ¾" nylon furniture glides

CUTTING DIAGRAM

2x4 (1½ x 3½) - 96 (5.3 Bd. Ft.)

A	A	

2x4 (1½ x 3½) - 96 (5.3 Bd. Ft.)

A	A	

2x4 (1½ x 3½) - 96 (5.3 Bd. Ft.)

C	C	

2x4 (1½ x 3½) - 96 (5.3 Bd. Ft.)

D	D	

2x6 (1½ x 5½) - 96 (8 Bd. Ft.)

B	B	

The Glue-Up Station consists of two identical wood frames that are hinged together at the top. (I used "two-by" Douglas fir for all of the wood parts.)

Note: These frames are designed to hold 36"-long pipe clamps. If you prefer, you can alter some of the dimensions to hold other sizes.

LEGS. Each frame starts off with a simple pair of legs (A) *(Fig. 1)*. To tilt each frame at an angle so a workpiece is able to sit flat against the pipe clamps, a 20° miter is cut on each end of each leg *(Fig. 1a)*. Make sure all four legs end up the same length.

TOP RAIL. The legs are held together with a top rail (B) that's ripped to width to match the legs and at a 20° angle on each edge (see End View in *Fig. 1*).

The front edges are angled so when you attach broom clips (later) they'll be able to grab the pipe clamps. And the same angle on the back edges keeps the top rails on each frame from binding when you fold up the station for out-of-the-way storage.

STRETCHER. After attaching the top rail of each frame to the legs with lag screws, I added a stretcher (C) to prevent the frame from racking. This stretcher is cut to fit between the legs and is screwed to the top rail of each frame *(Fig. 1b)*. Here again, I used a lag screw at each end to fasten the stretcher to the legs *(Fig. 1c)*.

BOTTOM RAIL. All that's left to complete each of the basic frames is to add a bottom rail (D) to the legs *(Fig. 2)*. Holes drilled in the top edge of this rail

act as a "pocket" for the bottom end of each pipe clamp.

To make it easy to remove the clamps and set them back in place, these holes are slightly larger than the outside diameter of the black clamp pipe. (I drilled $1\frac{1}{8}$"-dia. holes to accommodate $\frac{3}{4}$" black pipe.)

BROOM CLIPS. Now that the holes are drilled for the clamps, it's just a matter

of screwing metal broom clips to the top rail. To keep the pipe clamps aligned, the clips are centered over the holes in the bottom rail *(Figs. 2 and 3)*.

Finally, tacking a pair of nylon glides to each bottom corner makes it easy to open and close the Glue-Up Station *(Fig. 2)*. For sources of hardware, including broom clips and nylon glides, see page 126.

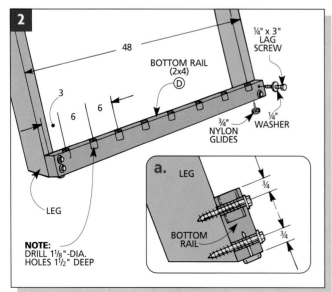

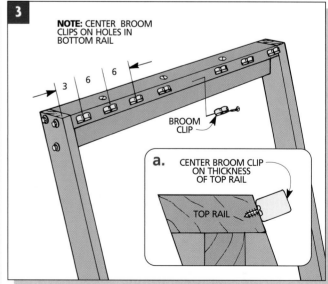

DESIGNER'S NOTEBOOK

If floor space is limited in your shop, you can build this wall-mounted version of the Glue-Up Station. Simply build one half of the original station design, and then add support at the bottom of the wall.

CONSTRUCTION NOTES:

■ First cut two arms (E), each with a curve at one end to keep the support from binding *(Fig. 1b)*. The other end is mitered so it fits tightly against the wall.

■ Add the support bar (F) between the arms *(Fig. 1)*. This 1½"-dia. dowel fits into holes drilled in the arms.

■ Attach the support to the frame with hex bolts *(Figs. 1a and 2)*.

■ Tack nylon glides to the bottom and mount the station to the wall. Use a piano hinge with one leaf screwed to the top and the other screwed to the wall *(Fig. 2a)*.

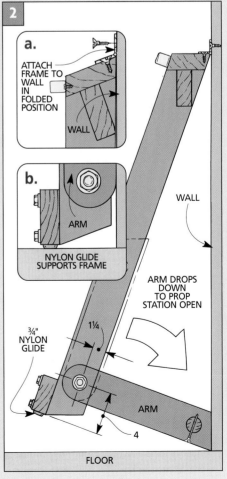

WALL-MOUNTED
STATION

MATERIALS LIST

NEW PARTS
E	Arms (2)	1½ x 3½ - 16
F	Support Bar (1)	1½ dowel x 44⅞

HARDWARE SUPPLIES
(8) No. 8 x ¾" Rh woodscrews
(5) No. 8 x 3" Fh woodscrews
(10) ¼" x 3" lag screws
(10) ¼" washers

(1) 1½" x 48" piano hinge w/ screws
(8) Broom clips
(2) ½" x 4" hex bolts
(6) ½" flat washers
(2) ½" lock nuts
(2) ¾" nylon furniture glides

Note: Only need 2 of part A and 1 each of parts B, C, and D.

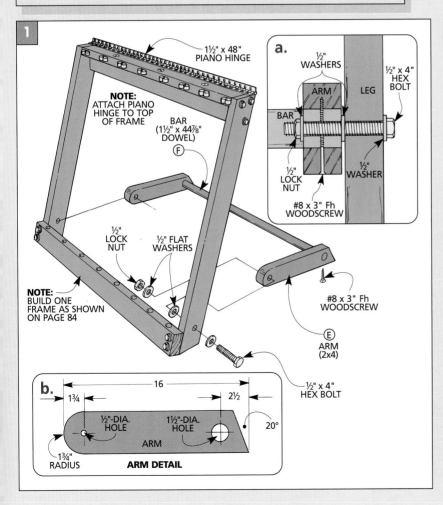

With the two separate frames completed, they're ready to be assembled.

Note: The directions here are for a double frame (as shown in the photo and Exploded View on pages 82-83). However, if you only built one frame for mounting against a wall, refer back to the Designer's Notebook on page 85 for instructions on mounting it with different hardware.

HINGE. I wanted to make it easy to fold the Glue-Up Station so it would take up a minimal amount of storage space.

To accomplish this, the frames are held together with a piano hinge that's screwed to the inside edge of each top rail (B) *(Figs. 4 and 4a)*.

Note: Mounting this piano hinge flush with both the top rails creates a flat surface that is ideal for holding glue and supplies.

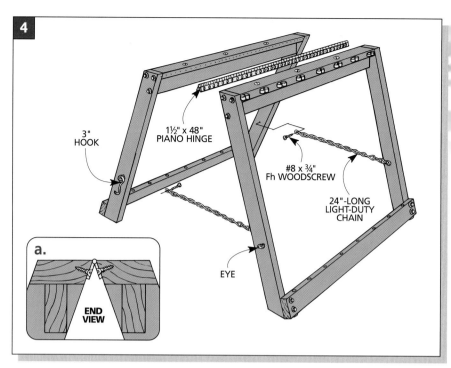

4

3" HOOK

1½" x 48" PIANO HINGE

#8 x ¾" Fh WOODSCREW

24"-LONG LIGHT-DUTY CHAIN

EYE

a.

END VIEW

TECHNIQUE .... *Using the Glue-Up Station*

When using this Glue-Up Station to put together a solid wood panel, it's easiest to adjust each clamp first for the width of the panel *(Steps 1 and 2)*.

Note: I like to position the clamp heads ½" farther apart than the width of the panel.

Then it's just a matter of stacking the individual pieces on the station and applying glue *(Step 3)*.

Finally, after tightening the back clamps, position additional clamps on the *front* of the panel. This will help ensure that you apply even clamping pressure *(Step 4)*.

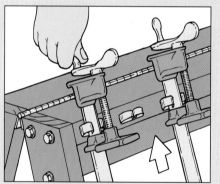

1 *Start by backing off the top clamp heads until they hit the bottoms of the broom clips.*

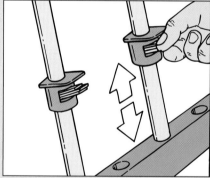

2 *Next, adjust the bottom clamp heads to allow for the width of the panel you'll be gluing up.*

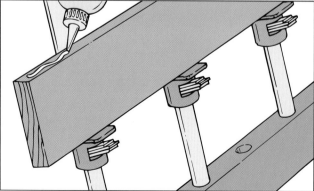

3 *Now you can lay the individual workpieces on the pipe clamps, and apply glue to each one as you work your way toward the top of the panel.*

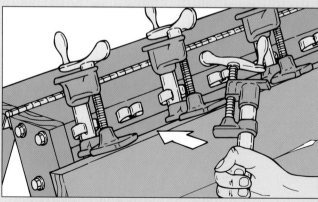

4 *After the last workpiece is positioned, tighten the pipe clamps along the back, then add another row of clamps across the front of the panel.*

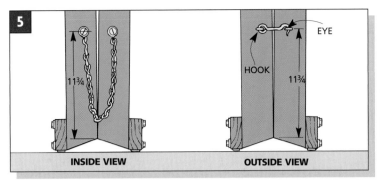

INSIDE VIEW | **OUTSIDE VIEW**

ADDITIONAL HARDWARE. There are a couple more pieces of hardware to add to the station. First, to prevent the frames from spreading too far apart and damaging the piano hinge, I installed a light-duty chain on the inside face of each leg (see Inside View in *Fig. 5*).

Finally, attaching a hook and eye to the outside of each pair of legs lets you lock the Glue-Up Station together when it's folded for storage (see Outside View in *Fig. 5*). ■

TWO WORK SURFACES. *Each side of the Glue-Up Station is designed to hold pipe clamps. So to save time, you can glue up several panels at once.*

SHOP TIP . . . . *Protecting Wood From Clamps*

Sometimes the most frustrating tasks I face are the ones that seem the smallest and simplest. Take working with pipe clamps, for example. They're great for gluing up solid wood panels (made even easier with the Glue-Up Station). However, they present some special considerations that may seem insignificant but that can damage the project you're working on.

Below are two such problems having to do with the clamps themselves leaving their marks. Whether you want to avoid a crushed workpiece from the clamp heads or stains from the iron pipe, these simple tricks will help you.

Clamp Marks. *A common problem with pipe clamps is that it's all too easy to apply too much pressure and crush the workpiece.*

Plastic Padding. *One way to pad the jaws of a pipe clamp is to dip them in liquid plastic (available at most hardware stores).*

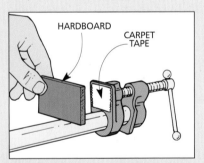

Wood Padding. *Another simple way to pad the jaws is to attach a small piece of hardboard (or scrap wood) with carpet tape.*

Stained Wood. *Pipe clamps can discolor a glued-up panel when the iron in the pipe comes in contact with the wet glue.*

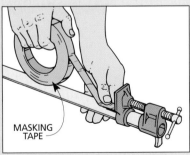

Masking Tape. *The quickest and easiest way to prevent discoloration is to isolate the pipe from the wood with masking tape.*

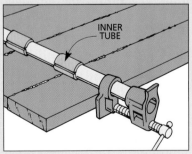

Inner Tubes. *A more permanent solution to preventing stains is to slide lengths of a bicycle tire inner tube over the pipe.*

BENCHES & CABINETS

Every shop, it seems, could use one more work surface or some extra storage. This section addresses those needs so that even the smallest shop can "work big."

For example, the saw cabinet and drop-down tool tray provide storage in spaces that are otherwise wasted.

Hung on the wall, the router bit cabinet holds more than bits, while the sharpening station dedicates storage and a work surface to the task of keeping a keen edge on your tools.

The modular tool bins offer customizable storage and can serve as a workbench base. The small workbench packs the features of its big brothers, and more, into a compact space.

Sharpening Station

Slicing through wood with a sharp tool is one of the greatest pleasures in woodworking. Keeping a fine edge on each of your tools is easy when your sharpening supplies are in one convenient spot.

Fighting a dull tool is just making work for yourself. Especially when you consider that it only takes a few minutes to sharpen a chisel or plane iron to a razor's edge.

Maybe the reason so many woodworkers put off sharpening their tools is the time it takes to round up sharpening supplies and clear a place to work. That's why I built this Sharpening Station. It gives me an area of my shop where my sharpening supplies are ready when I need them. By attaching the station to the wall, I can use the top both to mount my grinder and as a platform for sharpening tools by hand.

DUST-FREE. The enclosed cabinet keeps your supplies away from the dust that seems to settle on everything else in the shop. When you're ready to touch up a tool, simply slide the door to one side to get to your sharpening stones and accessories.

CONTAINER. One item that makes the entire sharpening process easier and cleaner is a plastic container like the kind you see at most discount stores (see photo). (I used an 8" x 13$\frac{1}{2}$" container that's 3$\frac{1}{2}$" deep.)

Filling the container with water creates a reservoir for storing my waterstones. And a shop-made stone holder

resting on the container keeps the waterstone from slipping around as I sharpen. (Refer to the Accessory box on page 93 for more about this stone holder.) Another benefit is that the lid snaps shut so water doesn't slosh out.

SHARPENING. To help you get the best edges possible on your tools, there is a Technique article on pages 94-95 that takes you step-by-step through the process of properly grinding and honing an edge on a chisel. While the process may look a bit involved, it really isn't. And you'll find it was time well spent the next time you make a cut with a razor-sharp tool.

EXPLODED VIEW

OVERALL DIMENSIONS:
30W x 15D x 12H

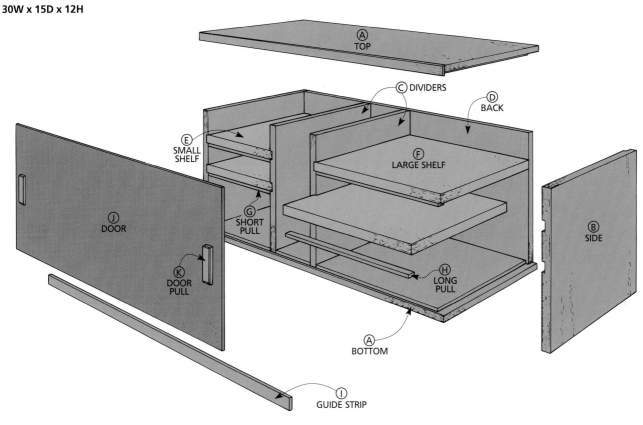

- Ⓐ TOP
- Ⓒ DIVIDERS
- Ⓓ BACK
- Ⓔ SMALL SHELF
- Ⓕ LARGE SHELF
- Ⓖ SHORT PULL
- Ⓙ DOOR
- Ⓚ DOOR PULL
- Ⓗ LONG PULL
- Ⓑ SIDE
- Ⓐ BOTTOM
- Ⓘ GUIDE STRIP

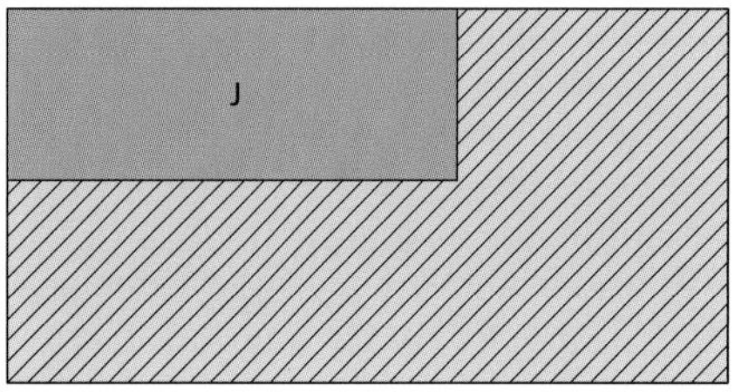

CUTTING DIAGRAM

¾ x 3½ - 36 (.9 Bd. Ft.)

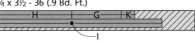

H   G   K

I

¼" HARDBOARD - 24 x 48

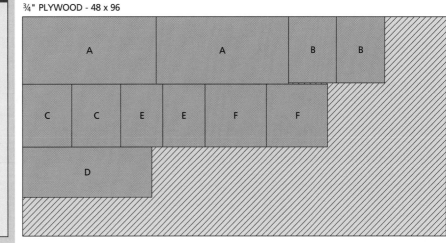

J

¾" PLYWOOD - 48 x 96

A   A   B   B

C   C   E   E   F   F

D

MATERIALS LIST

WOOD

A	Top/Bottom (2)	¾ ply - 14¾ x 30
B	Sides (2)	¾ ply - 14½ x 11
C	Dividers (2)	¾ ply - 13¾ x 11
D	Back (1)	¾ ply - 11 x 29
E	Small Shelves (2)	¾ ply - 13¾ x 9½
F	Large Shelves (2)	¾ ply - 13¾ x 14
G	Short Pulls (2)	¼ x ¾ - 8¹⁵/₁₆
H	Long Pulls (2)	¼ x ¾ - 13⁷/₁₆
I	Guide Strips (2)	¼ x ¾ - 30
J	Door (1)	¼ hdbd. - 10¹⁵/₁₆ x 30
K	Door Pulls (2)	¼ x ¾ - 2½

HARDWARE SUPPLIES
(28) No. 8 x 1½" Fh woodscrews
(4) ⅜" x 2" lag screws

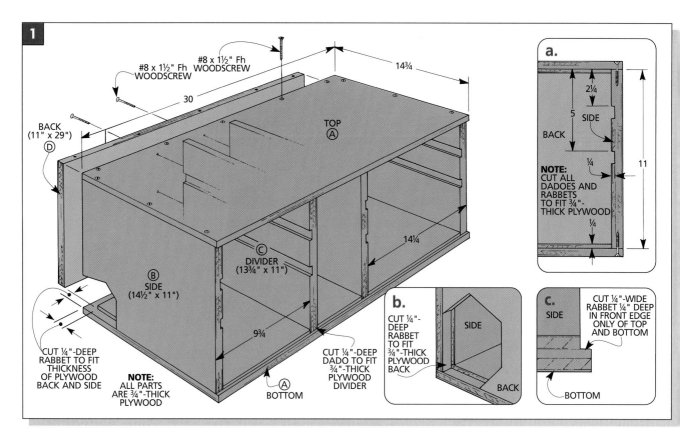

CABINET

The Sharpening Station is a plywood box with a sliding door and four pull-out shelves for easy access to grinding wheels, sharpening stones and other accessories (see photo below).

TOP AND BOTTOM. I started construction by cutting the top and bottom (A) of the box to size *(Fig. 1)*. Once this is done, they're rabbeted on all four edges *(Figs. 1 and 1a)*. Wide rabbets on both ends and along the back edge will accept the ¾" plywood sides and back (added later). And a narrow rabbet in the front edge forms part of the track for the sliding door. The width of this rabbet equals the thickness of the hardboard that will be used for the door *(Fig. 1c)*.

In addition to the rabbets, two dadoes are cut in each of the top and bottom pieces *(Fig. 1)*. Later, these dadoes will accept dividers that form individual compartments.

Note: You may need to alter the locations of these dadoes to accommodate your sharpening accessories.

SIDES AND DIVIDERS. The top and bottom are held together with two sides (B) and a pair of dividers (C). While the height (length) of these pieces is identical (11"), their widths are different.

To provide clearance for the sliding door, the sides are cut to width so they align with the shoulder of the rabbet in front and flush at the back (14½" in my case). But to allow for the back, the dividers are ¾" narrower (13¾").

With the sides and dividers cut to finished size, two dadoes are cut in one face of each piece to accept the shelves added later *(Fig. 1a)*.

Note: To keep the pieces properly oriented, I marked on each of the workpieces the position of each dado before cutting them.

Finally, the back edge of each side (B) is rabbeted to accept a plywood back *(Fig. 1b)*.

BACK. To determine the size of the back, dry-assemble the cabinet top, bottom, and sides. Then measure between the rabbets in the sides and the top and bottom. After cutting the back to size from ¾" plywood, you can assemble the box with glue and screws *(Fig. 1)*.

SHELVES

The next step is to add four sliding shelves to the case *(Fig. 2)*. Two small shelves (E) provide storage for the stone holders. And two large shelves (F) hold extra grinding wheels.

To make the shelves slide easily (yet still fit snugly), I cut them to fit their openings and then sanded the edges until they slipped smoothly in and out. While I was at it, I glued a thin strip of hardwood to the bottom of each shelf to serve as a pull (G, H) *(Fig. 2)*. Each pull is ¹⁄₁₆" shorter than the width of the opening *(Fig. 2a)*. I secured these with C-clamps while the glue dried.

DOOR

With the shelves in place, you're ready to add the hardboard door.

To determine the width of the door (J), measure the distance between the rabbets at the front of the case and subtract $1/16$" for clearance *(Figs. 3 and 3a)*. The door's length is the same as the cabinet's length (30″).

The door slides in a track that's formed by gluing narrow hardwood guide strips (I) to the front edges of the rabbets that were cut earlier in the cabinet's top and bottom *(Fig. 3a)*.

Before sliding the door in place, a couple of hardwood strips are glued to the door to act as door pulls (K).

Once the glue dries, slide the door into the track from one end and check that it slides smoothly. If the door binds slightly, trim it on the table saw. If it still binds, lightly sand the long edges of the door to round them over.

MOUNTING

All that's left to complete the Sharpening Station is to mount it to a wall. (You may need to enlist a helper to hold the cabinet while you position it.)

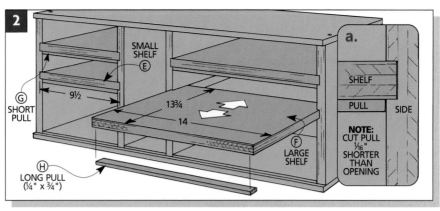

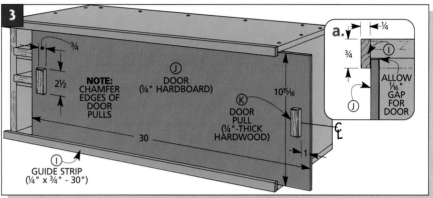

Make sure the top of the cabinet is at a comfortable working height. Then, to support the weight of a grinder, as well as the pressure exerted when sharpening by hand, I attached it to the wall studs with lag screws. ■

ACCESSORY . . . . *Stone Holder*

Making a holder for each of your sharpening stones solves two problems. First, it prevents the stone from slipping around. And second, it helps contain the mess, keeping clean-up to a minimum.

The stone rests on a wood base with two hardboard pieces attached to each end (see drawing). The holder then rests over a plastic container filled with water (see photo). This catches the "slurry" that's generated as you use the stone. (The stone can also be stored in the container to keep it moist.)

The bottom pieces of the holder butt tightly against the ends of the stone to keep it from moving. And the top (offset) pieces support the holder on the container. When attaching the hardboard, I used brass screws since they won't rust.

Note: A non-skid shelf liner (available at hardware stores) anchors the container while you use the stone.

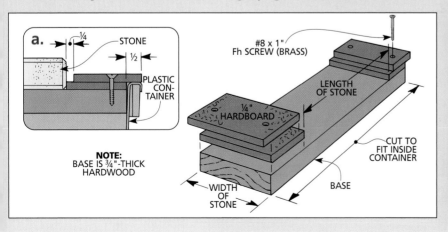

TECHNIQUE ..... *Sharpening a Chisel*

Just a grinder, a waterstone, and five minutes. That's all it takes to create a razor-sharp edge on a chisel.

HOLLOW GRIND. If a chisel is nicked or the end isn't square to the edges, I hollow grind the bevel first (see below).

By using a wheel, the bevel takes on a slight concave, or "hollow," shape. (The detail in *Step 2* on the opposite page shows an exaggerated hollow grind.)

HONE. Then I hone the edge to a mirror finish with a waterstone. The advantage to a hollow-ground bevel is that to get a sharp edge, you only have to hone the very tip of the bevel. This is easier than sharpening the entire bevel. Then as the cutting edge dulls, a quick honing will restore the sharpness.

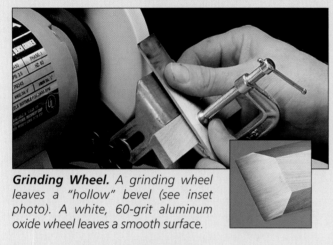

Grinding Wheel. *A grinding wheel leaves a "hollow" bevel (see inset photo). A white, 60-grit aluminum oxide wheel leaves a smooth surface.*

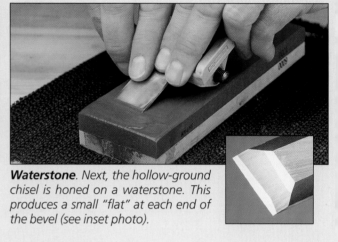

Waterstone. *Next, the hollow-ground chisel is honed on a waterstone. This produces a small "flat" at each end of the bevel (see inset photo).*

HOLLOW GRINDING

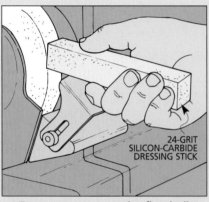

24-GRIT SILICON-CARBIDE DRESSING STICK

1 To ensure a smooth, flat hollow-ground bevel, first "square up" the wheel with a dressing stick.

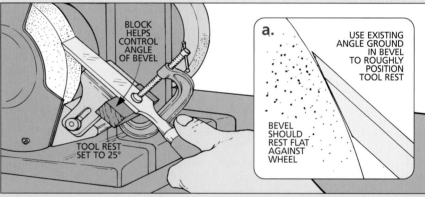

BLOCK HELPS CONTROL ANGLE OF BEVEL

TOOL REST SET TO 25°

a. USE EXISTING ANGLE GROUND IN BEVEL TO ROUGHLY POSITION TOOL REST

BEVEL SHOULD REST FLAT AGAINST WHEEL

2 Now position the tool rest to grind a 25° angle (see detail 'a'). Place the chisel with its bevel flat against the wheel. Then to help guide the chisel across the wheel and maintain the proper angle, clamp a small block of wood to the base of the chisel.

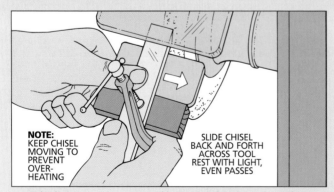

NOTE: KEEP CHISEL MOVING TO PREVENT OVER-HEATING

SLIDE CHISEL BACK AND FORTH ACROSS TOOL REST WITH LIGHT, EVEN PASSES

3 Take light, even passes and keep the chisel moving. This way the metal can't overheat and ruin the chisel. To keep the tool cool, dip the tip occasionally in a "quench cup" filled with water.

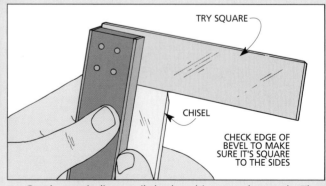

TRY SQUARE

CHISEL

CHECK EDGE OF BEVEL TO MAKE SURE IT'S SQUARE TO THE SIDES

4 Continue grinding until the bevel is ground smooth. Then check the edge with a try square to make sure it's flat and square to the sides.

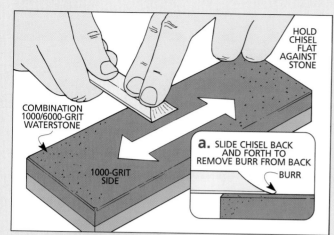

COMBINATION 1000/6000-GRIT WATERSTONE

HOLD CHISEL FLAT AGAINST STONE

1000-GRIT SIDE

a. SLIDE CHISEL BACK AND FORTH TO REMOVE BURR FROM BACK

BURR

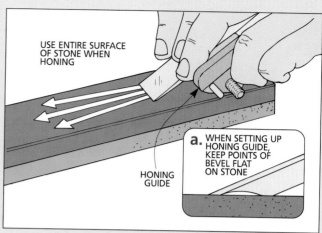

USE ENTIRE SURFACE OF STONE WHEN HONING

HONING GUIDE

a. WHEN SETTING UP HONING GUIDE, KEEP POINTS OF BEVEL FLAT ON STONE

1 To hone the edge, first flatten the back of the chisel using a 1000-grit waterstone. (This will also remove any burr created by a grinding wheel.) The back will become shiny as it's polished.

2 Next, place the two points of the grind flat on the stone (see detail 'a'). Use a honing guide (see photo below) to maintain the angle as you sharpen the bevel by sliding the chisel.

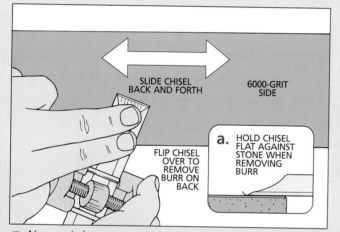

SLIDE CHISEL BACK AND FORTH

6000-GRIT SIDE

FLIP CHISEL OVER TO REMOVE BURR ON BACK

a. HOLD CHISEL FLAT AGAINST STONE WHEN REMOVING BURR

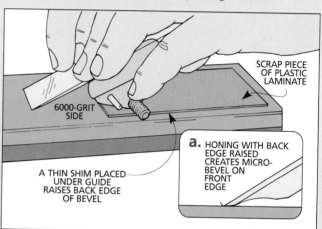

SCRAP PIECE OF PLASTIC LAMINATE

6000-GRIT SIDE

A THIN SHIM PLACED UNDER GUIDE RAISES BACK EDGE OF BEVEL

a. HONING WITH BACK EDGE RAISED CREATES MICRO-BEVEL ON FRONT EDGE

3 Now switch over to a 6000-grit waterstone to remove the burr created when the edge was honed and to polish the back of the chisel. Press the chisel flat to the stone. You're after a mirror-like shine on the back.

4 After the back of the chisel is polished, I hone a micro-bevel on the front edge — it makes a chisel cut better and stay sharp longer. Just lift the back edge slightly for a couple of passes. (I put a piece of laminate under the guide as a shim.)

HONING GUIDES

When honing a chisel, you could free-hand it across a stone. But it wouldn't be long before the angle of the bevel was altered. And this would make it more difficult to get a sharp edge.

To maintain the same angle throughout the life of a chisel and get it as sharp as possible, I recommend using a honing guide (see photo at right and *Step 2* above).

Honing guides are designed to hold a chisel firmly and securely in place at the angle the bevel was originally ground. This makes it easy to touch up a bevel quickly. Most guides also have some type of roller system so you can slide a chisel back and forth across the surface of the stone. And most guides

let you change the angle at which the tool is held in the guide so you can hone the proper angles on different types of plane irons.

There are two basic types of honing guides. The one I prefer is small and compact and rides directly on top of the stone (on the right in photo). The other is larger, a bit more complicated to set up, and requires more room to roll since it rides on the bench behind the stone. One advantage to this is that it allows you to use the full length and width of the stone for sharpening.

Both types are available through woodworking mail-order catalogs or you might find them at larger home centers. See Sources on page 126.

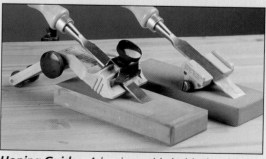

Honing Guides. *A honing guide holds the chisel at the proper angle for sharpening. The guide will hold chisels of different widths and also plane irons.*

Router Bit Cabinet

Box joints at the corners of this cabinet let you show off your craftsmanship. Behind the frame and panel door is room for up to twenty router bits, plus a handy drawer to hold accessories.

Considering the price of router bits these days, it just makes sense to invest the time to protect them. This cabinet is designed to organize your bits while safeguarding them, too.

SPACING. The bits are spaced apart and held upright in a pair of shelves (see photo). Since the bits can't bump into each other (as they used to when I kept them in a drawer), the sharp cutting edges don't get nicked. The space between the bits also makes it easy to

grab hold of the one you need. There's even a unique approach to holding the bits in the shelf. It prevents the bits from binding as the shelf expands or contracts with changes in humidity.

DOOR. This cabinet also has a door to keep the bits clean and free from dust and dirt. And I added a pullout drawer inside the cabinet to store and protect wrenches and other accessories.

WALL MOUNT. A simple two-piece mounting system makes it easy to hang

the cabinet in a convenient spot near your router table. And if you take your router out of the shop to do some work, the cabinet lifts off the hanger so you can take the bits with you, too.

JOINERY. I chose to make the cabinet case and the drawer with box joints. They're strong and also decorative. But if you don't have a box joint jig, a different version of the cabinet using simpler joinery is shown in the Designer's Notebook on page 101.

EXPLODED VIEW

OVERALL DIMENSIONS:
10W x 4¹³/₁₆D x 13H

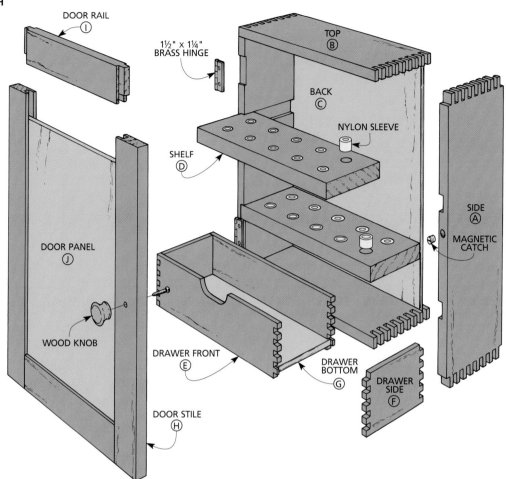

DOOR RAIL
I

1½" x 1¼"
BRASS HINGE

TOP
B

BACK
C

NYLON SLEEVE

SHELF
D

SIDE
A

MAGNETIC
CATCH

DOOR PANEL
J

WOOD KNOB

DRAWER FRONT
E

DRAWER
BOTTOM
G

DRAWER
SIDE
F

DOOR STILE
H

MATERIALS LIST

WOOD

A	Sides (2)	½ x 4¼ - 13
B	Top/Bottom (2)	½ x 4¼ - 10
C	Back (1)	¼ ply - 9½ x 12½
D	Shelves (2)	¾ x 3¾ - 9½
E	Drawer Ft./Bk. (2)	¼ x 2½ - 8¹⁵/₁₆
F	Drawer Sides (2)	¼ x 2½ - 3¾
G	Drawer Bottom (1)	¼ ply - 3½ x 8¹¹/₁₆
H	Door Stiles (2)	½ x 1½ - 13
I	Door Rails (2)	½ x 1½ - 7¾
J	Door Panel (1)	¼ ply - 7¾ x 10¾
K	Cabinet Cleat (1)	¼ x 2½ - 9
L	Wall Cleat (1)	¼ x 2½ - 8¹⁵/₁₆

HARDWARE SUPPLIES

(1) No. 4 x ⅜" Fh woodscrew
(1) ¾"-dia. wood knob w/ screw
(1) ⁵/₁₆"-dia. magnetic catch
(2) 1½" x 1¼" brass hinges w/ screws
(*) ¼"-I.D., ½"-long nylon sleeves
(*) ½"-I.D., ½"-long nylon sleeves
* Quantity will vary depending on your
collection of bits.

CUTTING DIAGRAM

½ x 7¼ - 72 (3.75 Sq. Ft.) **NOTE:** PARTS E, F, K & L ARE RESAWN AND PLANED TO ¼" THICK.

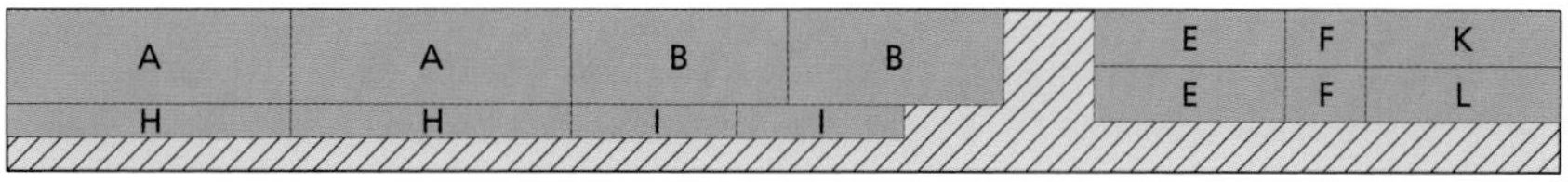

A	A	B	B		E	F	K
H	H	I	I		E	F	L

¾ x 5½ - 24 (1 Bd. Ft.)

D	D	

¼" PLYWOOD - 12 x 24

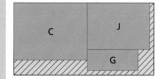

C	J
	G

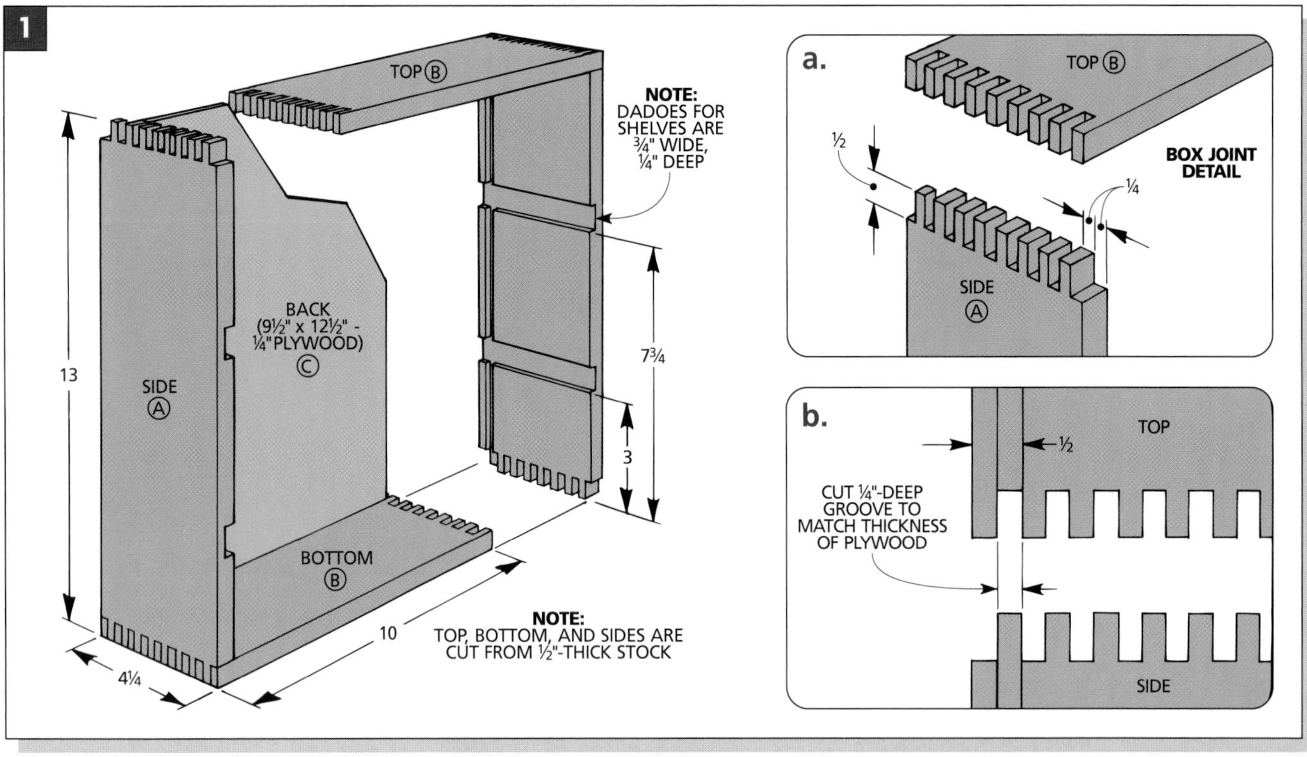
1
TOP Ⓑ
NOTE:
DADOES FOR SHELVES ARE ¾" WIDE, ¼" DEEP
BACK (9½" x 12½" - ¼" PLYWOOD) Ⓒ
SIDE Ⓐ
13
7¾
3
BOTTOM Ⓑ
10
4¼
NOTE:
TOP, BOTTOM, AND SIDES ARE CUT FROM ½"-THICK STOCK
a.
TOP Ⓑ
½
BOX JOINT DETAIL
¼
SIDE Ⓐ
b.
TOP
½
CUT ¼"-DEEP GROOVE TO MATCH THICKNESS OF PLYWOOD
SIDE

CASE

I started work on the cabinet by making the case. It's just a shallow box consisting of two sides (A), a top (B), and a bottom (B) *(Fig. 1)*. I cut these pieces from ½"-thick stock and used box joints to hold them together *(Figs. 1 and 1a)*.

SHELF DADOES. Once the box joints are cut, dadoes are cut in the sides for the shelves that hold the bits *(Fig. 1)*.

BACK. Next, to seal up the rear of the cabinet, I added a back (C) *(Fig. 1)*. It's just a piece of ¼"-thick plywood that fits into ¼" x ¼" grooves cut in the sides and top and bottom pieces *(Fig. 1b)*.

ASSEMBLY. Now the case can be glued together. When the glue dries, you'll need to plug the holes in the cabinet top and bottom that are left from cutting the grooves in the sides. (See the Shop Tip at the bottom of page 99.)

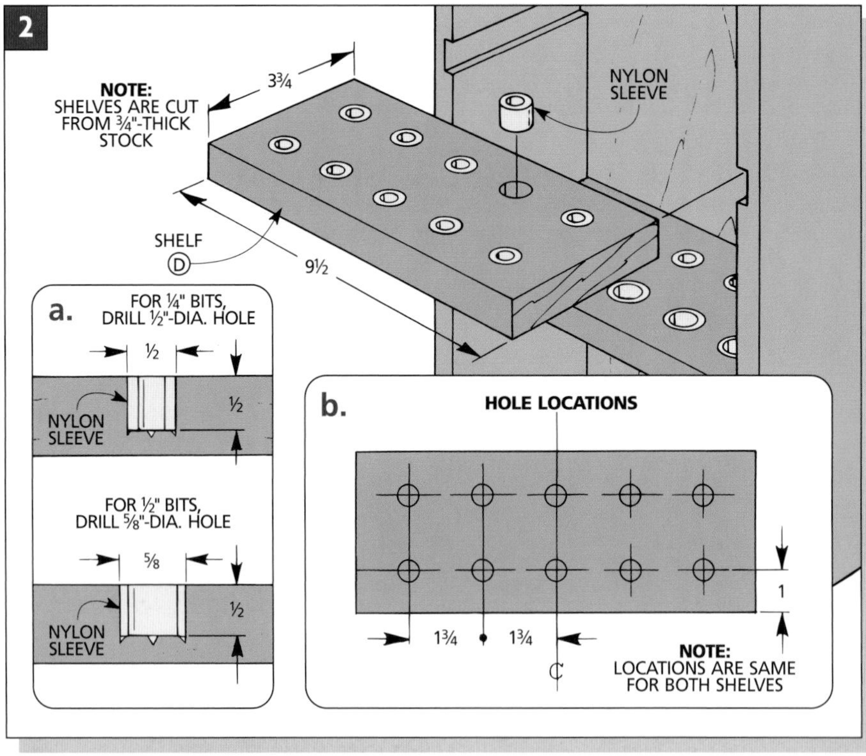
2
NOTE:
SHELVES ARE CUT FROM ¾"-THICK STOCK
3¾
NYLON SLEEVE
SHELF Ⓓ
9½
a.
FOR ¼" BITS, DRILL ½"-DIA. HOLE
½
½
NYLON SLEEVE
FOR ½" BITS, DRILL ⅝"-DIA. HOLE
⅝
½
NYLON SLEEVE
b.
HOLE LOCATIONS
1
1¾
1¾
℄
NOTE:
LOCATIONS ARE SAME FOR BOTH SHELVES

SHELVES

After the case is assembled, the next step is to make the shelves that hold the router bits. The shelves fit in the dadoes cut in the case sides earlier.

The shelves (D) are cut to length to fit between the sides. As for the width, trim them so they end up flush with the front edge *(Fig. 2)*.

BIT HOLES. After cutting the shelves to size, the holes for the router bits can be laid out *(Fig. 2b)*. But I didn't drill them to fit the shanks of my router bits. Instead, they're slightly larger.

SLEEVES. The reason is the nylon sleeves I used to line the holes (*Fig. 2a* and the Shop Tip at the top of page 99). They make it easy to get bits in and out.

Note: Before you start drilling, it's a good idea to buy the nylon sleeves first. A hardware kit containing these sleeves is available from *Woodsmith Project Supplies* (see Sources on page 126).

ASSEMBLY. Once the holes are drilled, the next step is to glue in the nylon sleeves. To do this, I squirt "instant" glue in each hole and insert a sleeve. Then to complete the case, glue the shelves flush with the front edge.

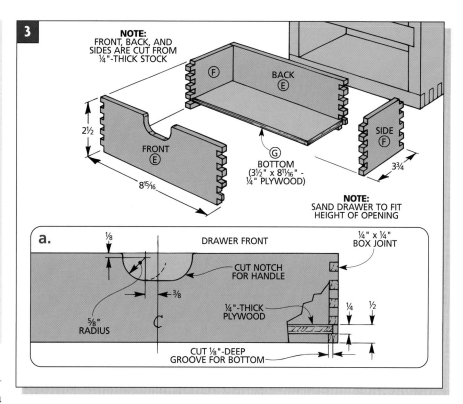

3

NOTE: FRONT, BACK, AND SIDES ARE CUT FROM ¼"-THICK STOCK

BACK (E)

F

2½

FRONT (E)

8¹⁵⁄₁₆

SIDE (F)

3¾

G

BOTTOM (3½" x 8¹¹⁄₁₆" - ¼" PLYWOOD)

NOTE: SAND DRAWER TO FIT HEIGHT OF OPENING

a.

⅛

DRAWER FRONT

¼" x ¼" BOX JOINT

CUT NOTCH FOR HANDLE

⅜

¼"-THICK PLYWOOD

¼   ½

⅝" RADIUS

CUT ⅛"-DEEP GROOVE FOR BOTTOM

DRAWER

After completing the case, I added a small drawer that slides into the bottom opening of the case *(Fig. 3)*. This makes a handy place to store larger bits, wrenches, and other accessories.

BOX JOINTS. The drawer is made up of a front and back (E) and two sides (F) with box joints at each corner *(Fig. 3)*. But since the drawer pieces are cut from ¼"-thick stock, the box joints will be ¼" x ¼" *(Fig. 3a)*.

DRAWER PIECES. To find the height (width) of all the drawer pieces, measure the height of the opening (2½"). Normally, at this point I would subtract ¹⁄₁₆" for clearance. But this would mess

up the ¼" spacing for the box joints. So instead, I cut the pieces to full height (2½") and then sanded the drawer to fit the opening after it was assembled.

The length of the front and back (E) pieces equals the width of the drawer opening, less ¹⁄₁₆" for clearance (8¹⁵⁄₁₆") *(Fig. 3)*. And since I wanted the drawer to be flush with the case front, the sides (F) are cut to match the depth of the opening (3¾").

NOTCH. To make a simple "handle" for the drawer, I cut a centered notch in the top edge of the drawer front *(Figs. 3 and 3a)*. I did this by roughing out the

opening with a jig saw, then sanding up to the line with a drum sander.

Once this notch is cut out, box joints can be cut to join the drawer pieces together *(Fig. 3a)*.

BOTTOM. The next step is to cut a groove in each drawer piece for a ¼"-thick bottom (G) *(Figs. 3 and 3a)*. Here again, you'll need to plug holes after you've glued up the drawer.

TEST FIT. After filling the holes, test the fit of the drawer in the case. If necessary, sand the top or bottom edges of the drawer to achieve a fit that's snug but still slides in and out easily.

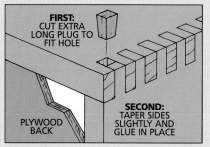
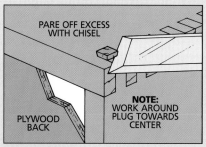

DOOR

With the drawer complete, the next thing is to add a door to keep your router bits free from dust and dirt. The door is just a hardwood frame that fits around a plywood panel *(Fig. 4)*.

FRAME PIECES. All the frame pieces are cut from $1/2$"-thick stock and are the same width ($1 1/2$"). The only difference is their length. The stiles (H) are 13" long, and the rails (I) are $7 3/4$" long.

STUB TENON AND GROOVE. The frame (and panel) is held together with a simple joint — a stub tenon and groove. The first step when making this joint is to cut a $3/8$"-deep groove centered in each piece *(Fig. 4a)*. This groove accepts a $1/4$"-thick plywood panel (J). It also serves as the mortise for the short (stub) tenons cut on the ends of the rails *(Figs. 4 and 4a)*. When cutting the tenons, flip the rail between passes so you make cuts on opposite faces and sneak up on the tenon's final thickness. This automatically centers the tenon on the rail's thickness.

ASSEMBLY. After the stub tenons are cut, the door can be glued and clamped up. When the glue is dry, you can mount the door on the case. It attaches to one side with a pair of hinges *(Fig. 5)*.

Note: The hinge mortises are cut in the case to match the thickness of one hinge flap. This leaves about $1/16$" clearance between the door and the case for a magnetic catch that's added next.

CATCH. With the door in place, the next step is to add a knob and a magnetic catch *(Fig. 5a)*. To keep the gap between the door and case to a minimum, I used a No. 4 x $3/8$" flathead woodscrew instead of the thick strike plate that came with the catch *(Fig. 5a)*. It still provides plenty of "pull" and can be adjusted in or out easily.

HANGING SYSTEM. Finally, to mount the case to a wall, I used a unique two-piece system *(Fig. 5b)*. A cabinet cleat (K) is glued to the back of the case. And a wall cleat (L) is screwed to the wall. The mating edges are beveled at 45°. The advantage of this system is it allows you to lift off the cabinet and take it wherever you need it in the shop. ■

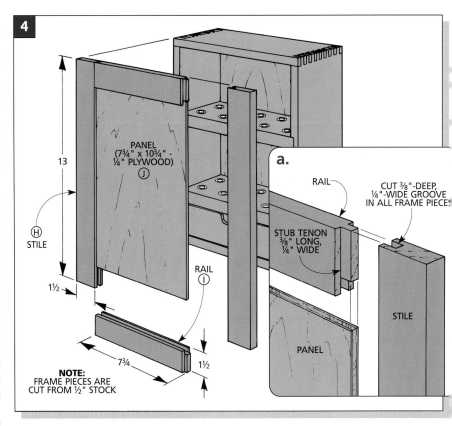

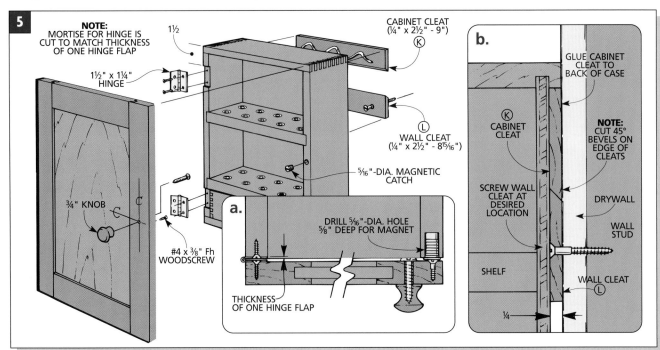

DESIGNER'S NOTEBOOK

Simpler joinery and an open front make this version of the Router Cabinet easier to build. It features slide-out shelves, an easy-to-access storage tray, and it can sit on a bench or be wall mounted.

CONSTRUCTION NOTES:

■ Start by cutting the sides (A), top (B), and bottom (B) to size *(Fig. 1)*.
■ To accept the top and bottom, rout rabbets on the sides (A) *(Fig. 1)*.
■ Next, cut grooves in the sides, top, and bottom to hold the back (C) *(Fig. 1)*.

MATERIALS LIST

CHANGED PARTS

A	Sides (2)	½ MDF - 4¼ x 14
B	Top/Bottom (2)	½ MDF - 4¼ x 14
C	Back (1)	¼ hdbd. - 13½ x 14

NEW PARTS

M	Shelf Bases (2)	¼ hdbd. - 5 x 14
N	Tray Lip (1)	¼ hdbd. - 1 x 13½
O	Bit Holders (2)	½ MDF - 3¾ x 12½
P	Filler (1)	¼ hdbd. - 2 x 13½

HARDWARE SUPPLIES

(2) No. 8 x 1½" Fh woodscrews
(8) No. 8 x 1¼" Fh woodscrews
Note: Don't need parts D, E, F, G, H, I, J, K, L.

■ Also cut a groove near the front edge of the bottom (B) for a lip added later.
■ Before assembling the case, cut two dadoes in each side to hold the shelf bases (M) *(Fig. 1)*.
■ Now you can dry-assemble the case and cut a back (C) to fit between the grooves. Then glue and screw the case together.
■ Cut a tray lip (N) to fit between the case sides and glue it in place *(Fig. 1)*.
■ To make the shelves, start by cutting two shelf bases (M) to shape *(Fig. 2)*.
■ A bit holder (O) is glued to each shelf base. Cut these from ½" MDF, then

drill holes to hold your bits *(Fig. 2)*. (Nylon inserts aren't used, since MDF won't swell or shrink like solid wood.)
■ Finally, add a hardboard filler strip (P) to the back so the cabinet can be hung on a wall *(Fig. 1)*.

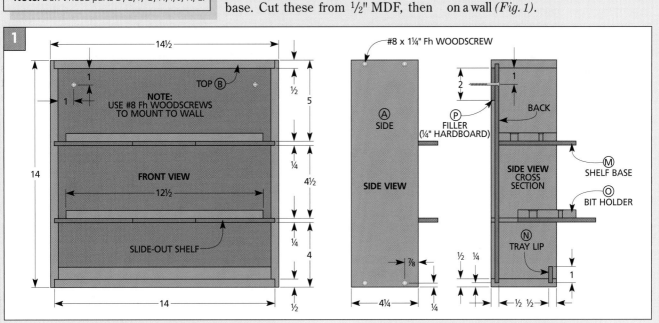

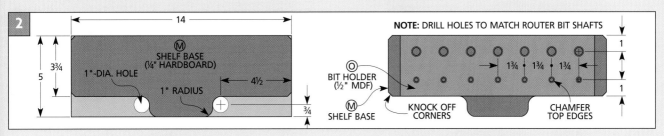

OPEN CABINET

Saw Cabinet

Table saw accessories should be stored out of the way, yet close at hand while you work. This cabinet provides just the place under the saw's wing, where they're easy to reach when you need them.

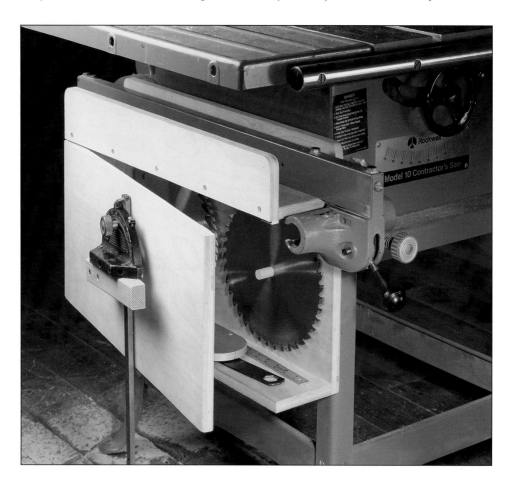

It's no secret that the table saw is the workhorse of most shops. Whether cutting pieces to size or forming joinery, I'd be lost without my table saw. But to do all that work, the table saw requires a number of accessories, from the rip fence and miter gauge to different types of blades and the wrench used to change them.

To keep these items close at hand, I built a cabinet that hangs on the side of my table saw, taking advantage of the space below the table extension.

RIP FENCE STORAGE. When I need to switch from the rip fence to the miter gauge, there's convenient storage for the fence right nearby. On top of the cabinet, there's a channel. It's open at both ends so the head can hang below the top and the rest of the fence can extend out the back. And there's usually some space left beside the fence to store my push sticks.

DOOR. The cabinet has a door which effectively doubles the storage space — allowing you to store the arbor wrench, saw blades, and other accessories inside. The miter gauge hangs in a quick-access holder on the outside of the door. It's designed so you can easily store the miter gauge, even if you have a long auxiliary fence fastened to it. (The

Accessory box on the opposite page has details on making an auxiliary fence.)

BLADE HOLDERS. Inside the cabinet are two pegs to hold saw blades. This keeps them out of the way so the teeth don't get chipped. The pegs are long enough that they will hold several blades each or even a full dado blade set with chippers.

OPTIONAL TRAY. I've noticed that other items tend to pile up around the saw as I work. So I designed an optional add-on tray to hold things like push sticks, safety glasses, and rulers. Details for building this tray are in the Designer's Notebook on page 105.

EXPLODED VIEW

OVERALL DIMENSIONS:
6W x 23D x 15½H

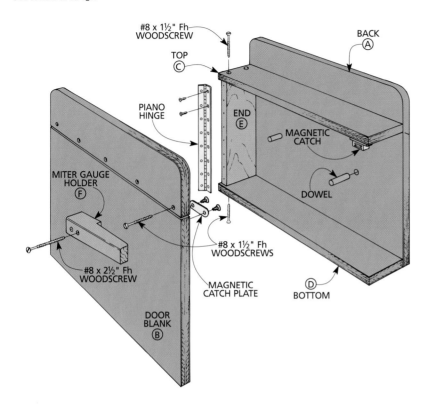

#8 x 1½" Fh WOODSCREW

TOP Ⓒ

BACK Ⓐ

PIANO HINGE

END Ⓔ

MAGNETIC CATCH

MITER GAUGE HOLDER Ⓕ

DOWEL

#8 x 1½" Fh WOODSCREWS

#8 x 2½" Fh WOODSCREW

MAGNETIC CATCH PLATE

BOTTOM Ⓓ

DOOR BLANK Ⓑ

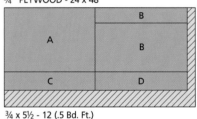

CUTTING DIAGRAM

¾" PLYWOOD - 24 x 48

A	B
	B
C	D

¾ x 5½ - 12 (.5 Bd. Ft.)

| E |

ACCESSORY . . . . *Adjustable Miter Fence*

One of the best accessories I have for my table saw is an adjustable fence for my miter gauge *(Fig. 1)*. (I designed a holder on the Saw Cabinet to hold the miter gauge with a fence.)

The fence is made of two interlocking parts — a short rabbeted top piece that's screwed to the miter gauge. And a long, rabbeted bottom piece with a tall face glued to its front. When the machine screws are tightened, the long piece is pinched against the miter gauge.

To make the fence, start by ripping a piece of ¾"-thick stock 1¼" wide. Then cut a ½" rabbet in one edge exactly half the thickness of the piece (⅜") *(Fig. 1)*.

Now cut a 6"-long piece from one end. This is the top piece that will be screwed to the miter gauge. The long piece will form the bottom of the fence.

To create the pinching action, sand or plane ⅟₃₂" off the rabbeted face of the top piece *(Fig. 2a)*.

Next, install threaded inserts in the top piece so they align with the holes in the miter gauge face *(Fig. 2)*.

Now, to form a U-shaped channel, glue a 2"-wide front face to the front edge of the long rabbeted piece (but not to the short piece) *(Fig. 2)*.

1

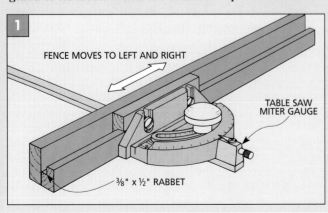

FENCE MOVES TO LEFT AND RIGHT

TABLE SAW MITER GAUGE

⅜" x ½" RABBET

2

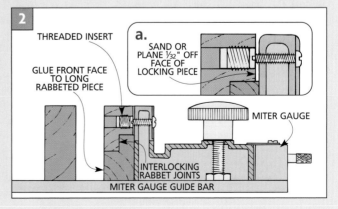

THREADED INSERT

GLUE FRONT FACE TO LONG RABBETED PIECE

a. SAND OR PLANE ⅟₃₂" OFF FACE OF LOCKING PIECE

MITER GAUGE

INTERLOCKING RABBET JOINTS

MITER GAUGE GUIDE BAR

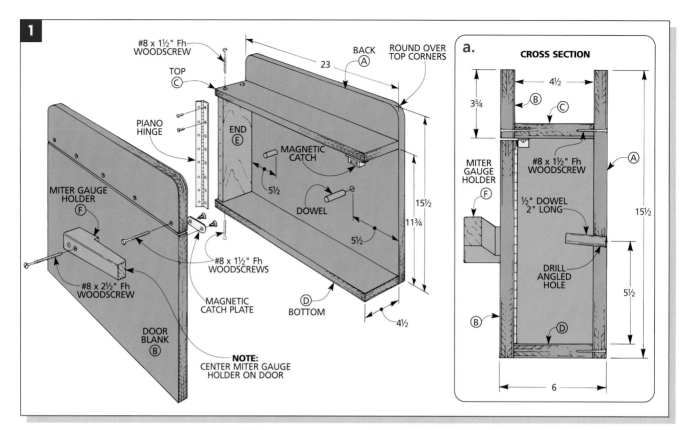

CONSTRUCTION

To build the cabinet, I started by cutting the back (A) and the door blank (B) from ³⁄₄"-thick plywood *(Fig. 1)*. I cut both pieces 15¹⁄₂" wide by 23" long (large enough to store 10"-dia. saw blades side by side).

TOP AND BOTTOM. The door and the back are joined together with the top and bottom (C, D). Cut both of these pieces to the same length as the back and 4¹⁄₂" wide *(Fig. 1)*.

Note: The 4¹⁄₂" width will accommodate most saw fences, but you can change the width to fit your fence.

After the top and bottom are cut to size, drill shank holes through the back piece and pilot holes into the top and bottom (C, D). Then screw the top and bottom to the back piece *(Fig. 1)*.

END PIECE. To mount the door, an end (E) is cut to fit between the top and bottom pieces *(Fig. 2)*. To provide more holding power for the hinge screws, I cut this piece from ³⁄₄"-thick hardwood (not plywood).

The width of this piece has to allow for the hinge that's attached later. So measure the width of the bottom (4¹⁄₂") and subtract the thickness of the hinge. After the end is cut to size, screw it between the top and bottom.

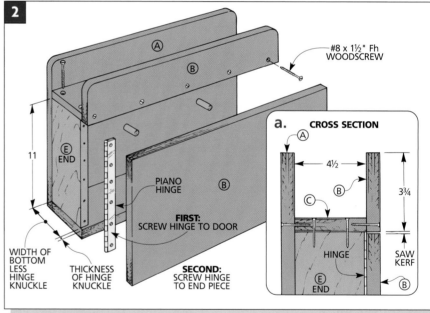

DOOR BLANK. Before the door can be mounted, the door blank is ripped into two pieces. One piece becomes the door. The other piece is screwed to the top to complete the channel for the rip fence *(Fig. 2)*. Rip the top piece 3³⁄₄" wide *(Fig. 2a)*. When the door is mounted to the case later, the saw kerf provides clearance for the door to open.

BLADE HOLDERS. Before installing the door, I drilled two ¹⁄₂"-dia. holes for

dowels that hold the blades inside the cabinet *(Fig. 1a)*. These holes are angled to keep blades from falling off.

MOUNT DOOR. When you're ready to mount the door to the cabinet, cut a piano hinge the same length as the door. Then screw the hinge to the door *(Fig. 2)*. Next, screw the other flap of the hinge to the end (E). Finally, to help keep the door closed, add a magnetic catch under the top (C) *(Fig. 1)*.

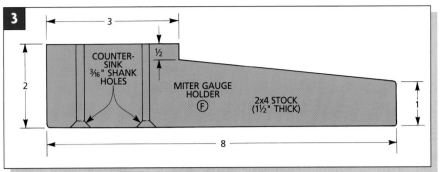

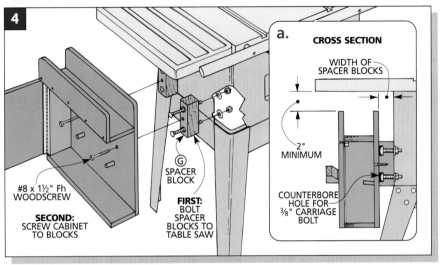

MITER GAUGE HOLDER

One of the most awkward things to store is a miter gauge — especially when it has a long auxiliary fence attached to it. Storing it becomes even more of a problem if you want easy and quick access when you need it.

One solution is this simple quick-access miter gauge holder (F) that mounts to the front of the cabinet door. It's just a bracket with a tapered notch.

I cut mine from a scrap piece of 2x4 8" long (Fig. 3). Then, I ripped it to a width of 2".

Next, lay out the tapered notch and cut it out with a jig saw or on a band saw. Also, drill two countersunk shank holes through the thickest portion of the holder. Before mounting the holder, ease the sharp edges with sandpaper.

When mounting the holder to the door, center it on the door's length so an auxiliary fence won't stick past the front of the cabinet. Also, tilt it at a slight angle to keep the miter gauge from sliding off the front (open) end.

MOUNTING

With the cabinet complete, all that's left is to mount it to the saw.

As you position the cabinet, make sure you leave enough room below the wing to allow you to place the rip fence in the channel (Fig. 4a).

If the angle of the legs on your table saw interferes with mounting the cabinet, add a couple of spacer blocks (G) between the cabinet and the saw. Counterbore holes in the blocks, and use carriage bolts to fasten them to the side of the saw (Fig. 4). Now just screw the cabinet to the blocks and start organizing your accessories. ■

DESIGNER'S NOTEBOOK

ACCESSORY TRAY

■ This optional tray provides a place to put smaller accessories. It consists of a hardboad front (I) and back (K), and a ³/₄" hardwood bottom (J) that are glued to two tray ends (H) cut from ³/₄"-thick hardwood (see drawing).

■ The back (K) is taller than the front (I) to allow you to screw the tray flush with the top edge of the Saw Cabinet (see drawings).

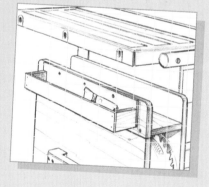

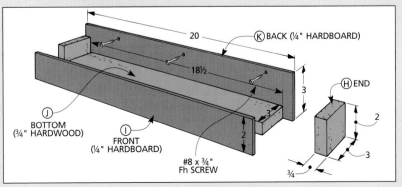

Modular Tool Bins

Here's storage that's as easy to make as it is versatile. Set them side by side or stack them up to fit the space in your shop. The shelves adjust so you can organize the compartments to suit your needs.

Storing portable power tools is always a problem. They usually end up in a pile on a shelf somewhere. And the power cords unwind and weave together like spaghetti.

To solve this, I built these Modular Tool Bins. It's really a tool storage system that you can customize easily to fit your needs. The cabinets are open in the front to keep the tools right at hand. A set of shelves creates a series of bins — each bin a "home" for a specific tool or accessory. The shelves can be moved up or down to make each opening a custom fit. And since it's easy to access

the shelves, I find I'm more likely to put a tool back where it belongs instead of just setting it down.

ADAPTABLE. I also wanted a system that could be adapted to fit a variety of shop layouts. So I built two smaller cases instead of one large cabinet. This way I could stack the bins (see left photo), place them side by side (see right photo), or use them as stand-alone units in separate areas. By adding a work surface between them, they can even be used as the base for a workbench. There's more about this option in the Designer's Notebook on page 111.

SHELVES. To store the widest possible variety of power tools, the shelves are two different widths. And in keeping with the simple design, there's no hardware needed to hold the shelves. Instead they fit in a set of dadoes in the sides. This makes it easy to rearrange the shelves to accommodate different tools and accessories. I even customized several of the shelves to hold specific tools. (For more on this, see the Designer's Notebook on page 110.)

Even though there are 24 dadoes for the shelves, I'll show you a trick for cutting them quickly.

EXPLODED VIEW

OVERALL DIMENSIONS:
23¾W x 15¾D x 36H

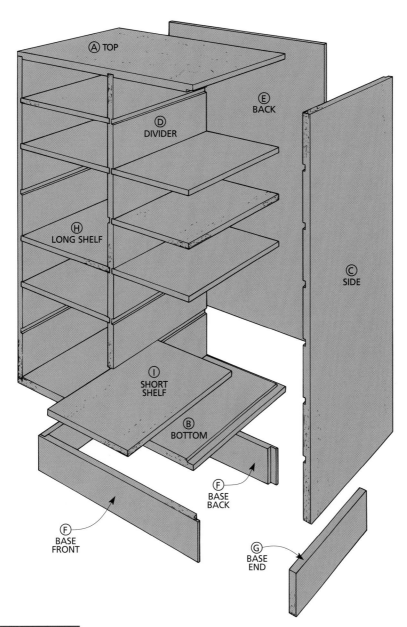

A TOP
E BACK
D DIVIDER
H LONG SHELF
C SIDE
I SHORT SHELF
B BOTTOM
F BASE BACK
F BASE FRONT
G BASE END

MATERIALS LIST

WOOD

A	Tops (2)	¾ ply - 15¾ x 23¾
B	Bottoms (2)	¾ ply - 15¾ x 23¾
C	Sides (4)	¾ ply - 15¾ x 31½
D	Dividers (2)	¾ ply - 15¼ x 31½
E	Backs (2)	½ ply - 22¾ x 31½
F	Base Ft./Bk. (2)	¾ x 3½ - 21¾*
G	Base Ends (2)	¾ x 3½ - 13¼
H	Long Shelves (8)	½ ply - 15¼ x 12¾
I	Short Shelves (8)	½ ply - 15¼ x 9¾

* Length for single base.

HARDWARE SUPPLIES

(44) No. 8 x 2" Fh woodscrews
(4) No. 8 x 1¼" Fh woodscrews
(24) No. 4 (1½") finish nails
(8) No. 6 (2") finish nails

CUTTING DIAGRAM

¾ x 3½ - 72 (1.75 Bd. Ft.) (Base For One Single-Wide Case)
F F G G
¾ x 3½ - 72 (1.75 Bd. Ft. Each) (Base For One Double-Wide Case)
F G
F G
¾" PLYWOOD - 48 x 96
A A B B
C C D
C C D
½" PLYWOOD - 48 x 96
E E
H H H H I
H H H H I
I I I I I I

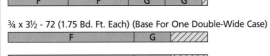

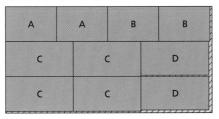

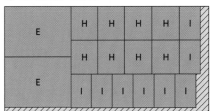

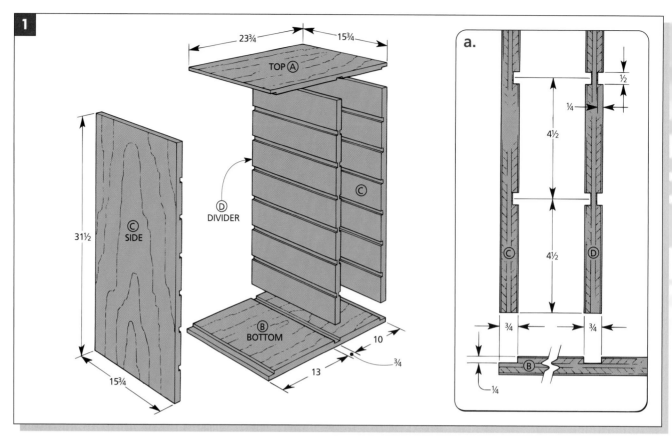

CASE

The modular tool bins consist of two identical cases. Each case is just a plywood box with a divider *(Fig. 1)*.

All of the $3/4$"-thick plywood pieces for both cases are cut from a single sheet (refer to the Cutting Diagram on page 107). Since these pieces are all the same width ($15^3/4$"), I started by ripping the sheet into three $15^3/4$"-wide strips.

TOP AND BOTTOM. Once the case pieces are cut to width, the top (A) and bottom (B) pieces can be cut to their finished length ($23^3/4$") *(Fig. 1)*.

Then the ends are rabbeted to accept the side pieces *(Fig. 1a)*. And a dado is cut in each piece for a divider added later. Note that this dado is offset on the length of the top and bottom *(Fig. 1)*.

SIDES AND DIVIDERS. The next step is to cut the sides (C) and dividers (D) to

length ($31^1/2$") *(Fig. 1)*. To accept the adjustable shelves (added later), $1/2$"-wide dadoes are cut in the inside faces of the sides (C), and both faces of the dividers (D) *(Fig. 1a)*.

CUT IN PAIRS. That's a lot of dadoes to cut (24 per case). To cut these quickly, I use a special technique. I cut the dadoes in pairs starting near the ends and working towards the center *(Fig. 2)*. This cuts your set up time in half and ensures the dadoes will align.

Start by attaching a long auxiliary fence to your miter gauge *(Fig. 2)*. Then clamp a stop to the fence and cut the first dado. Now turn the workpiece end for end and cut a second dado *(Fig. 2)*.

Once you've cut matching pairs of dadoes in all four sides and both dividers, then reset the stop and cut the next set of dadoes.

Note: For each divider (E), flip the piece over and repeat the cuts on the other side.

BACK

To strengthen the case and prevent it from racking, I added a back (E) made from $1/2$" plywood.

RABBET. To hold the back in place, I cut rabbets on the inside edges of the top, bottom, and side pieces (A, B, C) *(Figs. 3 and 3b)*.

TRIM DIVIDER. But before you can assemble the case, you'll need to trim $\frac{1}{2}$" off the width of the divider (D). This way it won't interfere with the back when it's installed later *(Fig. 3)*.

ASSEMBLE CASES. Now you're ready to assemble the cases. To do this, apply glue, then screw the top and bottom to the sides and divider *(Figs. 3 and 3a)*.

Note: Make sure that the case is square, and the front of the divider (D) is flush with the front of the case.

ADD THE BACK. Finally, cut a back (E) to fit in the rabbets in each case. Then glue and nail the back in place *(Fig. 3b)*.

BASE

To make the bottom bin more accessible and keep the case up off a damp floor, I added a base *(Fig. 4)*.

The base consists of four pieces of 1x4 stock: a front and back (F), and two ends (G). The front and back pieces are rabbeted to accept the ends *(Fig. 4a)*.

CUT PIECES. The length of the ends is the same ($13\frac{1}{4}$"). But the length of the front and back depends on how you arrange the cases. If the base is for a single case (or you're going to stack them), the front and back pieces are $21\frac{3}{4}$" long. If the cases are side by side, they're $45\frac{1}{2}$" long.

ASSEMBLY. The base is assembled with glue and a couple of nails at each corner *(Fig. 4a)*. Then it's centered under the case (this allows a 1" overhang) and screwed in place *(Fig. 4b)*.

A series of dadoes allows the shelves to be adjusted or even removed to accommodate tools of various sizes.

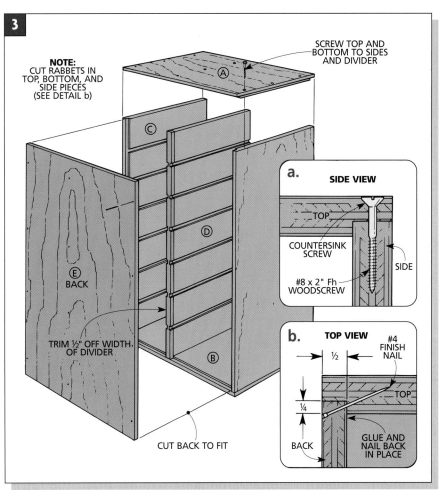

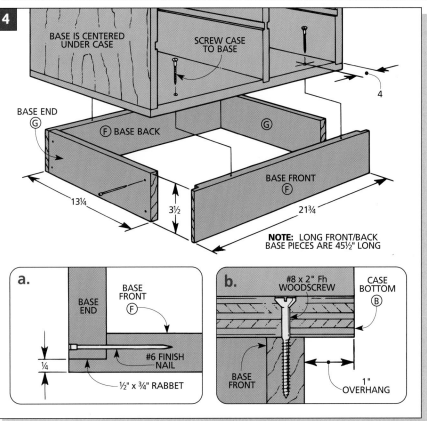

The only thing left to complete the tool bins is to add the adjustable shelves *(Fig. 5)*. These ½" plywood shelves are cut to fit in between the dadoes in the sides and divider.

TWO SIZES. The depth of the shelves (distance from front to back) is the same (15¼"). But the lengths (distance from side to side) are different *(Fig. 5)*. (Note the grain direction.)

In my case, the long shelves (H) are 12¾" long, and the short shelves (I) are 9¾" long.

Note: The ½" plywood that remains from cutting the backs (E) will allow for eight shelves of each size. Make as many shelves as you need.

CHAMFER AND BEVEL. To prevent chipping and to make it easier to slide the shelves in and out, I took them to the router table and chamfered their front and back edges *(Fig. 5a)*. Then I beveled the front edge of each dado in the cabinets *(Fig. 5a)*. This can be done with a chisel, a file, or with sandpaper.

CUSTOMIZE. Finally, I took the time to customize some of the shelves to hold specific tools, as shown in the Designer's Notebook below. ■

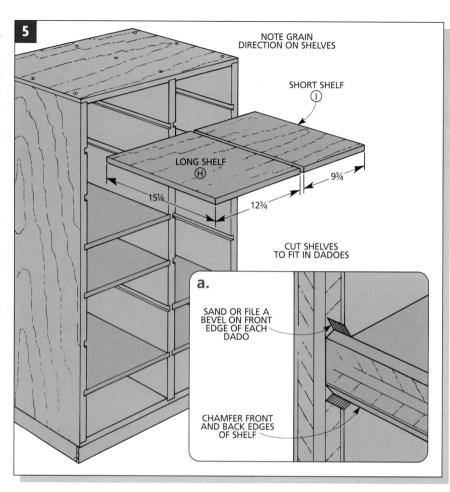

5

NOTE GRAIN
DIRECTION ON SHELVES

SHORT SHELF
(I)

LONG SHELF
(H)

15¼

12¾

9¾

CUT SHELVES
TO FIT IN DADOES

a.

SAND OR FILE A
BEVEL ON FRONT
EDGE OF EACH
DADO

CHAMFER FRONT
AND BACK EDGES
OF SHELF

DESIGNER'S NOTEBOOK

Different tools have different storage needs. These modifications give each tool a custom-fit home.

CUSTOMIZING THE SHELVES

Circular Saw. *To keep the saw from tilting when it's set on a shelf, I cut a long rectangular slot wide enough to fit the blade guard. This allows the saw to sit flat. An easy way to lay out this slot is to trace the opening in the saw's baseplate.*

Drills. *To make it easy to reach in and grab an electric (or cordless) drill, notch the front end of one of the shelves. Each notch is cut to fit the handle and holds the drill upright. The cord for the electric drill can be coiled up on the shelf below.*

DESIGNER'S NOTEBOOK

An easy-to-make work surface placed across two of the Modular Tool Bins can serve as a workbench. The hardboard top can be removed for quick replacement when it becomes worn from use.

CONSTRUCTION NOTES:

■ Start by cutting a base (J) from $3/4$" plywood to a width of 18". This allows for a $1^1/8$" overhang on the front and back (see detail 'a' in drawing). To provide some "knee room" between the bins, I cut my base to a length of 72". You can make yours longer or shorter to fit your space.

■ A hardboard cover (K) is cut to the same size as the base (J) (see drawing).

■ Hardwood edging is added to each side of the base to hide the edges of the plywood. The edging also extends above the top of the base to form a "lip" to hold the hardboard in place (see detail 'a' in drawing).

■ The edging (L, M) is $3/4$"-thick stock ripped to a width of $1^1/2$". I cut each piece about 1" over finished length to allow me to sneak up on the final length as I mitered the ends.

■ When "wrapping" a workpiece with mitered trim on all four sides, I like to start with the front piece, then cut the side pieces (M) to length. I cut and attach the back piece last. This way, any slight gap in the miters will be at the rear where it's less noticeable. Of course, I cut a number of test joints first to get the best fit possible before starting to miter the trim.

■ When the trim is mitered to length, it can be fastened to the base. Before doing this, I set the base on top of the Tool Bins to provide clearance since the trim extends below the bottom edge (see detail 'a' in drawing).

■ I used a scrap of $1/4$" hardboard as a gauge to help position the trim above the top edge of the base. A couple of

finish nails in each piece help hold it in position as you clamp it (see detail 'a').

■ Before setting the cover (K) in place, drill a finger hole through the base (J) centered on its length (see drawing).

This lets you lift the cover so you can replace it if it becomes worn.

■ Secure the work surface to the Tool Bins by driving screws through the top of the bins up into the base.

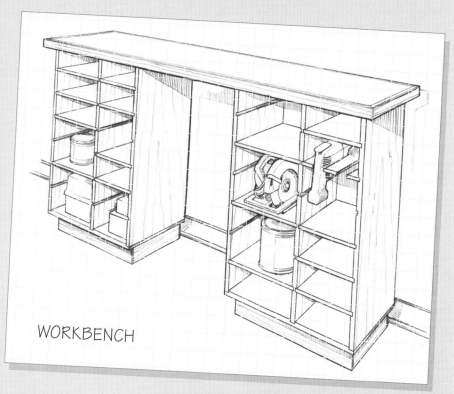

WORKBENCH

MATERIALS LIST

NEW PARTS

J	Base (1)	$3/4$ ply - 18 x 72
K	Cover (1)	$1/4$ hdbd. - 18 x 72
L	Long Trim (2)	$3/4$ x $1^1/2$ - $73^1/2$
M	Short Trim (2)	$3/4$ x $1^1/2$ - $19^1/2$

HARDWARE SUPPLIES

(8) No. 8 x $1^1/4$" Fh woodscrews
(8) 4d ($1^1/2$") finish nails

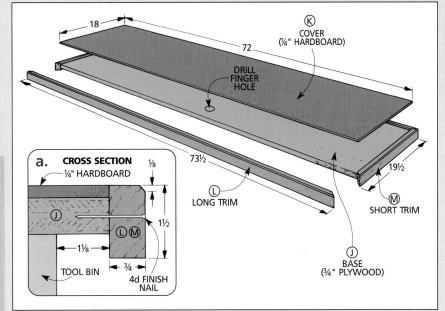

a. CROSS SECTION
$1/4$" HARDBOARD
$1/8$
$1^1/8$
$3/4$
$1^1/2$
TOOL BIN
4d FINISH NAIL

18
72
DRILL FINGER HOLE
$73^1/2$
$19^1/2$
COVER ($1/4$" HARDBOARD) ⓀK
LONG TRIM ⓁL
SHORT TRIM ⓂM
BASE ($3/4$" PLYWOOD) ⒿJ

Drop-Down Tool Tray

The deep lid of this workbench-mounted tray holds tools and keeps dust out. But making a lid to fit a box is difficult — unless you use a simple technique that guarantees a perfect match.

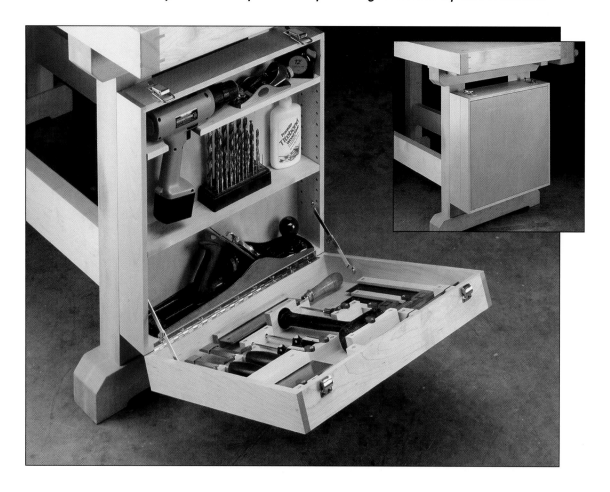

Keeping my bench top clear sometimes seems like a losing battle. Even when I'm working on a simple project, tools and materials have a way of piling up on top.

Usually, this clutter just gets in the way. But every once in awhile, one of my tools gets knocked to the floor. In fact, I was picking up a chisel (freshly sharpened, of course) when the idea for this tool tray hit me.

UNDERBENCH STORAGE. The tray hangs under the bench in a space that usually just goes to waste. The lid drops down to put the tools I use most within easy reach. And when I'm done using a

tool, it's easy and convenient to slip it back into the tray — out of the way.

LID. Building a lid to fit a box *exactly* can be difficult. So I didn't. Instead, I simply built an enclosed box and cut the lid from it. This is a simple procedure on the table saw.

HOLDERS. The lid of the tray is extra-deep so tools can be kept in it. But tools stored in the lid would fall out if they weren't secured somehow. Custom holders lock each tool in place. The Designer's Notebook on page 117 has more about making these tool holders.

SHADOW LINES. The case is held together with tongue and groove

joinery. Usually when I cut this joint, I cut the tongues to fit the grooves perfectly, so the pieces fit together tightly. But this time, I cut the tongues on the panels a bit long. This forms a decorative shadow line around the panel on the case lid (see inset photo above).

HARDWARE. The hardware for this project should be available at most hardware stores and home centers (or check the mail-order sources on page 126). In addition to a few screws, you'll need a length of piano hinge. To keep the lid from opening too far, supports secure the lid to the case. And a couple of draw catches hold the lid closed.

EXPLODED VIEW

OVERALL DIMENSIONS:
20W x 6D x 20H

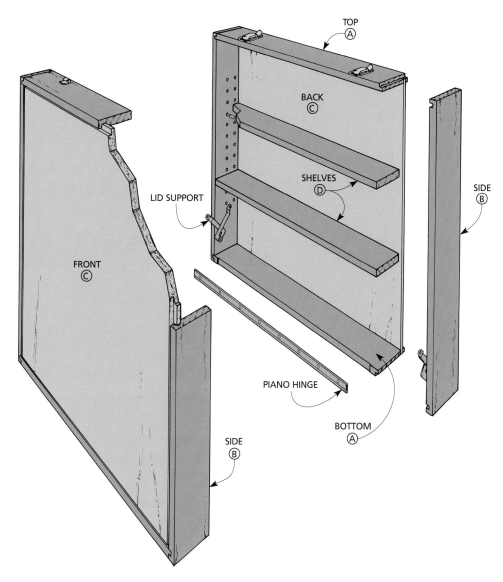

TOP
Ⓐ

BACK
Ⓒ

SHELVES
Ⓓ

SIDE
Ⓑ

LID SUPPORT

FRONT
Ⓒ

PIANO HINGE

BOTTOM
Ⓐ

SIDE
Ⓑ

MATERIALS LIST

WOOD
A Top/Bottom (2) $\frac{1}{2}$ x 6$\frac{1}{8}$ - 19$\frac{1}{2}$
B Sides (2) $\frac{1}{2}$ x 6$\frac{1}{8}$ - 20
C Front/Back (2) $\frac{1}{2}$ ply - 19$\frac{1}{2}$ x 19$\frac{1}{2}$
D Shelves (2) $\frac{1}{2}$ x 3 - 18$\frac{7}{8}$

HARDWARE SUPPLIES
(4) No. 10 x 1$\frac{1}{4}$" Fh woodscrews
(1) 1$\frac{1}{16}$" x 18"-long piano hinge w/ screws
(2) 7"-long lid supports w/ screws
(2) 3$\frac{1}{2}$" x 1$\frac{1}{4}$" draw catches w/ screws
(8) Shelf support pins

CUTTING DIAGRAM

$\frac{1}{2}$" PLYWOOD - 24 x 48

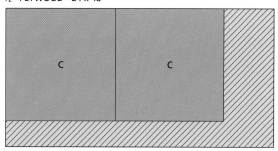

$\frac{3}{4}$ x 7$\frac{1}{4}$ - 96 (5 Bd. Ft.)

| A | A | B | B | |

$\frac{3}{4}$ x 3$\frac{1}{2}$ - 48 (1.2 Bd. Ft.)

| D | D | |

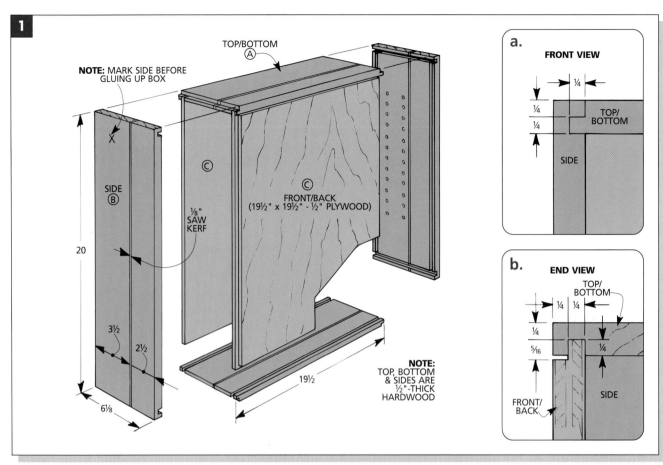

1

NOTE: MARK SIDE BEFORE GLUING UP BOX

TOP/BOTTOM
Ⓐ

SIDE
Ⓑ

X

Ⓒ

⅛"
SAW
KERF

Ⓒ
FRONT/BACK
(19½" x 19½" - ½" PLYWOOD)

20

3½

2½

6⅛

19½

NOTE:
TOP, BOTTOM
& SIDES ARE
½"-THICK
HARDWOOD

a.

FRONT VIEW

¼

¼

¼

TOP/
BOTTOM

SIDE

b.

END VIEW

TOP/
BOTTOM

¼ ¼

¼

5/16

¼

FRONT/
BACK

SIDE

CASE

The tray consists of two parts: a box that holds two adjustable shelves, and the drop-down lid. But rather than make each part separately, I built a single, fully-enclosed box and then cut it apart to form the lid. This ensures a perfect fit between the box and the lid.

TONGUE AND DADO. I started building the tray by cutting a top (A), bottom (A) and two sides (B) to size *(Fig. 1)*. (I used ½"-thick maple.) These pieces are then held together with tongue and dado joints *(Fig. 1)*.

When cutting this joint, I like to cut the dado first. That way, I can sneak up on the final thickness of the tongue to get a tight fit. So after setting up a ¼" dado blade in the table saw, I cut a ¼"-deep dado across each end of each side (B) *(Figs. 1a and 2)*.

To cut the tongues, I attached a wood auxiliary fence to my rip fence and positioned it next to the blade. Then I cut tongues on the top and bottom (A) to fit the dadoes *(Fig. 1a)*.

GROOVES. Once you've completed the basic joinery for the top, bottom, and sides, you'll need to cut a pair of grooves in each piece to accept the front and back (C) of the box (added next).

The grooves in the top and bottom are simple enough. They run along the entire length of the workpiece. But if you cut the grooves the full length of the sides (B), they'll be visible at each end and need to be filled with wood plugs. So instead, I stopped the grooves at the dadoes cut earlier *(Fig. 2)*.

An easy way to do this is to rout them with a straight bit in the router table. But first, you need to know where to start and stop each groove.

To do this, make two marks on the router fence — each one ⅜" from the edge of the bit *(Fig. 3a)*. (I used a ¼"-straight bit.) The extra ⅛" provides a "fudge factor" so you don't accidentally rout the grooves past the dadoes.

Now you're ready to rout the grooves. First, start the router, then carefully lower the workpiece onto the spinning bit so the end aligns with the starting point *(Figs. 3 and 3a)*. Then rout the groove until the opposite end aligns with the stop mark, and shut off the router *(Fig. 3b)*. To rout the opposite groove, turn the workpiece end for end and repeat the process.

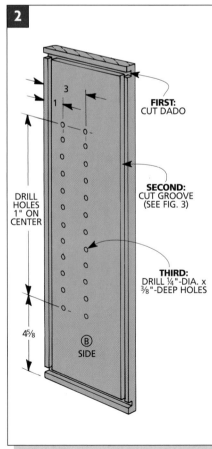

2

3

1

DRILL
HOLES
1" ON
CENTER

4⅝

Ⓑ
SIDE

FIRST:
CUT DADO

SECOND:
CUT GROOVE
(SEE FIG. 3)

THIRD:
DRILL ¼"-DIA. x
⅜"-DEEP HOLES

Once the grooves were routed in the sides, I cut the full-length grooves in the top and bottom (A).

DRILL HOLES. The next step is to drill holes in the sides for the shelf support pins *(Fig. 2)*. It's important that each set of four holes aligns. Otherwise, the shelf will rock. An easy way to locate the holes is to make a template from pegboard. Mark the holes you want to drill through, and cover the others with masking tape. Then drill through the holes. When doing the other side (B), make sure you keep the same edge of the template to the rear of the case.

Keep in mind that you won't know which part of the box the holes are drilled in once it's assembled. So to keep from accidentally cutting through the holes when you separate the lid from the box, it's a good idea to mark the part that has the holes *(Fig. 1)*.

FRONT/BACK. All that's left to complete the basic box is to add a plywood front and back (C). (I used 1/2"-thick birch plywood.) The edges of these pieces are rabbeted to form tongues that fit the grooves in the box pieces. But these tongues are a bit different from those cut on the top and bottom pieces. To create a decorative "shadow line" around the edges of the front and back, I cut the rabbets 1/16" wider than the

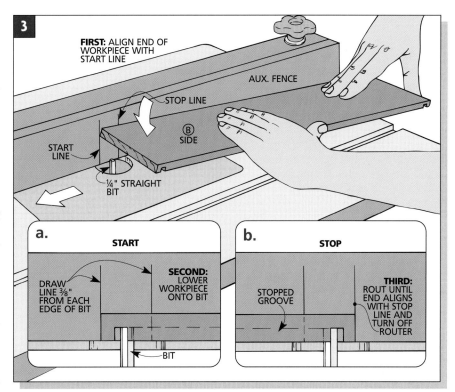

depth of the grooves (5/16") *(Fig. 1b)*.

Note: To reduce splintering, I put masking tape on the face of the plywood before cutting the rabbets.

ASSEMBLE BOX. Now it's just a matter of gluing and clamping the pieces of the box together. First, assemble the top and bottom (A) with the front and back panels (C). Then add the sides (B). Check that the case stays square as you apply the clamps.

Once the glue dries, cutting the lid from the box is a simple process. The Shop Tip below shows how to do this.

SHOP TIP . . . . *Cutting a Lid from a Box*

There's nothing complicated about using a table saw to cut a lid from a box.

The first step is to set the rip fence to the width of the lid. (For the Drop-Down Tool Tray, this is 2 1/2".)

Then the key is to set the blade so it's slightly

less (1/16") than the thickness of the box side *(Fig. 1)*. This leaves a thin membrane that holds the box together and keeps the kerf from pinching the blade.

Note: Use a piece of scrap the same thickness as the sides to set the height of the blade.

Once all four sides are cut, you can sever the membrane by making a series of *light* passes with a knife *(Fig. 2)*. Then use the knife and a scrap block to remove the ridges left behind *(Fig. 3)*. Finally, a light sanding cleans up the mating edges.

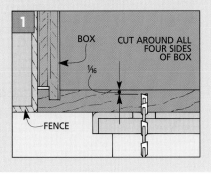

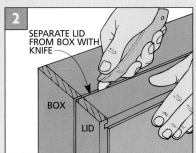

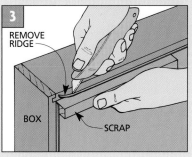

At this point, the tool tray is just an empty box with a lid. But adding a few pieces of hardware and a pair of adjustable shelves lets you take advantage of the storage space inside.

HINGE. The box and lid are held together with a piano hinge *(Fig. 4)*. To allow the lid to shut tightly, it's recessed into a shallow notch routed in the back edge of each part *(Fig. 4a)*. Note that the notch is only as long as the hinge. It doesn't run the full width of the case.

LID SUPPORTS. After screwing the hinge in place, I installed a pair of lid supports *(Fig. 5)*. They bear the weight of the lid and the tools inside. To provide easy access, the supports are positioned so they hold the lid open at a slight angle *(Fig. 5a)*.

DRAW CATCHES. Next, to hold the lid closed, I added a pair of draw catches *(Fig. 6)*. The trick is to position each catch so the bail draws the lid tight. To do this, start by mounting the catch. Then, with the catch in the raised position, set the strike in place so it's snug against the bail on the catch *(Fig. 6a)*. Mark the locations for the screws and install the bail.

SHELVES. After installing the draw catches and attaching the tray to the bench (I screwed it to the legs of the bench), all that's left is to add two shelves inside the tray.

The shelves (D) are ½"-thick pieces of hardwood that rest on four shelf support pins *(Fig. 7)*.

Note: You may want to customize a shelf to hold one of your tools (see the photo below).

Then you can add tool holders in the lid as shown in the Designer's Notebook on the opposite page. ■

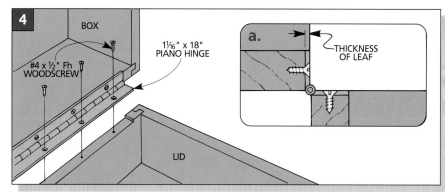

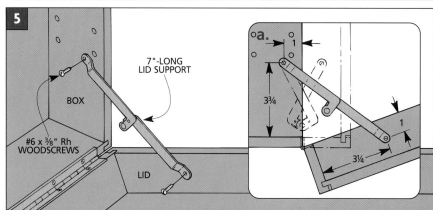

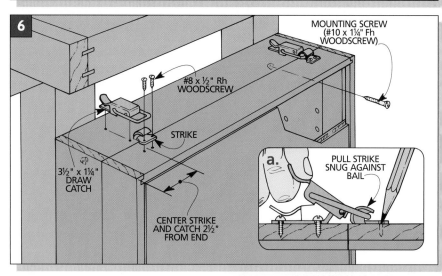

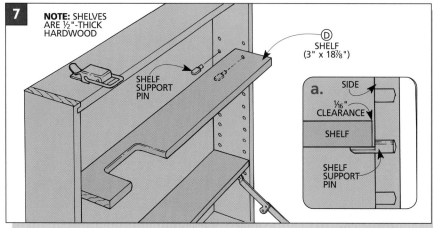

To make a convenient holder for a cordless drill, just cut a simple notch in one of the shelves to fit the handle. It will stay dust-free inside the tool tray.

DESIGNER'S NOTEBOOK

The lid of the Drop-Down Tool Tray offers plenty of storage — you just have to make sure things stay put when you close it up. These shop-made holders will keep your tools in place.

CONSTRUCTION NOTES:

■ For my screwdrivers, mallets and awl, both ends of each tool are captured between two blocks (*Fig. 1* and drawing at right).

■ One block has a hole that creates a pocket for the blade (or the handle of the mallet) *(Fig. 1)*. The other has a curved notch that fits the shape of the opposite end of the tool.

■ A wood turnbuckle is added to lock the tool in place *(Fig. 1)*.

■ Since chisels get shorter as they are sharpened, the bottom of the tool hangs below the bottom of the hanger

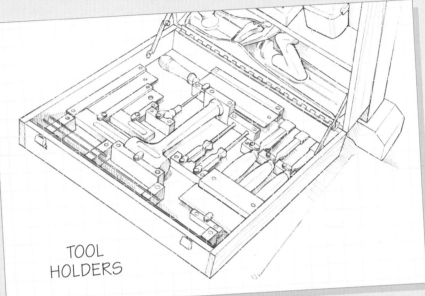

TOOL HOLDERS

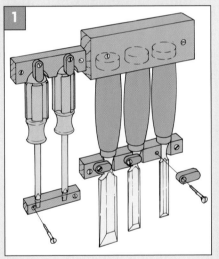

instead of resting in it *(Fig. 1)*.

■ To hold metal rules, simply cut a series of angled kerfs in some scrap blocks *(Fig. 2)*.

■ Varying the depth of the kerfs keeps rules of different widths flush at the top.

■ Position the blocks so the kerfs face up to keep the rules from falling out.

■ To hold a tool with a flat blade (like a square, scraper, or saw), all it takes is two pieces of scrap.

■ A kerf in one piece captures the blade

(Fig. 3). And a rabbet in the other one allows you to remove the tool easily and put it back in. To hold the blade flat, just be sure the bottoms of the kerf and rabbet align *(Fig. 3a)*.

■ To save space inside the lid, keep in mind that one piece can do double duty. For instance, the middle piece in *Fig. 3* acts as one part of the holder for two different squares.

■ Here again, wood turnbuckles are added to lock each tool in place.

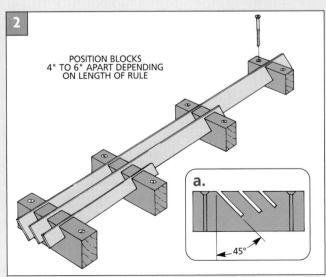

POSITION BLOCKS 4" TO 6" APART DEPENDING ON LENGTH OF RULE

a.

45°

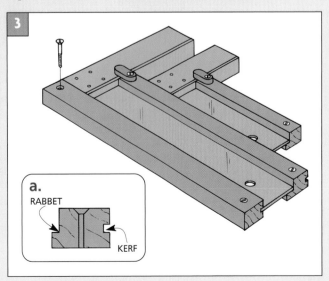

a.

RABBET

KERF

Small Workbench

Get the features of a full-size workbench without sacrificing a large portion of your shop. This bench boasts a rock-solid frame, a thick, sturdy top with two vises, and an optional storage cabinet.

When I built my first workbench, I didn't have much money. And I had even less space. So I rounded up some scrap pieces of "two-by" material and nailed a bench together that was no bigger than a card table.

In spite of the small size of the bench, there was still something about it I liked. With the bench tucked into the basement between the laundry area and shelves filled with fruit jam, I'd while away the hours — building a small box, getting a dovetail joint just right, or tuning up an old hand plane.

Well, it's funny how things work out.

That bench has come full circle. In fact, it's the idea behind this Small Workbench. The size is about the same as I remember it. Just right for a small shop or even an out-of-the-way corner of your house. Only this time around, there are a few improvements.

VISES. For instance, this workbench has two vises: a front vise and an end vise. Not your ordinary store-bought vises that are added onto the workbench after it's done. Instead, these vises are built into it.

By making each vise an integral part of the bench, you get a wide range of clamping options — more than with many benches that are twice this size.

HARDWOOD. Instead of scrap 2x4s, this time I used hard maple to make the bench as sturdy as possible.

STORAGE. This workbench has one other advantage over my old one — you can add storage. If you need to organize smaller items, the Designer's Notebook on page 124 shows how to make an optional cabinet that fits inside the base of the bench and keeps tools and materials within easy reach.

Even without the storage cabinet, there's room below the bench to store pipe clamps or short cutoffs on the stretchers between the legs.

EXPLODED VIEW

OVERALL DIMENSIONS:
33W x 24D x 29¾H

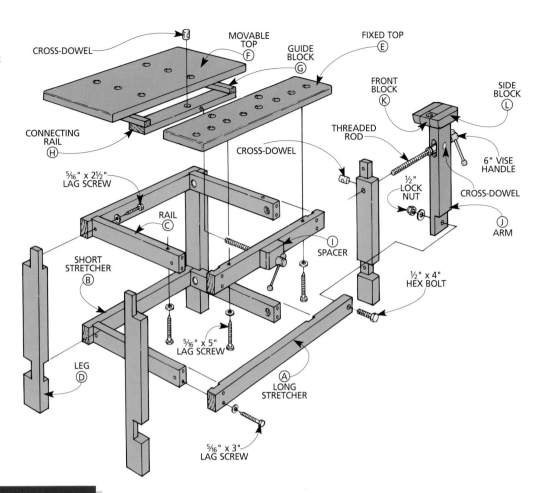

CROSS-DOWEL

MOVABLE TOP Ⓕ

GUIDE BLOCK Ⓖ

FIXED TOP Ⓔ

FRONT BLOCK Ⓚ

SIDE BLOCK Ⓛ

THREADED ROD

6" VISE HANDLE

CONNECTING RAIL Ⓗ

CROSS-DOWEL

½" LOCK NUT

CROSS-DOWEL

Ⓙ ARM

⁵⁄₁₆" x 2½" LAG SCREW

RAIL Ⓒ

SPACER Ⓘ

SHORT STRETCHER Ⓑ

½" x 4" HEX BOLT

⁵⁄₁₆" x 5" LAG SCREW

LEG Ⓓ

LONG STRETCHER Ⓐ

⁵⁄₁₆" x 3" LAG SCREW

MATERIALS LIST

WOOD

A	Long Stretcher (1)	1¾ x 3½ - 33
B	Short Stretchers (3)	1¾ x 3½ - 26
C	Rails (4)	1¾ x 3½ - 19
D	Legs (4)	1¾ x 3½ - 28
E	Fixed Top (1)	1¾ x 8½ - 30
F	Movable Top (1)	1¾ x 15½ - 30
G	Guide Blocks (2)	1¾ x 1¾ - 14
H	Connecting Rail (1)	1¾ x 3½ - 20¼
I	Spacer (1)	1¾ x 3½ - 4½
J	Arm (1)	1¾ x 3½ - 23½
K	Front Block (1)	1¾ x 1½ - 1¾
L	Side Blocks (2)	1¾ x 5 - 1¾

HARDWARE SUPPLIES

(16) ⁵⁄₁₆" x 3" lag screws
(8) ⁵⁄₁₆" x 2½" lag screws
(4) ⁵⁄₁₆" x 5" lag screws
(28) ⁵⁄₁₆" flat washers
(1) ⅜" x 11" threaded rod
(1) ⅜" x 14" threaded rod
(3) ¾" x 1¾" cross-dowels
(2) ⅜"-I.D. x 1"-long nylon bushings
(1) ⅜"-I.D. x 1"-long bronze bushing
(3) ⅜" fender washers
(3) ⅜" hex nuts
(2) ⅜" x 1⅛" coupling nuts
(1) ½" x 4" hex bolt
(1) ½" flat washer
(1) ½" lock nut
(2) 6" vise handles

CUTTING DIAGRAM

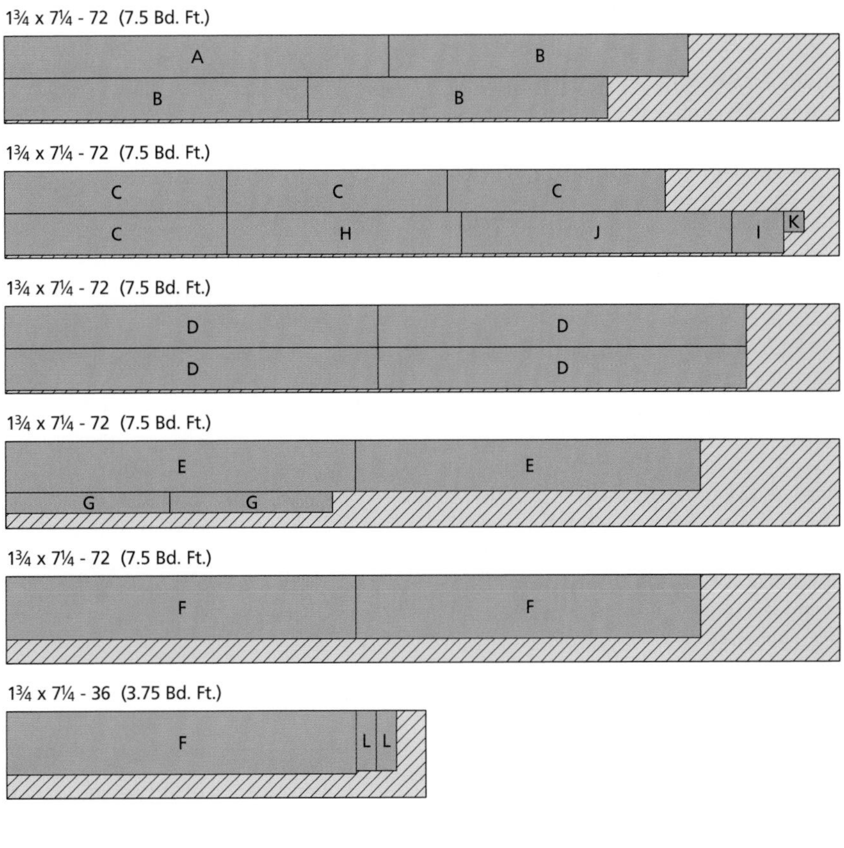

1¾ x 7¼ - 72 (7.5 Bd. Ft.)

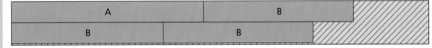

A	B
B	B

1¾ x 7¼ - 72 (7.5 Bd. Ft.)

C	C	C	
C	H	J	I / K

1¾ x 7¼ - 72 (7.5 Bd. Ft.)

D	D
D	D

1¾ x 7¼ - 72 (7.5 Bd. Ft.)

E	E
G	G

1¾ x 7¼ - 72 (7.5 Bd. Ft.)

F	F

1¾ x 7¼ - 36 (3.75 Bd. Ft.)

F	L / L

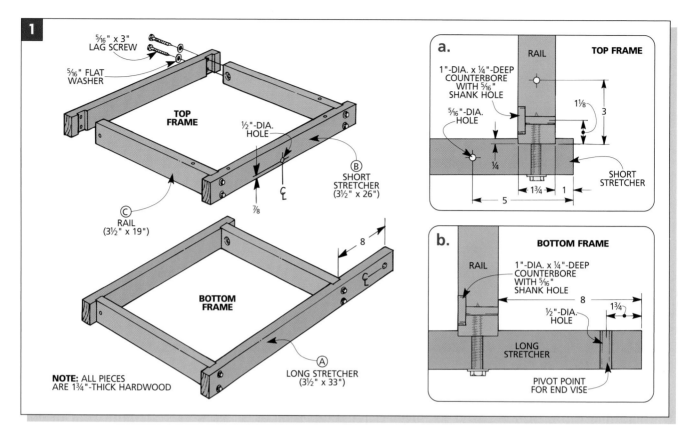

BASE

I started on the bench by making the base. It consists of a top and bottom frame and four interlocking legs — all made from 1¾"-thick hardwood (refer to *Fig. 3*). (I used maple.)

FRAMES. To support the end vise (added later), the bottom frame has a long stretcher (A) that cantilevers out past the base *(Fig. 1)*. But otherwise the short stretchers (B) and rails (C) of each frame are identical in size.

The rails fit in ¼"-deep dadoes near the ends of each stretcher *(Figs. 1a and 1b)*. But before assembling these pieces, it's best to drill a series of holes.

DRILL HOLES. A pair of counterbored shank holes in each rail provides a way to attach the frames to the legs *(Figs. 1a and 1b)*. And a hole near the end of the long stretcher (A) will serve as a pivot point for the end vise *(Fig. 1b)*.

There are also several holes drilled in the top frame only. To attach the fixed top later, I drilled two holes in the front stretcher and a single one in each rail *(Figs. 1 and 1a)*. And there's a hole near the bottom edge of the front stretcher for the front vise *(Fig. 1)*.

After drilling the holes, you can assemble the frames using glue and lag screws *(Fig. 1)*.

LEGS. With the frames complete, I started work on the legs (D) *(Fig. 2)*. The length of the legs determines the height of your workbench. To provide a comfortable working height, a good rule of thumb is to measure the distance between your wrist and the floor, then subtract the thickness of the

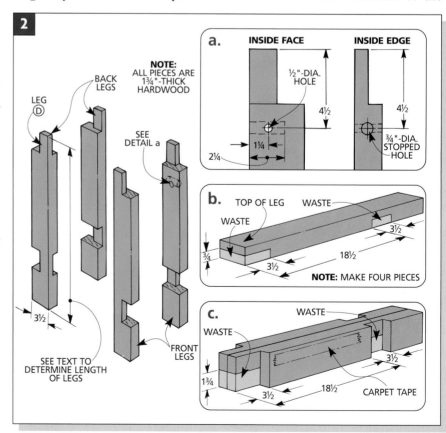

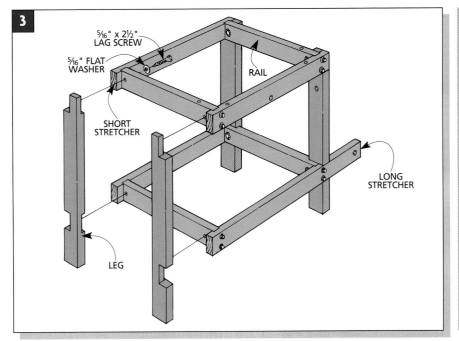

3

⁵⁄₁₆" x 2½"
LAG SCREW

⁵⁄₁₆" FLAT
WASHER

RAIL

SHORT
STRETCHER

LONG
STRETCHER

LEG

SHOP TIP
Bench Dogs

You can make a bench dog by cutting the threads off a large bolt and then grinding the sides of the head at a slight downward angle.

benchtop (1¾"). In my case, the legs were 28" long.

NOTCHES. The next step is to cut notches in the legs to accept the frames. Since both the front and the back pair of legs are mirror images, it's easy to cut a notch in the wrong place accidentally. So I used a simple technique to keep things straight.

Start by cutting a rabbet and a dado in each leg *(Fig. 2b)*. Then temporarily fasten the mirrored pairs together with carpet tape and cut notches in the edges of the legs *(Fig. 2c)*.

Before assembling the base, drill two intersecting holes in the right front leg for the end vise *(Fig. 2a)*. A large stopped hole is drilled in the inside edge. And there's a smaller through hole in the face of the leg.

ASSEMBLY. All that's left to complete the base is to attach the frames to the legs. They're held in place with glue and lag screws that pass through the holes in the rails drilled earlier *(Fig. 3)*.

TOP

The top of this workbench does more than provide a solid work surface. It also doubles as a vise.

To make this work, the top consists of two thick slabs that act as the "jaws" of the vise *(Fig. 4)*. The front part is attached to the base. And the back part slides back and forth to open and close the top. This means you can clamp a project between the two parts. Or use

bench dogs along with one of the vises to clamp work flat against the top.

GLUE-UP. To build the top, I started by gluing up the two slabs from pieces of 1¾"-thick hardwood. After sanding both workpieces nice and flat, it's just a matter of cutting the fixed top (E) and movable top (F) to size *(Fig. 4)*.

DOG HOLES. The next step is to drill holes for the bench dogs. (You can

make your own bench dogs easily. See the Shop Tip above.) Two rows of holes across the width of both top parts will be used with the front vise. And there's a single row along the length of the fixed top for the end vise.

After chamfering the holes *(Fig. 4a)* and outside edges of the top pieces, you can attach the fixed top. It's fastened to the base with lag screws *(Fig. 4b)*.

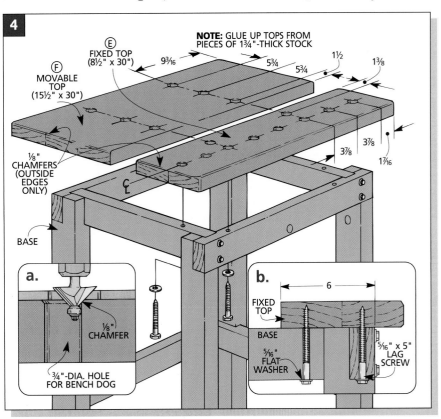

4

NOTE: GLUE UP TOPS FROM PIECES OF 1¾"-THICK STOCK

Ⓔ
FIXED TOP
(8½" x 30")

Ⓕ
MOVABLE
TOP
(15½" x 30")

9³⁄₁₆

5¾   5¾   1½   1⅜

⅛"
CHAMFERS
(OUTSIDE
EDGES
ONLY)

3⅞   3⅞

3⅞   1⁷⁄₁₆

BASE

a.
⅛"
CHAMFER

¾"-DIA. HOLE
FOR BENCH DOG

b.
6

FIXED
TOP

BASE

⁵⁄₁₆"
FLAT
WASHER

⁵⁄₁₆" x 5"
LAG
SCREW

With the top complete, you still need a way to make it open and close. That's the job of the front vise.

The operation of this vise is simple. A U-shaped guide assembly is attached to the movable top *(Fig. 5)*. As you turn a threaded rod that's connected to this assembly, it opens and closes the vise.

GUIDE BLOCKS. To prevent the vise from racking, two guide blocks (G) track the movable top along the rails (C) of the base *(Fig. 6)*. They need to be almost (but not quite) touching the rails to keep the vise from binding.

To locate the guide blocks, start by flipping the top and base upside down. Then use a scrap that's the same width as the maximum opening of the vise (3½") to position the movable top. With shims between the guide blocks and rails (I used playing cards), just screw the blocks in place *(Figs. 6a and 6b)*.

CONNECTING RAIL. The guide blocks are tied together with a connecting rail (H) *(Fig. 7)*. It transfers the rotation of the threaded rod to the movable top (refer to *Fig. 5*).

To make this work, you'll need to drill two intersecting holes in the connecting rail — one for the threaded rod and the other for a short, steel cross-dowel that's drilled and tapped to accept the threaded rod. (I cut a dowel from a length of steel rod. See the Shop Tip on the opposite page for details.)

To locate the hole for the rod, set the connecting rail on the guide blocks (with the top closed) and mark the centerpoint *(Fig. 7a)*. Then transfer this

centerpoint to the broad face of the connecting rail and drill a ¾"-dia. hole for the cross-dowel *(Fig. 7)*.

SPACER. The next step is adding a spacer (I) *(Fig. 7)*. It's just a block that allows the handle of the vise to clear the benchtop. Before attaching the spacer, you'll need to locate and drill a counterbored shank hole for the threaded rod and a nylon bushing *(Fig. 7b)*. Then chamfer the front corners and glue the spacer in place.

ASSEMBLY. Now you're ready to assemble the vise *(Fig. 5a)*. The handle is epoxied to the threaded rod. After installing two nylon bushings to support the rod (one in the spacer and the other in the top frame), it's captured

with a washer and two "jam" nuts. To complete the vise, slip the cross-dowel in place and thread the rod into it.

END VISE

To provide more clamping options, there's also a shop-made vise on the end of the workbench.

As you tighten this end vise, a long, vertical arm pivots on the long stretcher (A) and moves the clamp head toward the fixed top *(Fig. 8)*. So you can either hold a workpiece between the clamp head and the bench top. Or use bench dogs to clamp work flat.

ARM. The arm (J) is just a piece of 1¾"-thick hardwood with an oversize

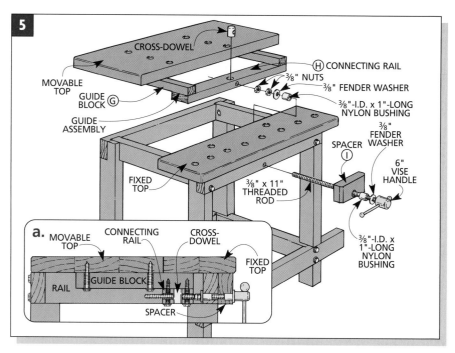

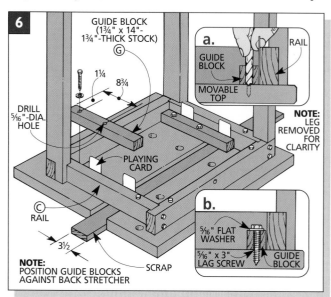

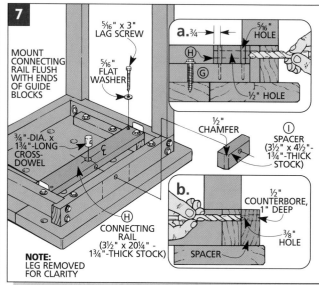

rabbet at the bottom *(Fig. 9)*. A hole near the bottom serves as the pivot point. And two intersecting holes at the top will be used to mount the vise. (The slotted hole allows the threaded rod to move up and down as the arm pivots.)

CLAMP HEAD. With the arm complete, the clamp head is built up around it using three hardwood blocks *(Fig. 10)*.

The front block (K) has an angled hole for a bench dog drilled in it before gluing it in place *(Fig. 10a)*. This ensures that the bench dog applies pressure downward so the workpiece will stay flat on the bench.

After gluing on the two side blocks (L), I sanded a slight curve on the face of the clamp head *(Fig. 10b)*. This way, the two clamping surfaces will be parallel, regardless of the position of the arm. So you'll always get good clamping pressure.

INSTALL VISE. After attaching the arm to the long stretcher with a bolt and lock nut, you can install the vise. As before, I used epoxy to fasten the handle to the threaded rod. But this time, the rod passes through two cross-dowels.

The one that fits in the leg produces the clamping pressure, so it's threaded *(Fig. 8a)*. But since the cross-dowel in the arm just keeps the rod aligned, I simply drilled an oversized hole but didn't tap threads in it.

This cross-dowel is sandwiched between a coupling nut and a spacer (bushing) on one side and another coupling nut on the other *(Fig. 8a)*. To capture the rod, thread on a hex nut so it's snug. Then to complete the vise, just thread the rod into the leg. ∎

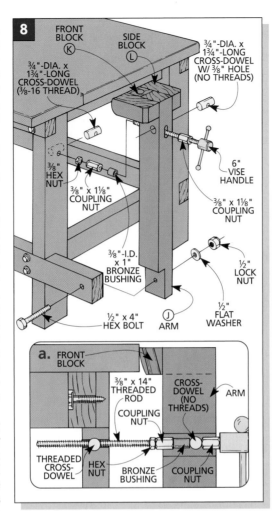

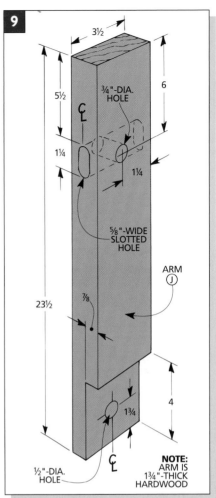

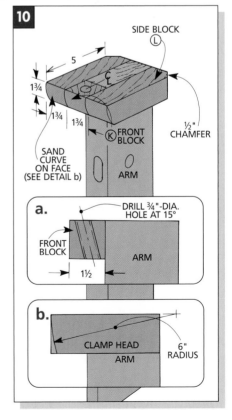

DESIGNER'S NOTEBOOK

Organize the space below the Small Workbench with this cabinet. Box-joint drawers slide open on aluminum angle drawer guides and European hinges let the doors open wide.

CONSTRUCTION NOTES:

■ The case consists of a top and bottom (M), two sides (N), and a divider (O) *(Fig. 1)*. Except for the divider, each piece is rabbeted on the back inside edge for a hardboard back that's added later *(Figs. 1 and 1b)*.

■ The pieces are held together with tongue and dado joints. But before cutting these joints, it's easiest to cover the exposed ends of the top and bottom. I just glued on ¼"-thick hardwood edging (P) *(Fig. 1)*.

■ After sanding or planing the edging flush with the faces of the plywood, you can cut the ¼"-wide dadoes in the top and bottom (M) *(Fig. 1a)*.

■ Then cut the tongues on the sides (N) and divider (O) to fit.

■ Before gluing the case together, you'll want to add the drawer guides. They're made from aluminum angle *(Fig. 2)*. The reason for this is simple.

The aluminum won't expand and contract with changes in humidity. So the drawers won't bind like they sometimes do with wood guides. And the alu-

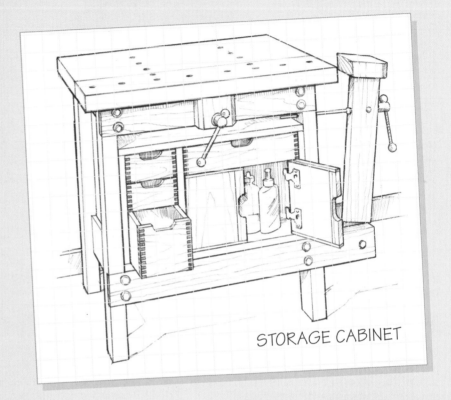

STORAGE CABINET

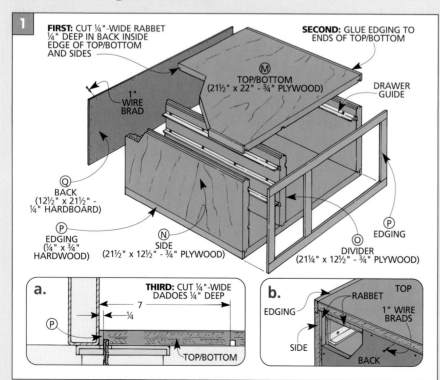

1

FIRST: CUT ¼"-WIDE RABBET ¼" DEEP IN BACK INSIDE EDGE OF TOP/BOTTOM AND SIDES

SECOND: GLUE EDGING TO ENDS OF TOP/BOTTOM

1" WIRE BRAD

Ⓜ TOP/BOTTOM (21½" x 22" - ¾" PLYWOOD)

DRAWER GUIDE

Ⓠ BACK (12½" x 21½" - ¼" HARDBOARD)

Ⓟ EDGING (¼" x ¾" HARDWOOD)

Ⓝ SIDE (21½" x 12½" - ¾" PLYWOOD)

Ⓞ DIVIDER (21¼" x 12½" - ¾" PLYWOOD)

Ⓟ EDGING

a.
THIRD: CUT ¼"-WIDE DADOES ¼" DEEP
7
¼
Ⓟ
TOP/BOTTOM

b.
EDGING
RABBET
TOP
1" WIRE BRADS
SIDE
BACK

MATERIALS LIST

CABINET
M	Top/Bottom (2)	¾ ply - 21½ x 22
N	Sides (2)	¾ ply - 21½ x 12½
O	Divider (1)	¾ ply - 21¼ x 12½
P	Edging	¼ x ¾ - 20 lineal ft.
Q	Back (1)	¼ hdbd. - 12½ x 21½

DRAWERS
R	Shallow Frt./Bk. (4)	½ x 3 - 5¾
S	Shallow Sides (4)	½ x 3 - 21¼
T	Small Bottoms (3)	¼ hdbd. - 5¼ x 20¾
U	Deep Frt./Bk. (2)	½ x 5¾ - 5¾
V	Deep Sides (2)	½ x 5¾ - 21¼
W	Wide Frt./Bk. (2)	½ x 3 - 14
X	Wide Sides (2)	½ x 3 - 21¼
Y	Large Bottoms (1)	¼ hdbd. - 13½ x 20¾
Z	Stops (5)	¼ x ¾ - 4
AA	Doors (2)	¾ ply - 5⅞ x 8⅛
BB	Wide Edging (2)	¾ x 1 - 8⅛

HARDWARE SUPPLIES
(32) No. 6 x ½" Fh woodscrews
(8) ½" x ½" - 20¾" aluminum angle
(2 pr.) 125° inset hinges
(26) 1" wire brads

minum angle is less expensive than manufactured drawer guides.

■ To make it easy to align the drawer guides, they fit in dadoes cut in the sides and divider *(Fig. 2)*. After drilling countersinks in the guides, they're simply screwed in place *(Fig. 2a)*.

■ All that's left is to assemble the case. To keep it square during glue-up, I cut a back (Q) to fit and used brads to hold it in place *(Fig. 1b)*. Then I glued edging (P) to the front edges of the case.

■ Once the case is complete, it's just a matter of building the drawers and doors to fit inside.

■ To provide storage for different size tools, there are two shallow drawers and a deep drawer on the left, and a wide drawer on the right *(Fig. 3)*.

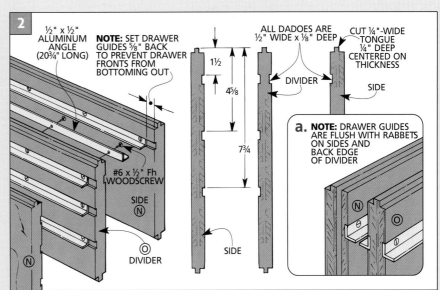

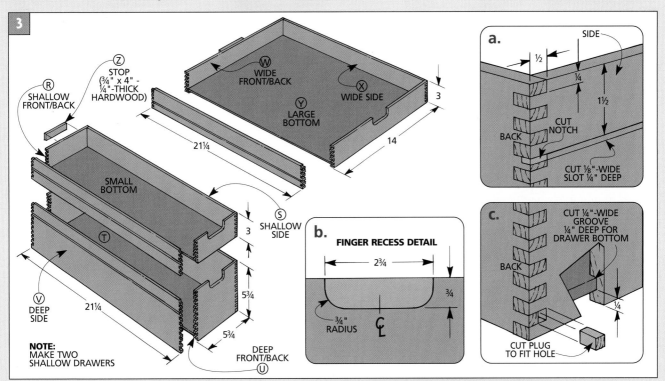

■ Each drawer is held together with box joints *(Fig. 3)*. Start by cutting the drawer fronts and backs (R, U, W) and sides (S, V, X) to size. (I used ¹/₂"-thick stock and allowed for a ¹/₈" gap all around the drawer.)

■ Now you can cut the box joints. To get the bottoms of the slots perfectly flat, I routed them using a straight bit.

■ Next, grooves are cut in the sides for the aluminum drawer guides *(Fig. 3a)*. Also, there's a groove in each piece for the drawer bottoms (T, Y) *(Fig. 3c)*.

■ Before gluing up the drawers, a finger recess is cut in each front *(Fig. 3b)*.

■ Then after the glue dries, cut a notch

in each back corner so the drawers can slide onto the guides *(Fig. 3a)*, and plug the holes in the sides *(Fig. 3c)*.

■ To complete the drawers, I glued a stop (Z) to the back of each one and planed it until the front was flush with the cabinet.

■ All that's left is to add the two doors (AA) *(Fig. 4)*. These are pieces of ³/₄" plywood that are trimmed with hardwood edging. A wide trim piece (BB) with a finger recess is glued to the inside edge of each door. And thin strips of edging (P) cover the other edges. After gluing on a stop (Z), I mounted the doors with European-style hinges.

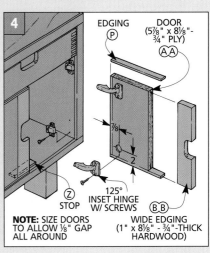

One thing we take into consideration when designing projects is whether the hardware is commonly available. Most of the supplies for the projects in this book can be found at local hardware stores or home centers, but sometimes you may have to order hardware through the mail. If so, we've tried to find reputable sources with toll-free phone numbers (see right).

Woodsmith Project Supplies also offers hardware for some projects (see below).

WOODSMITH PROJECT SUPPLIES

At the time this book was printed, the following project supply kits and hardware were available from *Woodsmith Project Supplies*. The kits include hardware, but you must supply any lumber, plywood, or finish. For current prices and availability, call toll free:

1-800-444-7527

Pegboard Storage
(pages 8-13)
Hardware kit...............No. 6827300

Includes all the hardware needed for the Pegboard Storage Cabinet.

Hardware Bin
(pages 14-17)
Brass label pulls .... No. 1005210

Miter Saw Station
(pages 52-59)
Hardware kit...............No. 6811200

Includes all the hardware needed to build the Miter Saw Station.

Benchtop Router Table
(pages 70-81)
Basic hardware kit.....No. 6845100
Deluxe hardware kit..No. 6845125

Basic kit includes hardware for table shown on page 73 in the Designer's Notebook. Kit includes a phenolic insert plate for mounting router. Deluxe kit includes hardware for basic table, plus dust collection hood, bit guard, featherboard, dual track, and a deluxe router plate with three different size inserts instead of phenolic plate.

KEY: TL08

MAIL ORDER SOURCES

Some of the most important "tools" you can have in your shop are mail order catalogs. The ones listed below are filled with special hardware, tools, finishes, lumber, and supplies that can't be found at a local hardware store or home center. You should be able to find many of the supplies for the projects in this book in one or more of these catalogs.

THE WOODSMITH STORE

2625 Beaver Avenue
Des Moines, IA 50310
800-835-5084
Our own retail store with tools, jigs, hardware, books, and finishing supplies. We don't have a catalog, but we do send out items mail order.

ROCKLER WOODWORKING & HARDWARE

4365 Willow Drive
Medina, MN 55340
800-279-4441
www.rockler.com
A catalog of hardware and accessories, including sharpening supplies, roller bearings, router table inserts, hinges, pulls, and dust collectors.

LEE VALLEY TOOLS LTD.

P.O. Box 1780
Ogdensburg, NY 13669-6780
800-871-8158
www.leevalley.com
Several catalogs actually, offering pulls, hinges, dust collection systems (including remote and automatic switches), roller bearings, and more.

WOODCRAFT

560 Airport Industrial Park
P.O. Box 1686
Parkersburg, WV 26102-1686
800-225-1153
www.woodcraft.com
This catalog has all kinds of hardware, including lazy Susans, hinges, pulls, and label holders. You'll also find router table inserts, dust collection systems and accessories.

We've also listed manufacturers for multi-purpose woodworking machines as mentioned on page 23

Note: The information below was current when this book was printed. August Home Publishing does not guarantee these products will be available nor endorse any specific mail order company, catalog, or product.

GARRETT WADE

161 Avenue of the Americas
New York, NY 10013
800-221-2942
www.garrettwade.com
The "Bible" for hand tools, but also a source for sharpening stones, honing guides, lazy Susan bearings, hinges, label holders, pulls, and more.

WOODWORKER'S SUPPLY

1108 North Glenn Road
Casper, WY 82601
800-645-9292
You'll find a good selection of pulls and hardware, sharpening supplies, and dust collection items.

The following manufacturers offer multi-purpose machines for woodworking (refer to page 23).

LAGUNA TOOLS

17101 Murphy Avenue
Irvine, CA 92614
800-234-1976
www.lagunatools.com

SHOPSMITH, INC.

6530 Poe Avenue
Dayton, OH 45414
800-543-7586
www.shopsmith.com

SMITHY CO.

170 Aprill Drive
P.O. Box 1517
Ann Arbor, MI 48106
800-476-4849
www.smithy.com

INDEX

AUGUST HOME
PUBLISHING COMPANY

President & Publisher: Donald B. Peschke
Executive Editor: Douglas L. Hicks
Creative Director: Ted Kralicek
Senior Graphic Designer: Chris Glowacki
Associate Editor: Craig L. Ruegsegger
Assistant Editors: Joseph E. Irwin, Joel Hess
Graphic Designers: Vu Nguyen, April Walker Janning, Stacey L. Krull
Design Intern: Heather Boots

Designer's Notebook Illustrator: Mike Mittermeier
Photographer: Crayola England
Electronic Production: Douglas M. Lidster
Production: Troy Clark, Minniette Johnson
Project Designers: Ken Munkel, Kent Welsh
Project Builders: Steve Curtis, Steve Johnson
Magazine Editors: Terry Strohman, Tim Robertson
Contributing Editors: Vincent S. Ancona, Jon Garbison, Bryan Nelson
Magazine Art Directors: Todd Lambirth, Cary Christensen
Contributing Illustrators: Mark Higdon, David Kreyling, Roger Reiland,
Kurt Schultz, Cinda Shambaugh, Dirk Ver Steeg

Director of Finance: Mary Scheve
Controller: Robin Hutchinson
Production Director: George Chmielarz
Project Supplies: Bob Baker
New Media Manager: Gordon Gaippe

For subscription information about
Woodsmith and *ShopNotes* magazines, please write:
August Home Publishing Co.
2200 Grand Ave.
Des Moines, IA 50312
800-333-5075
www.augusthome.com/customwoodworking

Woodsmith® and *ShopNotes*® are registered trademarks of August Home
Publishing Co.

Photo of Shopsmith multi-purpose machine on page 23 courtesy
of Shopsmith, Inc.

Oxmoor House®

Oxmoor House, Inc.
Book Division of Southern Progress Corporation
P.O. Box 2463, Birmingham, Alabama 35201

ISBN: 0-8487-2682-0
Printed in the United States of America

To order additional publications, call 1-205-445-6560.
For more books to enrich your life, visit **oxmoorhouse.com**